MEN
IN
FAMILIES

Edited by

Robert A. Lewis
Robert E. Salt

SAGE PUBLICATIONS
The Publishers of Professional Social Science
Beverly Hills   London   New Delhi

To the special men in our families:

Craig A. Lewis
David P. Lewis
Laurence G. Lewis
Richard L. Lewis
James T. Salt
William B. Salt

Copyright © 1986 by Sage Publications, Inc.

For information address:

SAGE Publications, Inc.
275 South Beverly Drive
Beverly Hills, California 90212

SAGE Publications India Pvt. Ltd.
M-32 Market
Greater Kailash I
New Delhi 110 048 India

SAGE Publications Ltd
28 Banner Street
London EC1Y 8QE
England

Printed in the United States of America

Library of Congress Cataloging-in-Publication Data

Main entry under title:

Men in families.

(Sage focus editions; v. 76)
Includes bibliographical references.
1. Husbands—Addresses, essays, lectures.   2. Father
and child—Addresses, essays, lectures.   3. Sex role—
Addresses, essays, lectures.   I. Lewis, Robert A. (Robert Alan),
1932-   . II. Salt, Robert E.
HQ756.M45   1985   306.8′5′088041   85-14330
ISBN 0-8039-2526-3
ISBN 0-8039-2527-1 (pbk.)

FIRST PRINTING

MEN
IN
FAMILIES

SOME OTHER VOLUMES IN THE
SAGE FOCUS EDITIONS

6. **Natural Order**
   Barry Barnes and Steven Shapin

8. **Controversy (Second Edition)**
   Dorothy Nelkin

14. **Churches and Politics in Latin America**
   Daniel H. Levine

21. **The Black Woman**
   La Frances Rodgers-Rose

24. **Dual-Career Couples**
   Fran Pepitone-Rockwell

31. **Black Men**
   Lawrence E. Gary

32. **Major Criminal Justice Systems**
   George F. Cole, Stanislaw J. Frankowski,
   and Marc G. Gertz

34. **Assessing Marriage**
   Erik E. Filsinger and Robert A. Lewis

36. **Impacts of Racism on White Americans**
   Benjamin P. Bowser and
   Raymond G. Hunt

41. **Black Families**
   Harriette Pipes McAdoo

43. **Aging and Retirement**
   Neil G. McCluskey and Edgar F. Borgatta

47. **Mexico's Political Economy**
   Jorge I. Dominguez

50. **Cuba**
   Jorge I. Dominguez

51. **Social Control**
   Jack P. Gibbs

52. **Energy and Transport**
   George H. Daniels, Jr., and Mark H. Rose

54. **Job Stress and Burnout**
   Whiton Stewart Paine

56. **Two Paychecks**
   Joan Aldous

57. **Social Structure and Network Analysis**
   Peter V. Marsden and Nan Lin

58. **Socialist States in the World-System**
   Christopher K. Chase-Dunn

59. **Age or Need?**
   Bernice L. Neugarten

60. **The Costs of Evaluation**
   Marvin C. Alkin and Lewis C. Solmon

61. **Aging in Minority Groups**
   R.L. McNeely and John N. Colen

62. **Contending Approaches to World System Analysis**
   William R. Thompson

63. **Organizational Theory and Public Policy**
   Richard H. Hall and Robert E. Quinn

64. **Family Relationships in Later Life**
   Timothy H. Brubaker

65. **Communication and Organizations**
   Linda L. Putnam and
   Michael E. Pacanowsky

66. **Competence in Communication**
   Robert N. Bostrom

67. **Avoiding Communication**
   John A. Daly and James C. McCroskey

68. **Ethnography in Educational Evaluation**
   David M. Fetterman

69. **Group Decision Making**
   Walter C. Swap and Associates

70. **Children and Microcomputers**
   Milton Chen and William Paisley

71. **The Language of Risk**
   Dorothy Nelkin

72. **Black Children**
   Harriette Pipes McAdoo and
   John Lewis McAdoo

73. **Industrial Democracy**
   Warner Woodworth, Christopher Meek,
   and William Foote Whyte

74. **Grandparenthood**
   Vern L. Bengtson and Joan F. Robertson

75. **Organizational Theory and Inquiry**
   Yvonna S. Lincoln

76. **Men in Families**
   Robert A. Lewis and Robert E. Salt

77. **Communication and Group Decision-Making**
   Randy Y. Hirokawa and
   Marshall Scott Poole

78. **The Organization of Mental Health Services**
   W. Richard Scott and Bruce L. Black

CONTENTS

Preface   7

Introduction: What Men Get Out of
    Marriage and Parenthood
      Robert A. Lewis   11

PART I.   MEN AS HUSBANDS   27

  1. Why Men Get Married: More and Less
     Traditional Men Compared
      Bruce Nordstrom   31

  2. Why Some Men Do Not Marry
      Stephen F. Duncan   55

  3. Characteristics of Husbands' Family Work
     and Wives' Labor Force Involvement
      Patrick C. McKenry, Sharon J. Price,
      Philip B. Gordon, and Nancy M. Rudd   73

  4. Husbands' Responsibility for Household
     Tasks in Older Marriages: Does
     Living Situation Make a Difference?
      Timothy H. Brubaker and Linda Ade-Ridder   85

  5. Husbands' Jealousy
      Bram Buunk   97

  6. Husbands, Lovers, and Loneliness
      Jenny De Jong-Gierveld   115

PART II.   MEN AS FATHERS   127

  7. Delayed Childbearing: Men's Thinking
     About the Fertility Decision
      Kristine M. Baber and Albert S. Dreyer   131

8. Effects of Increased Paternal Involvement
   on Children in Two-Parent Families

   *Michael E. Lamb, Joseph H. Pleck,
   and James A. Levine*   141

9. Some Parenting Attitudes of Young
   Black Fathers

   Michael E. Connor   159

10. Black Fathers' Relationships with Their
    Preschool Children and the Children's
    Development of Ethnic Identity

    John Lewis McAdoo   169

11. Parent-Child Relationships in
    Single-Father Families

    Shirley M.H. Hanson   181

12. Fathers' Supportiveness: Perceptions
    of Fathers and College Daughters

    Peggy S. Draughn and Mary L. Waggenspack   197

PART III.   MEN IN FAMILY, KIN, AND
            FRIENDSHIP NETWORKS   213

13. Family Life Events, Depression,
    and Black Men

    Lawrence E. Gary   215

14. Grandfathers: Making Up for
    Lost Opportunities

    Graeme Russell   233

15. Men and Their Friendships

    Peter J. Stein   261

16. Identity Change Among Older and
    Younger Men

    Mick Coleman and Jack O. Balswick   271

About the Contributors   283

PREFACE

The editors of this book have many things in common. We have the same first name. We are both men. As boys we grew up within the contexts of loving families. We both have fathers, still living, and a brother, one each. We know what some men do in families, because we both have had role models in our fathers, brothers, uncles, grandfathers, and other male relatives. We remember our grandfathers somewhat dimly now, but they were real people to us once: men who themselves grew up within families, had children of their own, and grandsons—us.

We are both social scientists at Purdue University who study families and share an interest in what men do in families. We are both also advocates of men having larger and more satisfying roles in their families. We promote active fathering when given an opportunity, such as this book of readings gives us. We therefore have proactive biases toward husbands' and fathers' greater involvement in their families. We want you, our readers, to know our biases. We work to keep science and advocacy separate, as we are primarily scientists who seek empirical truths; but we are also men concerned about other men in families.

We two are also very different. We are the products of different generations: There are nearly thirty years between us. We grew up in very different times. The older of us, Bob Lewis, was a boy during the end of the Great Depression, when men who could not support their families and who derived all their respect from their breadwinning role often lost that respect in the eyes of their wives and children. He remembers, as a child, the beginning of World War II, not so much as the time when men in his family went into service, but as the time when many women went outside the family to work in defense plants, to learn new skills, to earn money themselves, to experience new freedoms, and to begin the long climb toward equality with men in the marketplace and the boardrooms.

The other of us, Bob Salt, grew up in the 1960s, when some men were beginning to question the primacy of the breadwinning role. He saw the fulfillment available to men in their father role and the sadness best summed up in the popular song, "Cats in the Cradle," when men fail to experience the joys of interacting with their children until it is too late. He also remembers growing up in a family where both of his parents worked outside the home. His mother had often related the story of having trained a number of men to become bank managers during the 1950s while she herself was passed over for the position, only because of her gender. He also saw the need for fathers to be involved in their families to allow mothers the full opportunity to seek meaningful employment.

We know who we are. We are, fundamentally, two similar but also different men, each the product of his own family and his own time. But we are also men who derive great satisfactions from our family relationships and are concerned about the minority of men who do not.

We wonder who you, our readers, will be. We suspect that many of you will be women, because women experienced changes in work roles at least one decade before we men began to examine our own family roles critically. We also suspect that many of you will be women because whatever we men do or do not do within our families affects your roles and satisfactions too, as your role changes have affected ours.

We suspect that many of you will also be men, men of all ages and from different levels of education and income, but men at the edge of discovering new things about yourselves and your own family relationships. Some of you may be relatively new husbands or new fathers who are curious about the satisfactions as well as the strains that other men are experiencing in their families these days. Some of you are traditional men whose wives have changed their own roles, expectations, and attitudes toward men—especially you. Some of you have just experienced divorces and are trying to put the pieces of your lives back together, to risk other, close relationships with women again.

Some of you are perhaps members of men's therapy groups, men's support groups, or consciousness-raising groups. Perhaps you attended one of the national and regional Fatherhood Forums that were held last year (1984) in six major cities in the United States, including Chicago, Boston, Los Angeles, and Minneapolis. Perhaps these meetings lifted your outlook on what fathers can be to their children. Finally, some of you may be men taking academic courses in women's studies or sex-roles classes where the male point of view and male-oriented materials are needed for a balanced treatment of both female and male roles in contemporary society. Or you may be taking courses in one of the newest fields in the academic world—men's studies.

Men's studies appears to be the newest branch of gender scholarship, according to Brod (1983). A yet unpublished dissertation (S. D. Femiano, 1984, personal correspondence) has documented 27 academic courses on men's studies that are currently being taught at universities such as the University of Southern California, California State Universities in Hayward and Long Beach, Rutgers, the University of Massachusetts (Amherst), the University of Oregon, Brooklyn College, John F. Kennedy University, Mankato State (Minnesota), Old Dominion University (Virginia), the University of Tennessee, and the University of Alaska. We are planning to give a men's studies course next year at Purdue University.

Men's studies courses are being taught in the typical departments of psychology, sociology, and family studies. However, they are also being taught in English, history, and religion departments, such as at United Theological Seminary in Minneapolis; in health and human sexuality departments; and in Black studies programs. Femiano (1984) also has evidence that within a year fifty academics will either continue or begin to teach men's studies courses across the country.

There has been a research program to study men for a few years at Wellesley College in Massachusetts. Last year (1984), however, the Program for the Study of Women and Men in Society, an interdisciplinary program at USC, became the first department in the United States to hire a full-time academic committed to teaching and researching in men's studies. Last year also saw the creation of a master's program at Mankato State University, Minnesota, where there is a separate concentration in men's studies. Finally, in January 1984 a *Men's Studies Newsletter* and *Men's Studies Notes* were published by the Men's Studies Task Group of the National Organization for Men by Harry Brod and Joseph Pleck, respectively.

We suspect that the time is now ripe for a blossoming of critical research, especially research on men in families. We believe that this concentrated study of men in families will not take anything away from women's studies, but will indeed become a needed complement to women's studies. We leave that assessment to you, our readers, and to those who pursue the study of men in families.

—Robert A. Lewis
Robert E. Salt

REFERENCE

Brod, H. (1983). *The new men's studies: From feminist theory to gender scholarship.* Unpublished manuscript.

INTRODUCTION:
WHAT MEN GET OUT OF
MARRIAGE AND PARENTHOOD

Robert A. Lewis

A recent, controversial book by Barbara Ehrenreich, *The Hearts of Men: American Dreams and the Flight from Commitment* (1983), has articulated one of the major questions raised by this book: "Why do men want to be involved in marriage and parenthood?"

According to Ehrenreich, liberated women in the United States are not driving men away from the family; men have been deserting the family for decades. As an outcome, the family is an intrinsically unstable institution, because it rests on the "volition of individual men," that is, males accepting the breadwinner ethic, the belief that they *should* get jobs, get married, have children, and "move up" in the world. However, as more women are taking on outside employment and as the breadwinner ethic continues to erode in U.S. society, even more males, who are losing the status and pampering that are the rewards of being the sole breadwinner, have been rejecting formal marriage and parenthood. After all, why should contemporary men value and support marriage and the family?

In answer to this, Ehrenreich might argue that marriage used to provide males with guaranteed sex, emotional security, and laundry service; but now, liberated women are creating men who are impotent and anxious instead of secure, and who must do their own laundry. But if this is becoming a major trend, why do most males still get married and many males become parents?

THREE VALUE POSITIONS

Individual men vary greatly in the degree to which they support and value the institutions of formal marriage and parenthood. There are, however, at least three value positions that have been identified for men in recent times.

HIGH VALUE

One of these positions has been voiced by Jessie Bernard to the effect that men value and receive much through marriage and family life. Bernard (1972, 1976), in some of her writings, has strongly suggested that men may receive even more from marriage than do women: in other words, marriage is a better institution for men than for women. Some data seem to support this contention. For instance, a recent study by Jill Scheppler at the University of Florida revealed that for young adults aged 28-32 married men were more satisfied with their lives than were either single or married women. Single women were more satisfied than married women; single men were the least satisfied of all these four groups. This study has been preceded by a number of studies that reported married people happier than singles (De Jong-Gierveld, 1971, 1984; Gove, 1972).

Married men in the U.S. also live longer than do either single or divorced men (Gove, 1972; Gove & Hughes, 1980). Married men tend to be healthier, both physically and emotionally, than single men (Harrison, 1978). Of course, the direction of causation is most difficult to ascertain from correlational data. For example, marriage may prolong married men's lives because many of their basic physical and emotional needs are met in marriage, or, as De Jong-Gierveld has argued, marriage has a "protective status" for men. However, a drift theory of sociology might suggest that women tend to marry men who are already healthier, and who would live longer anyway. Thus the epidemiological data do not indicate the direction of causation. However, it is a reasonable assumption that one reason men continue to marry at high rates is that formal marriage still fulfills many of men's needs for affiliation, love, sex, and companionship—in other words, their needs for intimacy. Why would so many males continue to marry (one or more times), if marriage and parenthood did not continue to provide for many of their needs?

LOW VALUE

A second value position has been voiced strongly by Rita Liljestrom, a sociologist from Gothenburg, Sweden. She believes that men do not value marriage and the family very highly, because they do not receive much from it (Carlsson, 1983). Liljestrom has intuited a growing pattern for families around the world—mother-child dyads without permanently attached males. She predicts this future family pattern from trend data in Latin America, Scandinavia (especially Greenland), and the Caribbean, where many men are withdrawing from the family unit, reduced more or less to "sperm donors"—in other words, where men come and go, expand and then abandon the mother-child subsystem, and where men consequently are not an integral, continuing part of family life.

If you were to press Liljestrom further on these ideas, she would probably agree with Barbara Ehrenreich. Both suggest that men do not get much from marriage and family life, because marriage may bind men only temporarily to the mother-child dyad, often not long enough even to provide financially for the growing children. Liljestrom declares this in her own words: "The woman is the center of every family. She and the man create a sexual relationship, but as a mother she is biologically closer to the child than the man. . . . [Divorce then] . . . is often an active decision on the part of the woman, because she can get along without the man . . . [and often elects] to live alone with the children" (Carlsson, 1983, p. 59).

A number of both feminist and nonfeminist writers agree with Liljestrom's analysis. For example, Peter Wilson in *Man, the Promising Primate* recently reexamined the evidence for bonding or attachment among human beings as well as other primates. He concludes: "The primary bond of attachment in the human species is that between adult females and infants. There is no biological evidence for such a tie between adult males and infants" (Wilson, 1980, p. 48). Finally, data from Scandinavia, Hungary, and some other countries concerning the rising rates of cohabitation and lower rates of marriage can also be used to argue the value position that men may not receive as much from formal marriage today as they may have received in earlier times.

HIGHER VALUE FOR SOME MEN

Yet a third value position is being heard more frequently on this question of the extent to which contemporary males value marriage and the family in the United States. My own conclusion from studying men in their family relationships for over twenty years now is that some men are receiving even more today from marriage and family life than most men seem to have received for several decades. Increasingly, I see in my research how men of all ages are finding more fulfillment in the nurturing of their own children, wives, relatives, and friends. I continue to observe men who are role making, innovating, and playing out in their family lives many of the roles that were downplayed or forbidden to men in earlier decades. In the relative absence of empirical data, what may one conclude about American males' valuing of marriage and family life? One recent study of 71 traditional and nontraditional men (Nordstrom, Chapter 2 in this book) suggests that, contrary to some popular myths, most of these men want to be married. Further, the more traditional men were desirous to marry, not only more than the nontraditional men, but more than their intended wives. Certainly this is an area that ought to be explored further. In another recent study Arland Thornton and Deborah Freedman, following 916 mothers, 466 sons, and 450 daughters over an 18-year period, discovered that 90% of the sons expected to marry someday and three-fourths would be disappointed if they did not marry.

One explanation for some men investing more of their time and effort in their families seems to reside in men's greater psychological involvement in family life. Although there is still a popular stereotype that most men are more work oriented than family oriented, there is growing evidence that the contrary case is more often true (Adamek & Goudy, 1966; Campbell, Converse, & Rodgers, 1976; Rosenberg, 1957). Pleck and Lang (1978), in their analysis of the 1977 Quality of Employment Survey, also discovered that men's psychological involvement with marriage and family is greater than with their work. For example, 94% of the men in that study reported that the most important things that happened to them were in their marriage and family life, compared with 55% who had similar statements about their jobs. When controlling for education, family life-cycle stage, and spouse employment status, the positive effects of family are about 1.5 times greater than those for outside work. In effect, family experiences were seen as making greater contributions than outside work to overall well-being.

This evidence suggests that many fathers may be willing to increase their involvement with children (Pleck, 1983). Indeed, there is a growing body of data that suggests that men who value parenthood highly also are more involved with child care and find parenthood more satisfying than fathers who value it less (Owen, Chase-Lansdale & Lamb, 1982).

Increased participation of fathers in child care also seems to be associated with fathers' greater satisfaction in nurturing their children and in better understanding of their children (Gronseth, 1975; Russell, 1982).

In summary, it would seem that, whereas a growing minority of men are experiencing new highs in nurturing children and experimenting with other new roles in families, and although another minority of men may not be receiving much from marriage and family life, most men must receive enough from marriages and families to marry at least once. And even if men divorce, most will marry again and perhaps even invest in a second set of children.

THE MEANINGS OF FATHER AND HUSBAND POSITIONS

Just as men's values in marriage and family life in the United States seem to be changing, so also are the meanings attached to being fathers and husbands. One observation that must be made first is that the meanings attached to being a father or husband are not as clear as they once were. For example, what does the position of "father" connote? In more traditional times in the United States, fathering a child may have implied simply that a father had sired a child, that is, provided the sperm that fertilized an egg that developed into a child. This is all that was necessary to be a father in the most narrow sense of the term. If this is all that being a father connotes today, then I might agree with Liljestrom and Ehrenreich, that most men may not receive much from the institution of the family, since the coldest thing in the world is yesterday's orgasm.

In 1984 the U.S. Supreme Court made a landmark decision that surprisingly received little public attention. In a 6-3 ruling our high court declared that a father must be more than a biological parent to assure his right to challenge his child's adoption by someone else; that is, the mere existence of a biological link does not merit the same constitutional protection an unwed father earns by demonstrating a continuing commitment to all the responsibilities of parenthood.

So what is it to be a father? William Hurt, a young American actor who has a child but is not married to the mother of his child, was quoted recently by an interviewer as saying, "I don't know exactly what it means to be a father, but I'm crazy about my 8-month old son." Obviously, for some the position of father is a mystifying and gratifying experience, even though the meaning of fatherhood cannot be captured easily in words.

Quotations were given earlier from Peter Wilson's recent book, *Man, the Promising Primate*. It is he who firmly declares that the basic biological bond for all primate species is that between the adult female and her offspring. After tracing the "relationships" and "roles" (if you will allow the terms) of nonhuman primates, Wilson concludes that the attachment between a nonhuman female primate and her young is determined by the biology of birth and her continuing nurturance of her offspring. In contrast, most primate males are not even able to identify their own offspring (Wilson, 1980, pp. 48-49). However, Wilson declares that it is at this very point where evolution is discontinuous, that is, where human primates differ decidedly from nonhuman primates. In other words, there is no universal, instinctive form for basic human relationships. The options and forms for human relationships are wide open. Unlike other animals, human relationships depend somewhat upon one's own choosing and volition.

According to this line of thinking, the human father-infant bond therefore is *not* biologically determined. We may distinguish between the "real mother" and the "adoptive" mother, because being a real mother is invariate. But the father-child relationship varies more between and within cultures. As Wilson suggests, depending upon the culture, a man may be known as a father because he is the man with whom a woman is living at the time the child is born, because the infant resembles him or because the man and child have the same blood group. In some cultures it is believed that the fetus is fed and shaped through continuing sexual intercourse between the man and his pregnant partner. Because of the variability in the meanings of fatherhood, therefore, Wilson holds that the father-child relationship is a metaphor for or analogy to the female-infant bond. As such, it is also the first and basic kinship link in society, as distinct from the biological link between mother and child. As a human invention, "the father-child relationship is free from the constraints of nature, permitting great diversity and therefore more flexibility and adaptation for human survival in changing environments" (Wilson, 1980, p. 166).

In summary, we may note that very few family researchers have turned their thinking and studies to the most simple and yet most profound questions of what it means to be a father and a husband in a given society. Because the referents to fatherhood in even one society are so many and diverse, we ought to be as interested in the variability of meanings as in the median meaning or some other indicator of central tendency. Even though there has been a groundswell in the United States in the empirical study of fathers, especially new fathers, we still have little knowledge of how most men perceive fatherhood. We do not have even good descriptive studies of what fathers actually do in their families, because researchers typically are not present in homes when fathers are (Weisner, 1984).

WHY STUDY MEN IN FAMILIES?

Although there has been a spate of popular writings in the United States, there is also a scarcity of empirical research on men's contemporary family roles (Scanzoni, 1975). Consequently, we are not very sure what men do in their families. Something that is undeniably clear, however, is that more men are now playing atypical roles within families, roles that only a generation ago few men played and even fewer admitted playing. Even more clear is the observation that U.S. males have more role options than men had in earlier generations (Pleck, 1976).

As a personal aside, I can vividly remember washing the windows of our small apartment in the married student housing at the University of Minnesota during our graduate student days in the early 1960s. I remember this so well because I incurred more than once the derision of other graduate student fathers whose wives did not work outside the home or were not graduate students also, as my wife was. The greater role options and greater variation in roles played by some young husbands and fathers today in the United States make my own role-making experiences pale in comparison.

Unfortunately, most of the more exciting current descriptions of men's sex roles are, strangely, either not empirically derived or not particularly related to family life (Boyer, 1981; David & Brannon, 1975; Goldberg, 1979; Pleck, 1981; Pleck & Sawyer, 1974; Solomon & Levy, 1982). As described elsewhere (Lewis & Pleck, 1979), although male roles have been studied at least implicitly in family studies, men's changing roles in families have only recently been critically and sensitively examined. All too much of our knowledge about men's roles in families still comes from pollsters asking wives what their husbands feel and believe.

It was not until 1966 that men's changing roles in families became a focus of national interest. In that year William Smith, Jr., then president of the National Council on Family Relations, published an essay, "The Family Roles of Modern Man" (Smith, 1966). It was not until 1975, however, that a national conference allocated any significant time to a programmatic focus on men's changing roles in the United States. This program theme of the Groves Conference at Hot Springs, Arkansas, was more than a decade behind the much earlier study of women's changing work roles that had been supported by the most recent feminist movement. Generally speaking, empirical studies of men's roles, especially in the family, have lagged significantly behind studies of females' roles in the United States. Men's studies finally "arrived" when the central theme of the 1982 Groves Conference on Marriage and the Family was "Men's Changing Roles and Relationships."

With limited time and space it is impossible to summarize here all of the findings related to changes that have occurred in men's family roles. Those interested in assessing this field by themselves might read some of the special issues of scientific journals that have been focused on men's studies; for instance, the special issues in the *Journal of Social Issues* (Pleck & Brannon, 1978), *The Counseling Psychologist* (Skovholt, Gormally, Schauble, & Davis, 1978), *The Family Coordinator* (Lewis & Pleck, 1979), and the recent special issue on "Men's Changing Roles in the Family" (Lewis & Sussman, 1985) in *Marriage and Family Review*.

Those interested in specific topical areas within men's studies should locate the research bibliographies on male sex roles that have been published by the Men's Studies Collection of the MIT Humanities Library (Farriero, 1977) and the National Institute of Mental Health (Grady, Brannon, & Pleck, 1979). These and other resources are beginning to give documentation to the observations that more and more men in the United States are experimenting with as well as seriously playing roles day to day that a few decades ago only females would have played.

Just to whet the reader's appetite for information about men's changing roles, the following facts are offered:

(1) Did you know that a national time-use study of employed wives in 1976-1977 found that the wives spent only 12 more minutes a day in *combined* paid work and family work than their husbands spent? (Pleck & Rustad, 1981). Apparently, husbands' proportions of their total family work are increasing relative to their wives', because wives employed outside the home are now doing less work within the home. (Pleck, 1983)

(2) Did you know that a man's friends seem to be the major impediment to his taking on more responsibilities in the home? (Lein, 1979)

(3) Did you know that greater household involvement by males appears to assist men in their successful adaptation to retirement? (Keith & Brubaker, 1979)

In summary, as discussed above, we need more and better national studies of what men actually do in their own families. We need data especially about men (and women) in egalitarian marriages to discover how these relationships function and survive, because a growing number of both American men and women in younger cohorts are expressing interest in having marriages between equals. But above all, we need to know how much and why men in the United States value being husbands and fathers, because this is the ultimate and crucial examination of the social glue that binds men to their families.

PURPOSES OF THIS BOOK

Definitive conclusions about men's current values, meanings, and roles in marriage and family life in the United States have not been the major goal behind the writing of this chapter and book. Instead, the main purposes of this chapter and book have been as follows:

(1) To place the new, critical assessment and investigations of men within the context of families. This focus is somewhat "revolutionary" in comparison to the prevailing attention of the last two decades that has highlighted men as individuals, that is, men devoid of family contexts. We predict that men's studies will focus increasingly on men in their family environments. Viewing men within their most meaningful family relationships may well become a significant component of the growing field of men's studies.

(2) To investigate in depth the major positions and roles that men play in contemporary families. Although there have been a few excellent theoretical books and empirical books on fatherhood (Hanson & Bozett, 1985; Lamb, 1976; Lynn, 1974; Parke, 1981; Pedersen, 1976), there is no book of readings that collectively encompasses much of the recent research on most of the central positions and roles men play in their families. A unique objective of this book, therefore, is its comprehensive

inclusion of current analyses and descriptions of the wide spectrum of positions and roles that men play in contemporary families.

(3) To stimulate curiosity and encourage vital future research that some readers may be led to conduct on the ways in which contemporary men relate to other persons in their marital and familial relationships. It is clear to me at this time that men's values and roles in marriage and the family are being challenged and redefined at a rate greater than in the recent past. That which many husbands, fathers, stepfathers, grandfathers, and other male family members do within families is changing. More social scientists should be impelled to study what nearly one-half of the persons in families (males) value, believe, and do within these two institutions in our society.

As discussed elsewhere (Lewis, 1985), scholars and family advocates need to know more about the range of problems as well as the benefits that accompany the changes some men are experiencing in their family roles and in the conflicts that result from their internalizing the substantial demands of family and outside work. Unfortunately, some men are not only redefining for themselves what it is to be a husband and a father, but are already suffering from some of the things analysts of the family write about, especially those more interesting implications from research that filter through the media. For example, some writers have expressed their fears that, just as some women in the United States have taken on the roles of "super mom," so are some men trying to play out the roles of "super dad." There may be dangers in communicating heightened expectations to young fathers—for instance, that they can be more involved with their children and wives while not giving less to their careers or work outside the home.

In addition, we need to know more about the special problems men will experience as they establish and maintain egalitarian marriages (Osherson & Dill, 1983). Advocates of children and families must know the long-range results of fathers having sole or joint custody of their children following divorce, since there seems to be a small increase in this phenomenon. Even more important, we should know the short- and long-range results of co-parenting (fully shared caring for children), as this is becoming the most common pattern of dual-job marriages in the United States. Many of the chapters of this book delve into these and similar challenges for families where the adult male family member is adopting new roles, values, and meanings.

CONCLUSIONS

Men's values, expectations, and roles in families are changing. Nearly as dramatic has been the changing focus of social research as it has addressed the male members of families during the last fifty years. Robert Fein (1978) has characterized the study of fathers during the last five decades as the developing of three research paradigms. The *traditional* paradigm operated during the 1940s and 1950s, grounded in the psychoanalytic tradition and Parsons's dichotomy of instrumental versus expressive family roles. During this time researchers perceived fathers as distant and aloof, especially from their children. The father supported ("helped") the mother in her relationships with children. Because fewer mothers worked outside the home, mothers were central to their children's development; fewer fathers had direct relationships with their children.

Research during the 1960s, on the other hand, was guided by a more *modern* paradigm. Biller's and others' emphasis on fathers' absence from the home and political concerns with fathers' absence and the effect of Aid to Dependent Children produced a decade of growing awareness of the important effects that fathers had on their children, especially in terms of academic achievement, the prevention of delinquency, and the adoption of appropriate sex-role identities.

Even more recently, during the 1970s and 1980s, Fein identifies as an emergent paradigm an *androgynous* emphasis in research on the equal importance of fathers and mothers upon children's development. Researchers now see males as capable of a wide range of parenting skills and interests. For example, recent researchers have discovered that fathers can be good caregivers; young babies do not discriminate between their fathers and mothers; when fathers spend quality time with babies, the infants benefit significantly, especially on cognitive dimensions, and pick up more quickly on social cues (Sawin & Parke, 1979; Parke & O'Leary, 1976; Lamb, 1976; Lamb, Pleck, & Levine, 1985; Levine, 1976; Radin, 1972). Michael Lamb (1976) has contributed to and summarized much of this research with the conclusion that fathers can significantly influence their young children in unique and independent ways.

In summary, unless present social conditions change drastically, women who must or wish to work outside the home are not going to give up their gainful employment voluntarily. As William Goode (1982, p. 147) has written:

> I know of no instance when a group or social stratum gained its freedom or moved toward more respect and then had its members decide that they did not want it. Therefore, although men will not joyfully give up their rank; in spite of its burdens, neither will women decide that they would like to get back the older feminine privileges, accompanied with the lack of respect and material rewards that went with those courtesies.

Therefore, as more women continue to join the ranks of the gainfully employed, their men will either be pressed into "family work and services" or volunteer willingly to take their fair share of combined family and outside work. The sociological concept of reciprocal roles suggests that wherever women change their roles, either outside or inside the family, men in the family must change their own roles to complement those of their wives or role conflicts will proliferate, with accompanying stresses, until separation, divorce, or a system of complementary roles again prevails.

Men's roles in the family are changing. These changes are hinting at even greater equality between men and women in families. As William Goode (1982, p. 147) has also written recently:

> I believe that men perceive their roles as being under threat in a world that is different from any in the past. No society has yet come even close to equality between the sexes, but the modern social forces described here did not exist before either. At the most cautious, we must concede that the conditions favoring a trend toward more equality are more favorable than at any prior time in history. If we have little reason to conclude that equality is at hand, let us at least rejoice that we are marching in the right direction.

REFERENCES

Adamek, R., & Goudy, W. (1966). Identification, sex and change in college major. *Sociology of Education, 39,* 183-199.

Balswick, J. O. (1970). The effect of spouse companionship support on employment success. *Journal of Marriage and the Family, 32,* 212-215.

Balswick, J. O. (1981). Types of inexpressive male roles. In R. A. Lewis (Ed.), *Men in difficult times* (pp. 158-165). Englewood Cliffs, NJ: Prentice-Hall.

Balswick, J. O., & Peek, C. W. (1971). The inexpressive male: Tragedy of American society. *Family Coordinator, 20,* 363-368.

Bernard, J. (1972). *The future of marriage.* New York: World.

Bernard, J. (1976). Historical and structural barriers to occupational desegregation. In M. Blaxall & M. Reagan (Eds.) *Women and the workplace: The implications of occupational segregation* (pp. 92-93). Chicago: University of Chicago Press.

Boyer, K. D. (1981). Changing male sex roles and identities. In R. A. Lewis (Ed.), *Men in difficult times* (pp. 158-165). Englewood Cliffs, NJ: Prentice Hall.

Campbell, A., Converse, P., & Rodgers, W. (1976). *The quality of American life.* New York: Russell Sage.

Caplow, T., Bahr, H. M., Chadwick, B. A., Hill, R., & Williamson, M. H. (1982). *Middletown families: Fifty years of change and continuity.* Minneapolis: University of Minnesota Press.

Carlsson, B. (1983, December). You men are victims. *Scanorama,* pp. 57-61.

David, D. & Brannon, R. (1975). *The 49% majority: Readings on the male sex role.* Reading, MA: Addison-Wesley.

De Jong-Gierveld, J. (1971). Social isolation and the image of the unmarried. *Sociologia Neerlandica, 7,* 1-14.

De Jong-Gierveld, J. (1984). *Eenzaamheid* [Loneliness]. Deventer: Van Loghum Slaterus.

Ehrenreich, B. (1983). *The hearts of men: American dreams and the flight from commitment.* Garden City, NY: Anchor/Doubleday.

Erickson, E. H. (1950). *Childhood and society.* New York: W. W. Norton.

Farriero, D. (1977). *Men's studies bibliography* (3rd ed.). Cambridge: Massachusetts Institute of Technology, Humanities Library.

Fein, R. A. (1978). Research on fathering: Social policy and an emergent perspective. *Journal of Social Issues, 34,* 122-135.

Goldberg, H. (1979). *The new male: From self-destructiveness to self-care.* New York: William Morrow.

Goode, W. J. (1982). Why men resist. In B. Thorne (Ed.), *Rethinking the family.* New York: Longman.

Gove, W. R. (1972). Sex, marital status and suicide. *Journal of Health and Social Behavior, 13* (2), 204-213.

Gove, W. R., & Hughes, M. (1980). Reexamining the ecological fallacy: A study in which aggregate data are critical in investigating the pathological effects of living alone. *Social Forces, 57,* 1157-1177.

Grady, K., Brannon, R., & Pleck, J. (1979). *The male sex role: An annotated research bibliography.* Washington, DC: Government Printing Office.

Gronseth, E. (1975, July). *Work-sharing families: Adaptations of pioneering families with husband and wife in part-time employment.* Paper presented at the meeting of the International Society for the Study of Behavioral Development, Surrey, England.

Hanson, S.M.H., & Bozett, E. W. (1985). *Dimensions of fatherhood.* Beverly Hills, CA: Sage.

Harrison, J. (1978). Warning: The male sex role may be dangerous to your health. *Journal of Social Issues, 34,* 66-86.

Hite, S. (1982, November 14). The new, sensitive male: Is he too good to be true? *Family Weekly,* pp. 4-5, 7-8.

Keith, P. M., & Brubaker, T. H. (1979). Male household roles in later life: A look at masculinity and marital relationships. *Family Coordinator, 28,* 497-502.

Lamb, M. E. (1976). The role of the father: An overview. In M. E. Lamb (Ed.), *The role of the father in child development.* New York: John Wiley.

Lamb, M. E., Pleck, J. H., & Levine, J. A. (1985). Effects of paternal involvement on fathers and mothers. In R. A. Lewis & M. B. Sussman (Eds.), *Men's changing roles in the family.* New York: Haworth.

Lein, L. (1979). Male participation in home life: Impact of social supports and breadwinner responsibility on the allocation of tasks. *Family Coordinator, 28,* 489-495.

Levine, J. A. (1976). *Who will raise the children?* New York: Lippincott.

Lewis, R. A. (1981). *Men in difficult times.* Englewood Cliffs, NJ: Prentice-Hall.

Lewis, R. A. (1985). Men's changing roles in marriage and the family. In R. A. Lewis & M. B. Sussman (Eds.), *Men's changing roles in the family.* New York: Haworth.

Lewis, R. A., & Pleck, J. H. (Eds.). (1979). Men's roles in the family [Special issue]. *Family Coordinator, 28.*

Lewis, R. A., & Sussman, M. B. (Eds.). (1985). Men's changing roles in the family [Special issue]. *Marriage and Family Review.*

Lynn, D. B. (1974). *The father: His role in child development.* Monterey, CA: Brooks/Cole.

Miller, S. (1982). *Men and friendship.* Boston: Houghton Mifflin.

Osherson, S., & Dill, D. (1983). Varying work and family choices: The impact on men's satisfaction. *Journal of Marriage and the Family, 45,* 339-346.

Owen, M. T., Chase-Lansdale, P. L., & Lamb, M. E. (1982). *Mothers' and fathers' attitudes, maternal employment, and the security of infant-parent attachment.* Unpublished manuscript.

Parke, R. D. (1981). *Fathers.* Cambridge, MA: Harvard University Press.

Parke, R. D., & O'Leary, S. E. (1976). Family interaction in the newborn period: Some findings, some observations, and some unresolved issues. In K. F. Riegel & J. A. Meachan (Eds.), *The developing individual in a changing world* (Vol. 2). Chicago: Aldine.

Pederson, F. A. (1976). Does research on children reared in father-absent families yield information on father influences? *Family Coordinator, 25,* 459-464.

Pleck, J. H. (1976). *Men's new roles in the family: Housework and childcare.* Unpublished paper, Wellesley Center for Research on Women, Wellesley, MA.

Pleck, J. H. (1977). The work-family role system. *Social Problems, 24,* 417-427.

Pleck, J. H. (1981). *The myth of masculinity.* Cambridge: MIT Press.

Pleck, J. H. (1983). Husbands' paid work and family roles: Current research issues. In H. Lopata & J. H. Pleck (Eds.), *Research in the interweave of social roles: Vol. 3. Families and jobs.* Greenwich, CT: JAI.

Pleck, J. H., & Brannon, R. (Eds.). (1978). Male roles and the male experience [Special issue]. *Journal of Social Issues, 34.*

Pleck, J. H., & Lange, L. (1978). *Men's family role: Its nature and consequences* (Working paper). Wellesley, MA: Wellesley College Center for Research on Women.

Pleck, J. H., with collaboration of Rustad, M. (1981). *Wives' employment, role demands, and adjustment: Final report.* Unpublished paper, Wellesley Center for Research on Women, Wellesley, MA.

Pleck, J. H., & Sawyer, J. (Eds.). (1974). *Men and masculinity*. Englewood Cliffs, NJ: Prentice-Hall.

Quinn, R. & Staines, G. (1978). *The 1977 Quality of Employment Survey*. Ann Arbor: University of Michigan, Institute for Social Research.

Radin, N. (1972). Father-child interaction and the intellectual functioning of four-year-old boys. *Developmental Psychology, 6*, 353-361.

Redefining the role of fathers. (1983, June 13). *New York Times*, p. B-9.

Rosenberg, M. (1957). *Occupations and values*. New York: Free Press.

Russell, G. (1982). Shared-caregiving families: An Australian study. In M. E. Lamb (Ed.), *Nontraditional families: Parenting and child development*. Hillsdale, NJ: Lawrence Erlbaum.

Russell, G. (1983). *The changing role of fathers?* St. Lucia, Queensland: University of Queensland Press.

Sawin, D. B., & Parke, R. D. (1979). Fathers' affectionate stimulation and caregiving behaviors with newborn infants. *Family Coordinator, 28*, 509-513.

Scanzoni, J. H. (1975). *Sex roles, life styles, and childbearing*. New York: Free Press.

Skovholt, T., Gormally, J., Schauble, P., & Davis, R. (Eds.). (1978). Counseling men [Special issue]. *Counseling Psychologist, 7*(4).

Smith, W. (1966). The family roles of modern man. *Illinois Teacher of Home Economics, 10*(1), 1-17.

Solomon, K., & Levy, N. B. (1982). *Men in transition: Theory and therapy*. New York: Plenum.

Walker, K., & Woods, M. (1976). *Time use: A measure of household production of family goods and services*. Washington, DC: American Home Economics Association.

Weisner, T. S. (1984). Development during middle childhood: Ecocultural niches of middle childhood. In A. Collins (Ed.), *Development during middle childhood*.

Wilson, P. J. (1980). *Man, the promising primate: The conditions of human evolution*. New Haven, CT: Yale University Press.

PART I

Men as Husbands

As the introductory chapter of this book indicates, most men who are husbands value and receive much satisfaction from their marriages. In fact, as noted, there are data that suggest two things: Married men derive more satisfaction from their marriages and families than from their work, and they are also happier than single men, married women, and single women. What then are the benefits in marriage that lead most men in the United States to choose marriage?

Although some social motivators toward marriage are covert—for example, some social expectations—most men are aware of many reasons they marry. Some of these reasons are the same as for women: companionship, emotional support, sharing, and personal security. In the first chapter of this section, Bruce Nordstrom explores many of the reasons so many men want to get married. Although he finds some differences between men who have more and less traditional attitudes (for example, more traditional men wanting to get married in general and less traditional men wanting to marry a woman for her particular qualities), his basic conclusion is that both kinds of men do like being married.

In the second chapter, Stephen Duncan looks at the other side of the same coin. Duncan reports the results of his interviewing some men between the ages of 25 and 29, men who were just beyond the median age of marriage in the United States. In both his review of the literature and his own data, Duncan discovers that one of the most basic reasons for men in this age range staying single is that they are probably just delaying marriage until they have found the "right woman." He concludes his chapter with a series of six hypotheses for future testing: alleged reasons some men delay marriage and/or may never marry.

Even though most men in our society seem to value marriage highly, numerous social critics have been quick to point out that married men seem to spend little time at home or do little work within the home. Feminists and women in general over the last decade have decried reports of earlier research that men as husbands appeared not to do their fair share of work in the home. As noted in the introduction, more American husbands are now involved in home-related work and tasks.

The most recent research reveals that household participation by husbands is nowhere greater than in marriages in which wives are also gainfully employed. The reasons for greater participation by husbands in family work, however, have not been well understood. In their study of this area some years ago, McKenry, Price, Gordon, and Rudd (Chapter 3), although finding a relatively low level of husband participation in household tasks, found that there were very different reasons perceived by the husbands and the wives for the husbands' participation in family work. Since relatively few studies have asked men themselves why they do family work, this study is an important impetus to future studies that should attempt to "get inside men's minds," in order to determine those things that motivate men toward greater household participation.

Most studies of family development have found that one of the cohorts of men that reports the greatest marital satisfaction is the cohort of retired men aged 65 years and older. This is also the cohort that reports the highest levels of household participation. Brubaker and Ade-Ridder in Chapter 4 reexamine the reasons for retired men's participation in household tasks. In their study of retired husbands, these researchers found that the men expected to share equally with their wives and did so on two household tasks—washing dishes and cleaning the house. They suggest, however, that these expectations and behaviors may change for some men over time. They call for longitudinal research that may better illuminate these changes for husbands over time.

If husbands today value marriage more highly than do wives, husbands' jealousy in part could be better understood as arising from men's greater fear of losing their most valued relationship, their marriage. On the contrary, Bram Buunk reports in Chapter 5, after reviewing the literature and doing his own research, that not only do wives seem to be more jealous than husbands, but husbands' jealousy seems to be unrelated to factors indicating instability of their marriages. Other explanations will have to be sought for husbands' jealousy.

The final chapter of this section, by Jenny De Jong-Gierveld, examines more closely the notion that marriage for men has a function of "protection," that is to say, that marriage for men "protects" them from feelings of loneliness. In summary, this researcher found that loneliness scores were lower for men and women living with partners compared to single men and women. In addition, the loneliness of males was strongly associated with the perceived quality of only one relationship, that with a mate or female partner, whereas loneliness for females was strongly associated with the subjective evaluation of the social network in general.

1

WHY MEN GET MARRIED:
MORE AND LESS TRADITIONAL
MEN COMPARED

Bruce Nordstrom

Men do not want to get married. Women do, and so they have to talk or
trick men into marriages they would otherwise not willingly enter. This
at least is a popular theme in American culture and folklore, the basic
story line of many a movie, the assumption underlying the humor of
many a joke.

But in real life men seem to *want* to get married. Though men do
marry when slightly older than women, a greater proportion of men
than women eventually marry, husbands report being more satisfied
than wives with marriage (Bernard, 1973, pp. 3-58; Whitehurst, 1977,
pp. 22-24; Dizard, 1972; Renne, 1970), husbands enjoy more health
benefits than women by being married (Gove, 1972; Gove & Tudor,
1973; Gove & Hughes, 1979), fewer men than women try to get out of
marriage by initiating divorces (Pettit & Bloom, 1984; Jaffe & Kanter,
1976), and men remarry after divorce more often and more quickly than
women. Widowers even die more quickly after the deaths of their
spouses than do widows. This is scarcely what we would expect if men
were avoiding marriage at every turn, or saw it as an institution that
relentlessly domesticates them and costs them their freedom and
happiness.

This chapter examines how men really do feel about getting and being
married. All data and quotations are from a recent study I conducted
with 71 men, some more and some less traditional in their gender
behavior and attitudes.[1] Though more and less traditional men differ in
the kinds of women they choose to marry and in some of the things they

Author's Note: *An earlier version of this paper was presented at the Midwest Sociological
Society meetings, April 1982, in St. Louis.*

want out of marriage, *both* kinds of men, on the whole, like being married. As we hear men speak about their marriages, we'll understand why.

CHOOSING MARRIAGE

A few of the men in this study feel they either were pressured into marriage or drifted into it, but most say they wanted to get married. Some recall becoming so emotionally involved with someone they married her. But even more speak of being ready to marry or wanting to marry in general, and then searching for a wife. In either case, the men felt marriage would bring them a certain happiness, and certain benefits, that they would not find without it. Ironically, it is the men who might most be expected to avoid marriage according to conventional myth— the more traditional men—who seem most to have sought it.

Some men do speak of meeting a woman they were very attracted to or fell in love with whom they eventually married.[2] A draftsman in his fifties (a "traditional" man) says, "Well, I met her, fell in love, and we just decided to get married." A law student in his twenties (traditional) says:

> I really felt an instant attraction for her and I called her up. . . . and asked her out. . . . I knew after I talked with her that I was going to marry her. I told her that after we'd gone out for about two weeks, and she thought I was coming on a little strong. As it turned out, we did get married.

An engineer in his thirties (semitraditional) describes how he happened to get married when he did this way:

> I was going to school. And Margaret—she was quite young then, she was 18 and I was 21. And we started going out, about two and a half years. And for some reason or another I wanted to marry her. I say for some reason or another because when I told my friends I was getting married, they were amazed, because they thought I would be the very last person they could think of to get married. I thought of myself that way also—I'd always told myself I didn't want to get tied down, not for a long time anyway. But I guess it was a case of someone entering your life and changing your outlook on life. . . . I had been footloose, and the impact

Margaret was making on me, I figured I must be making the right decision, for a person to have that much impact. But I'm not sure whether it was Margaret or the stage I was at in my life—I'm not a sociologist! [laughs]

The idea that some men might marry for love is not unexpected. What is much more surprising is the idea touched in the last sentence quoted above: Some men marry at "the stage I was at in my life." In fact, the single largest category of men in this study explaining how they married is the group of men who felt a need or readiness for what they felt marriage would bring them at that point in their lives, and so who were seeking to marry. They were not pursued and caught by women, nor did they even meet women who aroused such emotion they wanted to marry them to keep them in their lives. Rather, it could almost be said that they wanted what they felt marriage would bring, and *then* sought women to marry. This theme is heard particularly from the more traditional men. Listen to a middle-age business executive, for example:

Well, I had this singular goal of finishing college that precluded almost anything else. And when I could see the light at the end of the tunnel, as they say, when I got into my senior year and saw that goal had just about been achieved, why I began to realize that I was going to have to shift gears a bit here. There were some other things that I was going to have to start participating in. And that was like going out with girls, thinking about where I was going to get a job. . . . And—something about my personality, I guess—I really was very interested in getting married, as I could see my college coming to an end. So psychologically I really was ready. . . .As things worked out, it just seemed like the right thing to do, get married. . . . 'cause I'd met my wife in February of my senior year, and we were married just a little over a year later.

A young government office clerk recalls:

I wanted to get married. . . . After I got out of the military, I was searching for someone to share my life with. . . . I was making myself aware that if the right girl did happen by, I wanted to settle down.

The readiness, even the eagerness, of many men to marry—rather than waiting to marry, grudgingly, upon being pursued and "caught," is highlighted by the fact that many men recall being not only anxious to marry but *more* anxious than their intended wives. And, just as more traditional men are more likely than less traditional men to talk about having been at the stage in their lives when they were ready to get married, so also are they more likely to say they were more anxious to marry than their wives. Some say they even had to talk their wives into it.[3] A middle-aged businessman recalls who wished to marry most:

> When I first met her she had no intention of ever getting married. . . . She had plans to be the ultimate old-maid school teacher, I guess. And even when we started talking about it . . . it took her a long time, really . . . to get all those things squared away in her mind
>
> [What do you think it was about you that changed her mind?]
>
> My persistence, I imagine! [Laughs] At that time, especially. She was not a noticeably assertive person at all. . . . She preferred to have someone . . . lend a direction or stability or whatever.

A bank manager recalls how he happened to get married:

> Talked her into it, I guess. [laughter] I—when I got back from Korea . . . she was a senior in high school at that time . . . and we started going together, and we went together while she was going through three years of college. During that time I had moved away from home, and was . . . "batching." And I got tired of that. I suppose . . . if she's got any regrets it's that she didn't finish college. And at the time that didn't seem important to me. But I was probably not thinking about her at that time.

To sum up: Most of the men in this study seem to have wanted to marry. Few just drifted into it or were talked into it. Most wanted to get married even before they met the women they would marry, and many wanted to get married more than their wives did once they did meet. This is particularly true for the more traditional men.

WHY MEN CHOOSE MARRIAGE

The things men marry for, the reasons a man may actively search for a wife even to the point of talking her into marriage, are anticipated in the quotes above. Each man, of course, has some of his own personal reasons for marrying. But it is remarkable how often men mention similar and interrelated reasons for marrying. Two of the words men use most often (both more and less traditional men) are "companionship" and "security."

COMPANIONSHIP

For many men, marriage provides a companion, a friend who is conveniently built into a man's life. This involves more than just having someone to keep company with: It means there is someone there to whom emotions and troubles can be expressed[4]—and for many men, their wives are the only such persons in their lives.[5] Expressed another way, men say they can be themselves at home, with their wives. A wife listens to and accepts a man and supports him in ways he rarely finds elsewhere. He doesn't have to compete or prove his worth or justify himself as he may feel he needs to do on the "outside." It feels very nice to be loved and wanted and "propped up" when needed. A deeper sharing of lives is possible than men experience outside the marriage. A young mill worker in his thirties (traditional) tells what he likes best about marriage:

> Just plain love. Somebody to come home to, somebody who'll be there when I get home, somebody to take care of the house, somebody to respond to, someone to talk to, someone that I can show emotions to, someone that helps me, helps me up when I'm down and pulls me down when I'm too high [laughs]. . . . She knows things I try to cover up—when I'm nervous, when I'm upset, when I'm depressed.

An engineer (traditional) says:

> I think right now what I enjoy best is the fulfillment in being close to her. The closeness that we have, there'd be no way to be that close to anyone but her. And it's a total acceptance of me by her. And a concern and a care for me that even my parents—they have a love for me that's different than hers. I think it's just the total acceptance she has of me as a person. And the closeness that we have.

An administrator in state government (traditional) in his fifties says:

> The kind of home that I like is a comfortable, open, togetherness kind of place, where things are all done together and you can speak out on

whatever's on your mind and expect to get a reaction from somebody. . . .
And where you can let go with your frustrations, express your exaspera-
tions as well as your pleasures, and usually expect some response. It's kind
of a small world, where that's where you are and the others around you are
close—that's the kind of home that I like.

A young administrative assistant in politics (traditional) likes marriage
because of

the freedom it gives me to really be myself with somebody. I don't have to
hold back any part of me. There's someone I can communicate with so
deeply that I can share myself. Plus the value of having someone who
gives me affirmation and reinforcement on a regular basis. That helps me
get past those times when I just really see myself as a big shmuck, and
wonder what I'm doing in this world.

When asked what he likes best about marriage, an engineer in his thirties
(semitraditional) says:

The ability to share thinking and feeling with another person, openly and
honestly—although I am guilty of not sharing enough, because I am a
closed person. I tend to keep things inside. When I feel bad, I tend to keep
it inside me, and Cheryl has to draw it out of me. And sometimes she does
draw things out of me and that makes it more comfortable for me to talk
about it. Like many times I want to talk about something but for some
reason I just can't talk about it, but she draws it out and I end up feeling
better.

For most men, the kind of companionship, sharing, and acceptance
described above, the deep sense of a place where one can be oneself, is
mentioned more often as a source of marital satisfaction than the
romance of marriage. For many, in fact, "love" has come to mean
precisely the qualities described above rather than the overtly romantic
and emotional feelings some felt when first married but which they say
have now "cooled." And those same qualities underlie and make
understandable what men mean by the "security" their marriages
provide.

SECURITY

The sense of being accepted and emotionally supported, of being listened to and taken seriously, of being able finally to relax at the end of the day in a place that is one's own and with a person one can really trust, all provide a sense of security for many men that they do not find elsewhere. The marriage and home are described by the men themselves as a base, a refuge, and a haven from which a man can go forth into a sometimes uncertain, capricious, judgmental, or even frightening world, and to which he can return for emotional and physical repairs. It is a bulwark against being alone, against having to face life's struggles by oneself.[6] When asked what he likes best about his marriage, a retired school administrator (traditional) says:

Oh, I always enjoyed home life. The security of having a home, someone you could lean on for support. And also lend support to.

A young forester (traditional) says:

I think a home is a kind of a security and a home-base you can go out from. I don't think it ties you down at all. I don't think there's anything I'd want to do [differently] if I weren't married. In fact, I'd probably want to find someone and get married again.

A draftsman in his fifties (traditional) says:

Oh, aside from the love that goes back and forth, I suppose [I like best] having a person that you can trust completely. It doesn't matter what the problem is, what you need to talk about, you can.

In short, both more and less traditional men find that companionship and security are two of the things they like best about marriage. Perhaps this isn't surprising—everyone needs an opportunity to be accepted and emotionally supported by others, to have others to open up to, to have relationships stable and secure enough so one can drop all but the most tenacious masks, to be able to have some significant degree of control over one's life. And for both more and less traditional men, a marriage is still the package deal society offers where all those things can come together and happen in some predictable and legitimate way.[7] Some of the other things more and less traditional men like best about marriage, however, do differ, and reflect some of the differences of the men themselves, how they organize their married lives, and how they see their wives.

THE IDEA OF MARRIAGE AND FAMILY LIFE

More traditional men, for example, are much more likely than less traditional men to find living up to the very *idea* of being a "family man" part of what they like about marriage. Being a good husband and father and responsible provider is usually much of what this type of man regards as being a mature adult male. Simply having the kind of home life society still holds out as ideal is in itself a source of satisfaction; marriage is not only personally respectable, but in some sense being single is odd or deviant as well.

THE RE-CREATION AND REPAIR OF ONE'S PAST

Another thing some traditional men like about being married is that it gives them a chance to re-create the kind of family life they enjoyed while growing up, and which they feel their parents would regard with pride. Or they enjoy being able to give their children what they missed when young. Traditional men seem to do this more than less traditional men, partly because they are more often from working-class backgrounds, where a father's ability to provide a stable and secure home life was problematic. Both moral maxims and practical emphasis have led men from these families to incorporate supporting a family as a valued goal, to be struggled for and not to be taken for granted.[8]

When a working-class man has come through a particularly traumatic childhood, creating a traditional family life is sometimes almost a form of self-healing, a closure for old wounds. A young warehouseman (traditional) says:

> I like companionship, I like having children, I like being a father. And I like attempting to give my children and my family those things that were lacking in my life. And it's probably my primary goal out of marriage . . . to provide a more comfortable situation and a continual family situation.

Even if there came a time when I felt that my wife and I were growing apart, I would not abandon my primary goal of providing for my children, what I feel was not provided for me. And that's important to me. And I don't have to make a lot of money to do that.

I just think the presence, the very act of being there, is probably the one thing I missed. I would like to have had a father . . . even if he didn't make excellent money the fact that he was [if he had been] a good person and loved my mother and did his damnedest to take care of us, that's what I would like my children when they get of age to sit back and say: "Well, we didn't have all the luxuries, but we did have a family. And it was good." And that's what I want.

THE STABILIZING AND SETTLING
EFFECTS OF MARRIAGE

While "setting down" has negative connotations in popular male imagery, in fact men who have had personally chaotic or unstable lives—who feel depressed at the ephemeral relationships of partying or drinking or checkered work history that has characterized their lives as single men—seem to value marriage as something that finally helps give their lives the purpose and stability that has eluded them on their own. Marriage ties these usually traditional men down in a positive sense, as an anchor keeps a boat from drifting away or a lifeline keeps a person from sinking—rather than serving as a ball and chain.

MARITAL "SUPPORT SERVICES"

Some traditional men mention their wives' cooking, cleaning, and child rearing as one thing they like about marriage. (Less traditional men, by definition in this study, are less likely to receive such services, sharing them instead.) A young mechanic talks about what he likes best about marriage:

Well, there's the companionship. But then again, there's also someone to do the wash, and the cookin' and so on. Which is fine, you know. I'll go out and earn the money, as long as the house is taken care of, and the kids, and everything, like that . . . and I kind of like having a full-time housekeeper. I can do a lot more other things and do more work than having to worry about taking care of those things, which if I'm a bachelor

I'm going to have to take care of. But I don't like it. I like being married
and have somebody else to do it, that's just a fact. That's all there is to it.

ENJOYMENT OF HIS WIFE AS A PERSON

Less traditional men, in contrast to more traditional men, mention
two additional sources of marital satisfaction. First, some men talk
about their wives being interesting and enjoyable people to spend time
with in a way traditional men usually do not. While traditional men
speak of companionship with their wives, of confiding in them or
receiving support from them, untraditional men also speak of simply
enjoying *talking* with their wives, exchanging ideas, learning from them,
even benefiting from their greater intelligence.[9] A college professor
(semitraditional) says:

> I guess I basically like the format it [marriage] offers for talking, having
> conversations. I of course like the intimacy and the sex, but I *love* to
> talk. . . . Jeanie is a good talker. I wouldn't get along well with anyone who
> was at a loss for words, who couldn't think of things to say, or who didn't
> like to talk. I think that's basically it—I love to talk to her, and share ideas
> with her. She is one of the few people I know who understands literature
> the way I do, and who has my taste in literature.

The wives of less traditional men more often have careers or outside
interests than do the wives of traditional men, and less traditional men
seem to enjoy what that enables their wives to bring to their shared life.
Traditional men praise their wives' patience, love, support, sensitivity,
homemaking, or skill with the children—"wifely" qualities, qualities
essentially connected to wives' relationships with and service to family
members—while less traditional men also mention intelligence, achievement, independence, and curiosity—qualities that single a woman out
for a man as a particular person over and above the roles she plays
within the family itself.[10] An older lawyer (semitraditional) says that
what he likes best about being married is "I think the—something
different. Her singing, her career, her kind of woman. Her sex—that's
always fun." A middle-aged mental health administrator says:

> I love her independence and I have a tremendous respect for her as a
> professional person. I'm very proud of her and her accomplishments, so I

sort of bask in the light of her successes. We share a lot of things—we like to travel together, we like to go places—we have a tremendously good time when we go away somewhere. And it's very easy—she's a very easy person in many ways, good-natured, good sense of humor, likes to experiment and try new things, even more than I do.

OPENNESS AND FREEDOM

A second thing untraditional men like about marriage that traditional men do not mention is the openness of their marriage, the lack of rigid expectations about what the husband and wife may be and do in the relationship, and the freedom less traditional men feel this gives them to be themselves.

Also, some men mention a second kind of freedom their less traditional marriages allow, a practical freedom from the burden of being sole provider, which has allowed them to make career shifts, return to school,[11] enter politics, or follow other interests—or simply not to worry about being fired.

CHOOSING A WIFE

The different things more and less traditional men like about marriage show up again, refracted through the prism of a different set of questions, as men talk about how they chose the women they married.

TRADITIONAL MEN

One of the things that strikes a listener as traditional men talk about how and why they chose their wives is that often these men really *don't know* why they married the woman they did. Asked how he picked out his wife to marry, a retired educator says, "She was the one I preferred—can't say why." An older draftsman agrees: [laughter] "I don't know!" A middle-aged businessman says:

There was obviously a certain amount of physical attraction at the start. And as I got to know her, I guess what I found, I found to be pleasant or enjoyable or satisfying, or what, I don't know. . . . In fact we certainly had very different images or visions or whatever of what a marriage was. I don't recall too much sitting down and talking point by point to clarify or come to a meeting of minds.

Some men respond to the question by talking about the physical characteristics of their wives. A law student says, "In the beginning it was a physical thing. . . . She was, and is, a very cute woman, and I was attracted to her physically. Her personality, she always seemed happy." But usually the wife's looks seem to be the reason her husband *noticed* her, what brought them together, rather than the basic *reason* he married her.[12]

Similarly, some men, in explaining why their wives were the right women for them, say in effect only "She wasn't the *wrong* one." A man may speak more of her not being "disqualified" than being actively, personally, or uniquely *chosen*. There was nothing wrong with her on an implicit—sometimes quite vague—checklist of compatibility. When asked how he knew his wife was the right woman for him, a middle-aged bank manager says:

> I don't know. Maybe it's a woman that has a good sense of values, one that you like to be with, one that you feel comfortable talking with, comes from a nice family. And it kinda helps if your folks like her too, you know.

An older fire department officer says:

> I don't know. She just seemed to have those qualities that suited me. She was always jokin', had a fairly good time wherever we went, whatever we done. She liked sports and I liked sports. She came from a fairly good-sized family too. And they were about a medium life-style [social class?] family like our parents were. We enjoyed bein' together and doin' things together.

Some traditional men say they knew their wives were the right women for them because they seemed to want the same kinds of family and lifestyle the men did. A business executive in his forties explains how he knew his wife was the right woman for him, for example:

> Well, I was very naive. [laughs] It didn't take much to convince me. We seemed to have a real affinity for one another. We really did. She was very

oriented to succeeding—it was real important to me to have a good job, and to do well, and have a nice family—all those things that I think were really strong in the fifties. I was really into that—and the same things were appealing to her.

A middle-aged dentist says, after a long pause:

We wanted the same things, basically. We wanted to get married, have a family, and settle down into a community, and do those things that had gone on in my family life.... I wanted essentially what I'd had when I was growing up, except I wanted it on a higher socioeconomic plane. So I guess that was a primary characteristic that drew us together. She was attractive to me physically, obviously. And she was successful, as far as being sought after and so on.[13]

The kind of woman who fit into the plans of these traditional men, of course, was one who herself was (or seemed)[14] fairly traditional—a woman who accepted the man's goals as her own and didn't seek to change him, who was more interested in becoming part of his life than in having some life of her own to which he would have to adjust, and who was personally supportive and would always "be there" for him. A corporate marketing manager in his forties who plans to remarry soon says:

I've known her and dated her steadily for a year, and she, her orientation, is toward the home—she wants to have kids—and I guess I've dated enough people in the last six years so that appeals to me. And it will work very, very well. It, it's, it's what—it's one of the things interestingly enough, it's one of the things that frustrated my former wife about me, that I wanted her to stay home, at least until the kids were past a certain age.

A utility lineman in his thirties explains why he picked his wife:

She listened. That's interesting—she listened to me more than anybody else. And my views were very important to her. And I loved it, being number one in somebody's book. And I was very moody then, and she always put up with it. Come through in a pinch, she was always someone I could count on. Whether we lost a football game or things were going great, she was always there. . . . She's not a real strong feeling [person], where she'll come right out and tell me or demand what she wants. We kind of mesh together, because if she *was* that kind of a person we'd have a personality conflict. I think I would resist a demand type of thing.

Another lineman says:

Well, I knew she was a person of quality. And she showed me that she was a person that accepted me. On my terms. For who I was. And she showed love for me. And I guess I couldn't turn it down!

An administrative assistant in his thirties says:

Sarah was interested in listening to me. She was an interesting person for me to be with. There was a lot about her—she laughed when I told jokes, I always thought that was good judgment on her part. And, uh, she seemed to be a very warm person, and made me feel comfortable. She still has a very inviting smile.

A young warehouseman says:

I think mainly the way she was so damned committed to me, the way she loved me. That really showed me that wow, I've got somebody here I could trust, and depend on, and always benefit from her loving me. . . . I realized I had something very special.

How do these responses help us understand why many traditional men are unclear why they chose particular women to marry? Remember that the situation underlying their responses is the fact that basically these men *wanted* to get married and were ready to get married. They were not confirmed bachelors who were tricked or swept off their feet by women to get them to the altar. To hear them talk, most of the men were looking forward to marriage, had decided to marry, and *then* were looking for someone to marry. This "someone" had mainly to meet only some fairly general (if nevertheless important) criteria for her to be suitable to marry: She had to have a similar social, educational, and sometimes religious background; to support and love him as a person; and to accept his ideas about what their family life would be like together. Her appearance might call his attention to her, or be a bonus, but does not seem to have been decisive in his choice. Traditional men may be uncertain about why they chose their wives because in one sense,

then, *it did not matter whom these men married.* The wish to marry led
to the woman, rather than the other way around: a meeting with a
particular woman leading to marriage.

There is also a second, related sense in which who the woman was
was deemphasized as the traditional men approached marriage. Remember, these men were looking not just for companions and wives, but
also for *housewives.* And given that to traditional men being housewives
is something that all women can do as part of their role *as* married
women (in fact, being wives and mothers is what women *are* to many
traditional men, not what they do), then in the broadest sense any
woman was suitable for marriage. These men needed mainly to
eliminate those women who were obviously incompatible with their
backgrounds and needs.

There is, finally, a third sense in which traditional men could ignore a
serious consideration of the particular qualities of the women they
might marry. Since they were marrying housewives, their future
lifestyles (income, place of residence, time for vacations, even choice of
friends) would not be determined by or depend on their wives. The wife
would be added to, and adapt to, the husband's lifestyle. He simply did
not have to pay close attention to her, and had the "luxury" of ignoring
many of the personal and practical things about her (potential income,
occupation, education, competence, and intelligence) that she more
likely had to consider when choosing him. He could afford to let his
impressions and emotions, aided only by vague objective guidelines,
guide his choice in a way she could not.[15]

This interpretation—that in at least three senses it doesn't matter
whom traditional men marry—would explain why a number of these
men say they do not really know why they chose to marry their wives. In
one sense, he did not choose her, *her in particular,* and so of course he
can't recall why he married her. He chose to marry, but circumstances
and chance chose her. Her appearance may stand out in his memory
partly because it was what led him to notice her among any number of
other women he might otherwise as likely have married; noticing her
looks was as much of a choice as he made (or felt he needed to make) and
so he recalls that as salient when asked how he chose her.[16] When he
talks about their similarity in backgrounds or values or expectations
about marriage he is not talking about how he chose *her* as much as the
category of women she happened to fit.[17]

Two findings are consistent with this argument that traditional men's
choices or decisions to marry seem to take precedence over whom to
marry. First, many of the more traditional men, when asked how they
knew their wives were the right women for them, or what they liked

initially about their wives, or even what their wives are like now, *do not describe their wives as people*. A man often fails to offer any description of his wife at all—even when he talks at some length about the marriage itself—or he describes her only in terms of her relationship to him or the roles she plays. There is rarely a description of the woman herself, or her personal qualities, apart from how she fits into his life or her role as wife and mother. Wife and mother may in fact be who she is to him; he almost cannot imagine her apart from those roles, and so can describe her only in terms of them (his thinking, as well as the marriage, is organized in terms of roles rather than in terms of individuals).[18] The listener often gets little sense of who the wife *is*, only what she *does*. Nearly half of the thirty more traditional men who are married in this study give little or no description of their wives (compared to almost none of the untraditional men)—sometimes *even when asked directly*. This is consistent with the idea that for these men it has been *being* married (having a wife) that is primary, and that *whom* they married (who fills the role of wife), while important, has been secondary.

The second finding in support of the above interpretation involves an apparent paradox. It is that those men who speak of romantic love leading to their marriages, while relatively few in number, are all among the more traditional men. The paradox is that these men, who were actually seeking to marry, and who if the above argument is correct could therefore have married almost any woman, yet seem to have actually experienced their initial involvement with their wives at least partly in terms of romantic love. And this love, rather than denying the woman's particular uniqueness, instead seems to revel in it—she was the "one woman" for him. How can this apparent contradiction be explained?

An administrator in state government remembers meeting his wife this way:

> I was sitting in this restaurant. . . . and she was sitting there. I looked at her, and I said I love that gal over there. I went and asked if I could sit down, later on I did sit down, and later on we married, a year later. I immediately—it's the first time in my life I ever thought I loved somebody immediately, and she thought the same thing immediately. It was love at first sight.

A middle-aged policeman recalls:

> I met my wife one day, and in a joking way but not so joking manner, I told a guy I was working with that I was going to marry her. . . . I asked her to marry me in two weeks, married her in one year, and though there have

been rocky times, I've been very happy with the choice God granted me. . . . I was lonely. . . . I was just so lonely. . . . She was lonely too. . . . She's a very beautiful woman—she's what I'd call the classic cheerleader. The type of woman that I felt I'd never have a chance to marry.

Superficially at least, these men found their "one and only," and it aroused feelings that led to marriage. A closer look, however, indicates that in fact it is really *nothing about the women themselves* that created the feeling of romantic love in the men who saw them—often even before they'd met! The men knew nothing about these women beyond the impression their appearance made. Their idealization of the women they married was based less on an exaggeration of the women's real qualities than an ignorance of them; the ignorance, in fact, made the idealization possible.

What seems to have happened is that these men brought latent, generalized romantic feelings to the situation with them, where something objectively superficial about the situation or the woman triggered them. These feelings, rather than existing in opposition to a prior and generalized desire to marry (as it might appear, since the feelings almost seem to spring up out of nowhere, grab hold of the man, and compel marriage), were rather a part of these men's desire to marry. On the one hand, they were one expression of their readiness to marry; on the other hand, they helped them choose partners (help they needed, because they didn't really know what women they'd like to marry) and served as an indicator or validation of that choice (she must be the one for me, or I wouldn't feel this way!).

LESS TRADITIONAL MEN

Less traditional men value marriage for some of the same reasons traditional men do, but they have different reasons as well. While they also find shared values and feelings and getting along well important in choosing a wife, these men, compared to the more traditional men, more often tend to describe their wives spontaneously, and to have married them for the qualities described. This difference reflects the different ways the groups of men see marriage itself.

Less traditional men speak of marriage as the coordination and mutual accommodation of *two* lives, whereas more traditional men seem to talk of the merger of one life (hers) into another (his). A consideration of a wife's qualities matters in the first case—attention must be paid to them—both because they have to be taken into account for practical reasons (an accommodation with them will have to be reached) and because they are part of why she is chosen as a wife. In the second case, however, it is mainly the wife's ability to merge with her husband's life that is relevant and described (she wants what I want out of life, she makes a good wife and mother, she loves me and accepts me).

In short, while more and less traditional men are both looking for some of the same specific qualities in the women they marry, and while both are generally looking for women who will share the kinds of lives they want to lead, there is an important difference in emphasis. The more traditional man is looking for a *wife*, with all that implies, including both his assumption that most of the accommodating to be done will be *hers,* and the long-range effect that *the* woman herself gets somewhat "lost" in the role she plays.[19] The less traditional man, on the other hand, is looking for an interesting woman to share his life with; this includes his assumption that the husband as well as the wife may have to sacrifice and accommodate if each person is to realize the goals each has brought separately to the marriage, and the effect that the woman herself "stands out," partly because she fails to conform to a predictable role and so must constantly be taken newly into account.

A mental health administrator, for example, explains how he knew his wife was the right woman for him:

> I just felt very positive about Pat, and about our relationship, and I do now, and the things we were able to do together. That doesn't mean we always had a smooth, easy relationship, or that we do now. Pat was 30, 31, had not been married, was very into her career, was good at what she did. She was a bright, competent person, she was very independent, a fact I liked. She didn't know whether she wanted to get married or not, and we lived together for a year. . . . But it's a good relationship, and one of the really fine things is that Pat really is an independent person. Very much her own person. *I* am very independent, very much my own person. But we can come together and it's really fine.

A supervisor for a food distributing company says of his wife:

> She is a very outspoken woman. She talked to me the way I would talk to—people! She pulls no punches. That's what—the conversation that took place was enough to set you back. It really showed me a lotta class. That's the way we went. . . . I just can't tell you how impressed I am by her—she's just a fantastic person. . . . I think she is the smartest person I have ever met in my life.

A divorced college professor says:

> I'm attracted to independent women who have their own careers, their
> own work, with whom I can enjoy getting together and talking, seeing
> each other. See each other and give each other support on a pretty equal
> basis. . . . The woman I'm seeing now, we're very similar in terms of our
> intellectual interests, politics, what we read, current isues. And then we
> like the same kinds of things in terms of theater, dance. And we get
> emotional support from each other. And then there's some sexual
> attraction. . . . But we're both completely independent. It's a very exciting,
> growing relationship.

A civil rights investigator for city government says:

> What I like about her is that she's very independent—feisty is a better
> word she's used. She has her own sense of vocation that she's confident
> with, good at, and gets a lot of strokes for—so that I don't have to prop
> her up. . . . She's witty, she has a good sense of humor, she's quick, her
> mind is quick—probably ten times quicker than mine. She has a good
> depth about her—what she doesn't have, she's game, she's willing to go
> look for it.

In short, less traditional men want some different things from
marriage than traditional men, and see marriage itself differently. These
differences are reflected in the kind of women they seek to marry and
how—even whether—they speak of them.

SUMMARY

Most men want to get married. Both traditional and untraditional
men find in marriage a degree of companionship, sharing, emotional
support, and personal security they cannot find as single men. Traditional men also enjoy simply being considered "family men," the
physical care and services provided by their wives, and sometimes the
chance marriage provides to settle down or create the kind of family life
some men missed as children. Less traditional men also enjoy just being
with and talking with their wives, and the freedom from rigid
expectations a marriage without set roles provides.

Both traditional and less traditional men look forward to marriage, but traditional men especially look forward to marriage in general. A traditional man commonly decides he wants to marry and looks for a wife, a wife who will take her part in the traditional family roles traditional men wish to play. Because she will become part of his life, because she will play the conventional roles of wife and mother, and because he is marrying the roles as much as the woman, exactly who she is and what she is like are secondary to him. He sometimes cannot recall what it was about her that he liked or how he picked her; his explanations—her looks, his love—involve no real knowledge of her. It surprises him later that they are different people, that he does not know her, that he's yet to discover her.

The less traditional man, on the other hand, while also wanting to marry, wants more to marry a woman for her particular qualities. Because he is not marrying her primarily for the roles she will play, his attention is on *her*; he recalls what it was about her that he liked, he describes the kind of person she is. He hopes for a marriage based on the coordination of two lives, and values the qualities—intelligence, competence, wit, humor, feistiness, independence—that make her interesting to him and that he fears would be swallowed up if she lived for him or the roles traditional women play.

NOTES

1. The men in this study were divided into five categories from most tradtional to most untraditional, based on both (a) their attitudes about men's and women's roles, masculinity, and the women's movement, and (b) whether their behavior within the family and their choice of occupation were more or less traditional. Behavior and attitudes were usually roughly similar, but when they were "out of sync" men were nearly always more liberal in their attitudes than in their personal lifestyles.

2. Whether these men fell in love and, as a result, married, is open to question. They do describe it that way. But, as will be proposed, it appears that it is particularly the more traditional men anxious to marry who "fall in love" in the love-at-first-sight, emotionally romantic sense. Hence the idea that men otherwise reluctant to marry decide to marry solely because they fall in love, or experience an overpowering emotion, should be taken with a grain of salt—even though it may be experienced and recalled by some men in that way.

3. Twelve of the twenty more traditional men who can recall say that they were the more eager to marry, compared to only two who remember their wives being the more interested, and six who say both were about equally interested in marriage. On the other hand, seven of the fifteen less traditional men who can recall say they were the more anxious to marry, compared to four who remember their wives as more anxious and four who feel they were both equally interested in marriage.

While these figures do support the idea that traditional men were more anxious to marry more often than less traditional men, still, a plurality of the less traditional men were more anxious to marry than their wives. The comparison is complicated by the fact that less traditional men were often interested in marrying less traditional women, some of whom were wary of marriage because of feminist belief or a failed traditional marriage or both. Hence less traditional men could be less interested than traditional men in getting married per se, and yet be more anxious to marry than their wives.

4. This is not quite the same as meaning that these husbands are necessarily always open with their wives. In fact, the difference is quite important. One complaint wives in many traditional marriages have is that the men don't share *enough* of their thoughts and feelings. What the men seem to be valuing is that their wives are people with whom all is shared. Some men seem genuinely uncomfortable about sharing deeply; for others, it is a matter of control—not just self-control, but control in family life in general.

5. Most of the men in this study, including the less traditional men, find having an emotionally intimate friendship with other men problematic.

6. One important, if implicit, source of resistance to change in the traditional family arrangement, in addition to men's beliefs about proper roles or the benefits they enjoy, is that for some men home and marriage is the only place they have as a haven, their wives the only ones they can trust and who accept them. So for some traditional men, any change in the marriage seems to threaten a loss of these things, and is resisted.

7. Work, where men spend most of their time away from home, while a source of important satisfactions for many men, usually does not involve the same kind of personal relationships marriage at least promises. Work relations are often superficial at best, and competitive and hostile at worst. Nor do most men find a full degree of control over their lives possible at work.

8. This is probably one important social structural source for some working-class men's traditional attitudes about marriage. Looking for this sort of connection is more fruitful than simply attributing traditional attitudes to ignorance, lack of education, dogmatism, lack of communication skills, and so on.

9. Traditional men sometimes say their wives are kinder or better persons than they, but none in this study ever said she was more intelligent or more competent.

10. These are also, in our culture, "male" qualities and "healthy mature adult" qualities (Giele, 1972, p. 308; Neulinger, 1968; Nowacki & Poe, 1973; Williams, 1973; Broverman et al., 1970). Less traditional men share family decision making with their wives more than traditional men not only because of different ideas about family roles and power, but also because less traditional men seem to have more respect for their wives as people who are capable and deserving of sharing decisions and who would have independent points of view to contribute.

11. Wives in traditional marriages sometimes work to put their husbands through school, but usually return to the home and children once their husbands finish and find jobs. In contrast, the pattern referred to here in less traditional marriages involves the wife having a long-term career undertaken for its own sake (rather than temporarily to support the family while the husband goes to school) and that enables the husband to return to school or risk the shift to a less well-paying job in his thirties or forties.

12. This is not meant to underestimate the role of a woman's appearance in a man's response to her. There is certainly a heavy emphasis in our society on women's looks and youthful sexiness (Hendrick & Hendrick, 1983, pp. 47-53). It may be that looks are decisive for some men—or at least necessary if not sufficient for them. This would be consistent with an argument made later that for some traditional men looking for a wife almost any woman will do, so that the choice may depend on objectively superficial things such as looks or chance.

13. Compare this interesting idea of what "success" involves for a woman with what less traditional men mean by success and achievement when describing their wives elsewhere.

14. Even"traditional" women are probably not as traditional as these men believe—or perhaps even as traditional as the women themselves thought they were before actually experiencing marriage. The fact that the women were often less anxious to marry than the men is one indirect indication of this; direct evidence includes the eventual dissatisfaction some traditional women come to feel with the completely traditional family roles some men try to preserve throughout the marriage life cycle.

15. This is part of why men on the whole test or report being more romantic than women (Rubin, 1973, pp. 204-206). It's not that women don't have strong feelings, but that women react to men with practical questions as well as emotions, while men can afford to let themselves be swept off their feet by a first impression or emotional rush.

16. Clinton Jesser (personal communication) has noted that this process might be compared with the way merchandisers attempt to differentiate among basically similar products by calling attention to relatively insignificant features of those products. Most advertising campaigns are intended simply to get a product noticed, and not to assess its qualities realistically in comparison to competing brands.

17. Perhaps one should not carry this interpretation too far. The case has been overstated here to make it clearly. It is, of course, not true that these men could have literally married almost anyone. Many had gone with other women whom they did not marry. Some degree of compatibility and attraction was important. The argument here is simply that they were not as important as one might expect. The men talk about being ready to marry, of being at the stage in their lives when it seemed important to marry, or feeling a need to marry—they sound like accidents waiting to happen.

18. Of course, many traditional men see themselves in terms of the roles they play, and some "lost themselves" in their work role in the same way they let their wives get "lost" in her wife/mother role.

19. This same effect shows up in the memories traditional men have about their parents. Asked what their parents were like in another part of this study, more traditional men rarely volunteered memories about their mothers; these women often seem to get "lost" in the daily round of traditional activities in which most of the men's mothers seem to have been engaged. This "getting lost" is not just an effect of playing a stereotyped role, of course, but of the nature of that role as well—fathers are remembered even though they, too, often played a stereotyped role in the family, but that role was powerful, interesting, somewhat mysterious (where does he go?), and often frightening to the son, and stands out in his mind. The mother's role was sacrificial and supportive, but also rather uninteresting, menial, servile, weak, and boring for many sons.

REFERENCES

Bernard, J. (1973). *The future of marriage*. New York: Bantam.

Broverman, I. K. et al. (1970). Sex-role stereotypes and clinical judgments of mental health. *Journal of Consulting and Clinical Psychology, 34*, 1-7.

Dizard, J. E. (1972). The price of success. In Louise Kapp Howe (Ed.), *The future of the family* (p. 192-201). New York: Simon & Schuster.

Giele, J. (1972). *Women and the future.* New York: Free Press.

Gove, W. R. (1972). The relationship between sex roles, marital status, and mental illness. *Social Forces, 51,* 34-44.

Gove, W. R., & Hughes, M. (1979). Possible causes of the apparent sex differences in physical health: An empirical investigation. *American Sociological Review, 44,* 126-146.

Gove, W. R., & Tudor, J. (1973). Adult sex roles and mental illness. *American Journal of Sociology, 73,* 812-835.

Hendrick, C., & Hendrick, S. (1983). *Liking, loving and relating.* Monterey, CA: Brooks/Cole.

Jaffe, D. T., & Kanter, R. M. (1976). Couple strains in communal households: A four-factor model of the separation process. *Journal of Social Issues, 32,* 169-191.

Neulinger, J. (1968). Perception of the optimally integrated person: A redefinition of mental health. *Proceedings of the 76th Annual Convention of the American Psychological Association,* San Francisco.

Nowacki, M., & Poe, C. A. (1973). The concept of mental health as related to sex of person perceived. *Journal of Consulting and Clinical Psychology, 40,* 160.

Pettit, E. J., & Bloom, B. L. (1984). Whose decision was it? The effects of initiator status on adjustment to marital disruption. *Journal of Marriage and the Family, 46,* 587-595.

Renne, K. (1970). Correlates of dissatisfaction in marriage. *Journal of Marriage and the Family, 32,* 54-67.

Rubin, Z. (1973). *Liking and loving.* New York: Holt, Rinehart & Winston.

Whitehurst, C. (1977). *Women in America: The oppressed majority.* Santa Monica, CA: Goodyear.

Williams, J. H. (1973). Femininity: A deviancy model of normal personality. *Catalog of Selected Documents in Psychology, 3,* 125-126.

2

WHY SOME MEN DO NOT MARRY

Stephen F. Duncan

From a very young age, males in the United States are taught that they must accept certain responsibilities. These responsibilities include attending school to prepare for a vocation and making eventual contributions to society. As they mature into adults, young men are particularly encouraged to seek out young women and get married; they receive assurances that happiness will then follow.

This high valuation of marriage and married life is perhaps responsible for the sometimes unsympathetic and critical attitude toward single men. Traditionally, both single men and single women have been described as social "misfits" (Havens, 1973) and as being among the "undesirables" (Macklin, 1980). Because the overt responsibility of initiating a marriage still rests primarily with the man, he is often the recipient of most of the criticism when he does not marry.

While it is the opinion of some researchers that singleness may be a choice (Adams, 1976; Havens, 1973; Preston & Richards, 1975), a recent national study has shown that the vast majority of Americans wish to be married (Simenhauer & Carroll, 1982). Among these are men who desire marriage but nevertheless find themselves single well beyond the median age of 25 years (U.S. Bureau of the Census, 1981). The central question that guided this research was this: What factors keep these men from marrying earlier, or at all?

FACTORS THAT MAY DELAY OR PROHIBIT MARRIAGE

FAMILIAL FACTORS

Childhood. Single men have been found to be two to three times as likely to report they had unhappy childhoods (Spreitzer & Riley, 1974).

One dimension of unhappiness reported was poor interpersonal relationships with parents and siblings. A higher degree of childhood stress has also been found among single men (Knupfer, Clark, & Room, 1966). Stressors include parental separation or divorce and perceived unhappiness in the parents' marriage. A single man's childhood home was generally devoid of a democratic decision-making style (Spreitzer & Riley, 1974) and he was more likely to come from a home where there was an alcoholic, unfaithful parent with poor credit or parents who were poor role models (Rallings, 1966). One understanding of this is that unhappy childhoods could extend hostile attitudes toward marriage and family life into adulthood sufficiently to deter these people from matrimony (Kuhn, 1948).

Socioeconomic status. The relative socioeconomic status of a man's family of origin has been found to affect his marriage plans. One analysis of marriages taking place over a five-year period led researchers to conclude that age at marriage increases with socioeconomic status (Burchinal & Chancellor, 1963). A national study found a similar relationship (Bayer, 1969). This relationship has also been found in many countries throughout the world (Bogue, 1969).

Birth order. Birth order has been suspected by other researchers. Those who are born later into a family are more likely to marry at a later age (MacDonald, 1967; Murdoch, 1969). As men delay marriage, many may find they prefer the single lifestyle and opt to remain single (Glick, 1975).

INDIVIDUAL FACTORS

Intelligence and occupational level. Men who have higher intelligence and occupational status are the least likely to remain single (Spreitzer & Riley, 1974). Dahl (1971) found that the single men in his study reported the lowest grade point averages when compared to single women and married persons. A more recent study comparing married and single persons found that single men demonstrated lower intellectual efficiency than married men (Thiesen & Cooley, 1979).

Personality characteristics. Single men have been found to be more passive in orientation and to exhibit isolationist tendencies (Knupfer et al., 1966). They report significantly less dominance, social presence, self-acceptance, and communality than married men (Thiesen & Cooley, 1979). Some single men express less desire for companionship

(Veroff & Feld, 1970) and report more loneliness than married men (Cargan, 1981; Willoughby, 1938). However, other studies have found that single men were not more alienated than married males, but in fact demonstrated equal or greater sociability than married men (Thiesen & Cooley, 1979; Willoughby, 1938).

Knupfer et al. (1966) discovered that a significant number of single men displayed overly strong attachment to their mothers. Many years ago, Kuhn (1948) called this tendency "mother fixation." Stone (1949) likewise held that single men were incapable of forming a strong emotional attachment to a mate because they cannot "divorce" themselves emotionally from their parents. They have little desire for companionship with female agemates, sex, home, and family, and hence lack the necessary motivations for marriage. These characterisitcs have been considered to be the result of a "deep-seated neurosis." Similar opinions were once held by Landis (1955), who stated that men who voluntarily delayed marriage past age 35 were sexually deficient, deficient in emotional development, and had physical handicaps or disfigurations or severe emotional problems. This research, however, could not confirm which were causes and which were effects.

Other studies have presented a very different view. Martinson (1959) found that single men had lower ego deficiency scores than married men. The differences in scores were particularly marked in the area of emotional adjustment. Single men have also been characterized as success and achievement oriented (Kelly, 1977) and self-confident (Willoughby, 1938). They are not single because of personality disorders, but because the situation has not been "right for marriage" (Darling, 1976).

Other research has reported that single men are more vulnerable to mental impairment. One study found high percentages of single men reporting a significant degree of mental impairment, greater than single women or married persons (Strole, Langer, Michael, Opler, & Rennie, 1962). Most of the studies conducted to determine the incidence of mental illness have reported higher percentages of single men so afflicted (Gove, 1972b). Knupfer et al. (1966) noted antisocial tendencies and severe neurotic symptoms among the single men in their study. Neuroticism has been associated with difficulty in attracting a spouse (Murstein, 1967). In Murstein's study, neuroticism was operationalized as hysteria, hypochondria, depression, anxiety, ego strength, and repression. He found that if a male exhibits neurotic, maladjusted tendencies, his relationship is more likely to be terminated than if the opposite is true.

In contrast, one group of researchers administered a health opinion survey to a large group and found single and married men to exhibit very similar scores (Warheit, Holzer, Bell, & Arey, 1976). In fact, those with the best scores could be either single or married.

Based on an analysis of trends during the years 1959-1961, Gove (1972a) concluded that being male and single is more predictive of suicide. Single people also have higher mortality rates than married people; single men were more vulnerable than single women (Gove, 1973). "These differences are particularly marked among the types of mortality where psychological states would appear to affect one's life chances" (Gove, 1973, p. 65).

Perceptions. In most studies, single men report they are less happy than other groups. Gurin, Veroff, and Feld (1960) conducted a national study to determine, among other things, their respondents' levels of happiness. After finding that married people reported greater happiness than single people, they also found some notable differences between single men and single women. Single men reported less happiness and more discomfort in their adjustment to singleness than did single women. Other studies have reported similar findings (Bradburn & Caplovitz, 1965; Bradburn, 1969). However, a more recent study has reported that single men did not report less happiness than did single women, while the differences between single and married men were maintained (Thiesen & Cooley, 1979).

Other reported perceptions center on various reported inadequacies. Many years ago, Hausheer and Moseley (1931) found that men perceived economic inadequacy as a leading factor contributing to their singleness. Hinkle (1949) stated that one reason men avoid marriage is because of the increased financial burden such a commitment would entail. More recently, Jenson (1974) found that one of the major reasons given by single adults for being single was that they did not have sufficient finances. Cutright (1970) concluded from 1960 census data that as income increased, the percentage of single men aged 25 to 54 decreased. Other felt inadequacies included a lack of confidence about one's ability to find a mate (Dahl, 1971) and an inadequacy in meeting the demands that marriage brings (Koos, 1953). However, others have reported very positive outlooks on marriage (Simenauer & Carroll, 1982).

Values. Some single men report a high valuing of personal freedom. Knupfer et al. (1966) found that single men reported a higher valuation of personal freedom than did single women or married individuals. Using a marital restrictiveness scale, Veroff and Feld (1970) found that single men viewed marriage as more restrictive than did their married peers. Several years ago, Hinkle (1949) suggested that one reason men avoid marriage is the restriction of their freedom. Most of the single men and women surveyed by Kelly (1977) reported a strong need for autonomy and independence and felt hesitant about making life changes that would alter their autonomous pattern.

Findings regarding religiosity have been mixed. Some research has reported that when compared to single women and married persons, single men show less commitment to moral codes (Knupfer et al., 1966; Jenson, 1974). Other studies have found that religious involvement is related to a later age at marriage for both sexes, particularly in the more orthodox religious groups, such as Jews and Catholics (Burchinal & Chancellor, 1963; Rosenwaike, 1972).

Higher educational aspirations have been associated with later marriage plans (Bayer, 1969). Carter and Glick (1976) cite 1960 census data as support for concluding that those who remain single include high percentages of people in both the lower and upper levels of educational achievement. In another study, a frequent reason given by single adults for being single was that they were too busy acquiring an education (Jenson, 1974).

Other values relate to men's perceptions of the desirability of marriage. Some men are single simply because they lack the desire to marry (Jenson, 1974; Bernard, 1972) and see opportunities for personal growth, increased friendships, and greater independence if they remain single (Stein, 1975). Others report they were single because marriage competes with other values (Koos, 1953), while others report a simultaneous desire for both intimacy and personal freedom, creating some ambivalence toward commitment, especially when centered around marriage (Kelly, 1977).

The relaxing of sexual attitudes for young people, creating a more accepting environment for premartial sexual involvement, has also been suggested as a factor in singleness (Lasswell, 1974). Those who condone premarital sexual expression and do not see marriage as the only acceptable sex outlet may see more viable lifestyles as a single person.

INTERPERSONAL FACTORS

Uncomplementary statuses. The current changing status of women may be producing interpersonal factors contributing to male singleness. Nowadays, because of their rising occupational status and income, women can "afford" to be single (Havens, 1973); they are freed from dependence upon a husband for financial support (Preston & Richards, 1975). Such independence may deter some men from actively seeking a mate because of inability to accept these status changes or even a woman's desire to seek employment outside the home (Cherlin, 1980).

As some men may seek wives who will enhance their dominant role (Strole et al., 1962), such assertion of female independence might contribute to their remaining single.

Mate selection. Bernard (1972) has explained singleness in terms of the mate selection process. Men typically marry "down" in terms of education and occupation, thereby rejecting high-status females as marriage partners. Those who remain single are low-status men and high-status women. If, as Strole et al. (1962) suggest, men desire to dominate in marriage, it is likely that a suitable woman would be more difficult to find within their field of eligibles.

Perceptions. Some men are perceived as unmarriageable by women with whom they interact (Popenoe, 1953). According to the women in this study, the men were unmarriageable because they were seen as excessively attached to their mothers or too much in love with themselves, maintained only superficial interactions with the opposite sex, were homosexual, or could not accept a woman on an equal basis. In other studies, some men reported that they found it difficult to meet members of the opposite sex (Hausheer & Moseley, 1931) who might be suitable as mates (Koos, 1953). Interestingly, a frequent major reason given for being single was having not found the right person (Koos, 1953; Jenson, 1974; Simenauer & Carroll, 1982).

SUMMARY

In summary, the literature on singleness presents contrasting and even some conflicting findings about the reasons for singleness among men. Some studies have reported that single men are socially and psychologically deficient, relatively unhappy, have higher suicide and mortality rates, and have less intelligence, lower occupational status, less education, and lower income than their married peers. They view marriage as restrictive and burdensome and avoid intimate female associations, thereby avoiding marital commitment. In summary, they have inadaquate feelings regarding themselves, their roles, and their marriageability.

Another group of studies report that single men are equally or even better adjusted than married men. Single men demonstrate greater ego sufficiency and are more sociable than their married peers. While singleness is for some a positive choice, others still maintain a positive outlook on marriage, even though their conflicting desires for intimacy and freedom create ambivalence toward marriage commitment. They are likely to come from higher socioeconomic strata, to have high educational aspirations and attainments, and to be success and achievement oriented. In summary, they are single because they have not found "the right person," not because of personality disorders.

THE STUDY

THE PURPOSE

Most of the research conducted to explore singleness in men has used a wide age span of males who vary from psychologically more modal to less modal. It therefore has been difficult to determine which factors were related to which age groups and to which population. Current data drawn from the perspective of the single individual himself have also been missing. Working from a symbolic interactionist perspective, it was assumed for the current study that male singleness could best be understood by learning the meanings and values these men attach to certain phenomena, because these variables are probably most directly related to the behavior (Burr, Leigh, Day, & Constantine, 1979).

In this study, the researcher was specifically interested in more psychologically modal men who delay marriage and who are only a few years older than the median age of marriage. It has been noted from the literature that concerns about economic security, a lack of risk taking in more permanent intimate relationships, and a value orientation favoring aloneness and freedom are factors that might explain why more modal men remain single. This study sought to verify, from the perspective of the individuals themselves, if these indeed were factors contributing to their singleness.

METHOD

SAMPLE SELECTION PROCEDURE AND CHARACTERISTICS

A sample of 30 men aged 25 to 29 were selected for participation in the study. All potential respondents were referred by professionally oriented women associated with these men. The women were asked to make a list of all the 25- to 29-year-old single men they knew whose psychological profiles they considered to be relatively normal (modal). All respondents were active members of the Church of Jesus Christ of Latter-day Saints (Mormons) and most were attending Brigham Young University in Provo, Utah, at the time of the study (Spring 1984).

DATA COLLECTION PROCEDURE AND ANALYSIS

Because this study sought to encourage the single men to verbalize their feelings and attitudes on matters relevant to the factors of interest, an interview approach was used. Each respondent was interviewed privately by the researcher. The question that began the interview was open-ended, asking the respondent to list the three major reasons he felt he was still single. If there were more than three reasons, he was encouraged to share those also. The questions that followed were a combination of both structured and open-ended questions designed to explore the respondents' concerns about economic security, risk taking in more permanent intimate relationships, and value orientation favoring aloneness and freedom.

Answers to the structured questions were coded and tabulated to produce frequency counts for each item. Answers to the open-ended questions were analyzed by means of theme analysis. Two researchers coded the open-ended responses into specific, mutually exclusive categories.

RESULTS

The particular themes were located within four broad categories. Within the larger categories were listed the more specific theme areas. Overall, as Table 2.1 shows, the most frequently given reason for remaining single was not having found the right person. That reason was also ranked as the most important reason for singleness. In fact, most of the men reported that all other reasons for being single would not matter if they found the right person. This response was followed in both response frequency and ranked importance by financial unpreparedness and educational pursuits. Other reasons were also given, but received fewer responses.

Most respondents reported a relatively high concern about economic security and listed various criteria of vocational and economic prep-

TABLE 2.1
Major Reasons for Remaining Single

Themes	Rankings					Totals
	1	2	3	4	5	
Fear						
fear of commitment	2	0	0	0	0	2
fear of failure in marriage	0	2	1	0	0	3
miscellaneous	0	0	0	0	1	1
totals	2	2	1	0	1	6
Felt inadequacy for marriage						
financial unpreparedness	4	5	3	0	1	13
emotional unpreparedness	1	1	3	0	0	5
miscellaneous	1	2	2	0	0	5
totals	6	8	8	0	1	23
Conflicting desires						
educational pursuits	0	5	3	0	0	8
career pursuits	0	1	1	1	0	3
desire for independence	0	2	2	1	0	5
miscellaneous	0	2	3	0	0	5
totals	0	10	9	2	0	21
Situational reasons						
have not found right person	20	4	3	1	0	28
miscellaneous	2	0	1	0	0	3
totals	22	4	4	1	0	31
Miscellaneous	0	5	5	2	0	12
Totals	30	29	27	5	2	

aration as prerequisites of marriage. Thus economic concerns may have had some impact on their marital delay.

Specific questioning in the risk-taking area revealed that nearly all of the men had at one time been close to marriage commitments. However, only two men were that close to marriage at the time of the interview. Many reported that experiencing a broken relationship had contributed to the fact that they were still single. This impact varied in degree from making them more cautious in relationships to its having had a damaging effect on their self-confidence. This appeared to be evidence of risk-taking concerns.

However, when asked specifically about their readiness to risk commitment in marriage, most reported readiness and many added that risk was not a problem given "the right person." Therefore, it appeared that risk-taking concerns were reduced given the perception that they were "risking" with the right one.

Instead of desiring aloneness and freedom, most of the men reported strong desires to marry. Many indicated that this was because of the potential companionship, personal fulfillment, family life, and other things marriage can offer. Most of them, however, reported that some life change was necessary in order to make marriage possible for them. The necessary changes were seen as centering on increasing involvement with the opposite sex and the development of skills felt to be needed in marriage. This apparent lack of involvement in a process that would enhance marriage chances was seen as further evidence of risk-taking concerns.

DISCUSSION

The focus of this study assumed that a symbolic interactionist perspective was useful in understanding why men remain single. It seems appropriate to use this framework as a vehicle to give meaning to the respondents' self-reports. The key explanatory concepts drawn upon were value, risk taking, generalized other, and expectations.

CONCERNS ABOUT ECONOMIC SECURITY

Respondents reported concern about economic security and advocated economic preparation for marriage in various ways. This verifies previous research (Hausheer & Moseley, 1931; Jenson, 1974) and also enlarges upon these earlier findings. In addition to identifying economic concerns as a factor contributing to marital delay, this study has also shed light on what specific economic criteria need to be fulfilled prior to marriage commitments. The relative influence that economic concerns have on marriage plans, at least for this group, has also been suggested. Although economic concerns ranked second in importance, most men claimed that all other reasons for remaining single would not matter given the right person. This suggests that, given the concurrent situation of economic uncertainty and the opportunity to marry the right one, these men would opt for marriage, unless by chance this was reported because it was perceived as a socially desirable response.

The reporting on economic concerns may be reflective of personal values. It has been found consistently that men who delay marriage come from higher socioeconomic strata (Burchinal & Chancellor, 1963; Bogue, 1969; Bayer, 1969). Men living in such environments are likely to have acquired the value of economic security. Through interaction with significant others living within a family system that is relatively

economically sound it is likely that these men have come to place value
on the possession of some degree of economic security. As values tend to
regulate behavior according to a specific standard (Faules & Alexander,
1978), it is possible that efforts to marry may be somewhat constrained
until a personally acceptable standard of economic security is reached.
Burr et al. (1979, p. 65) have proposed that "the greater the *perceived*
value of a phenomenon, the greater the effect it tends to have in social
processes." Applying this proposition to the above discussion, it can be
stated that the greater the perceived value of the attainment of economic
security before marriage, the greater the likelihood marriage will be
delayed.

The above relationship is influenced by what appears to be a value
that attaches greater importance to getting married (to the right one)
than to the attainment of economic security prior to marriage. Such a
value ordering is consistent with values taught by the religion of these
men. That is, men of marriageable age are strongly encouraged to marry
and begin their families and not to wait until schooling is completed.
(Over 70% of this sample were college students, during which time
economic resources were probably few.) But considering the overall
self-reports of these men, it is unlikely that any would marry without at
least some ability to meet the economic demands of marriage.

Therefore, the greater the perceived value of marriage (to the right
one), the weaker the relationship between concerns about economic
security and marriage delay.

RISK TAKING IN MORE PERMANENT
INTIMATE RELATIONSHIPS

Although findings regarding risk taking may be interpreted differently, there appears to be some evidence of risk-taking concerns. It is
possible that the high reporting of readiness to risk commitment (despite
effects of breakup experiences) was influenced by generalized other
expectations. Historically, the expected behavior of males has been that
they be strong, aggressive, assertive, dominant, silent, and success
oriented (Kirshner, 1981). It is important that a man portray an air of
toughness, confidence, and self-reliance to his audience to avoid the
appearance of vulnerability (David & Brannon, 1975). A disclosure that
a man is not ready to risk commitment might be seen by others as a sign
of weakness, inconsistent with the image he is expected to present
outwardly. Such a disclosure would also likely be perceived as
inconsistent with specific religious expectations. Mormon men are

expected to be making every effort to become married, and anything less is considered to be abnormal and antigrowth. A lack of readiness may be seen as a failure to follow church directives.

The risk-taking concerns noted in this current study appear to be different from those suggested by previous research (Kelly, 1977). It was noted in the Kelly study that the conflict resulting from simultaneous desires for intimacy and freedom created ambivalence toward commitment, especially when centered on marriage. This suggested that single men sense risk in committing to more permanent relationships because of the resulting loss of personal freedom such a commitment would entail. Given that in the current study only a few men listed the desire for freedom as a reason for remaining single, other reasons for risk-taking concerns must be involved.

Following broken relationships these men were probably more reluctant to risk becoming involved in intimate relationships. Such reluctance is suggested by the apparent lack of overt activity directed toward marriage (such as increases in opposite-sex involvement and the development of skills felt to be needed in marriage). Such a lack of activity could be related to the frequent reporting of the lack of the right person as a major reason for remaining single. Thus the greater the perception of risk in intimate relationships, the greater the likelihood that overt activity directed toward marriage will be decreased.

Other data noted in this study alter the above relationship. In the open-ended question that began the interview, most men claimed that all reasons for remaining single would not matter if they found the right person. And during more specific questioning regarding risk taking, many reported that risk is not a problem given the right person. This suggests that, given some perceptive guarantee of involvement with the right person (the probable spouse), risk-taking concerns are reduced. Thus the perception of involvement with the right person weakens the relationship between the perception of risk in intimate relationships and the lack of overt activity directed toward marriage.

VALUE ORIENTATION FAVORING
ALONENESS AND FREEDOM

A strong desire to marry was reported by most respondents. In the open-ended questions few men reported items reflecting a value orientation that favored aloneness and freedom. In addition, there was a high reporting of companionship and personal fulfillment as reasons for strong marital desires. Thus some previous research (Knupfer et al., 1966; Veroff & Feld, 1970) does not seem to be supported. Instead, our current findings suggest a high valuing of marriage, a value derived from the religious and social culture within which these men were enculturated. Because of the apparent lack of overt activity directed toward marriage, one might question the actual strength of marriage desires expressed by the men. However, this lack of activity instead seems to reflect risk-taking concerns already noted. Thus the greater the perception of risk in intimate relationships, the greater the likelihood that desires to marry will not be reflected in overt activity directed toward marriage. This relationship is weakened by the perceptive guarantee of the right one.

THE MAJOR REASON

The major reason given for being single—not having found the right person—together with financial unpreparedness and educational pursuits, repeated the reasons and rank ordering given in another study of a Utah Mormon sample (Jenson, 1974) that might differ from more heterogeneous samples drawn from different geographical areas. However, not having found the right person was also listed as the major reason for remaining single in another recent national study (Simenauer & Carroll, 1982).

Ideal mate image. But what does holding such an attitude mean? That it may reflect a risk-taking concern was noted earlier. If one considers the possibility of this response reflecting something other than a risk-taking concern, then one might entertain alternative interpretations. For example, Strauss (1946) theorized that human beings develop an ideal mate image that is a "blueprint" (Adams, 1979, p. 260) of the behaviors and traits they value in members of the opposite sex. This ideal mate image becomes the mentalistic criteria by which all potential mates are judged. It is possible that when a man reports he has not found the right person, he means he has not yet found one who fits his ideal mate image. As our males were older than the median age of males at marriage, it could be that they expected more from a prospective spouse than those who marry earlier. These higher expectations may lead to greater selectivity, prolonging the mate selection process. Thus the higher the expectations of a prospective spouse, the greater the likelihood marriage will be delayed (past the median age).

Divergent expectations. Particular expectations might have more influence than others. Although data on family dynamics were not collected in this study, there is evidence that single men come from homes where the father is the dominant decision-making figure (Spreitzer & Riley, 1974). Given that the men in this study reported active involvement in a religion that emphasizes the father as the head of the home, it is possible that they expect to play the dominant role in their future families. As a result, they may seek out women who will enhance their dominant role. However, given the changing attitudes regarding women's roles (Cherlin, 1980), women in their field of eligibles may favor a more egalitarian approach. Such divergence of expectations may create unresolvable difficulties. Accepting a woman as a fully equal partner may be perceived as too difficult (Popenoe, 1955). If a single man adheres to the need to dominate in marriage, finding the "right" one may become increasingly difficult. Therefore, the greater the expectation of dominance in marriage, the greater the difficulty associated with finding the right one, and hence the likelihood of marital delay.

Religious influences. Finding the right person may have a different meaning for these men when compared with more heterogeneous groups. In this connection, the further influence of their religious heritage must be noted. Some more orthodox faiths, Mormonism included, teach that marriage is sacred and permanent and is therefore to be pursued carefully (Otto, 1979). In addition, Mormon doctrine teaches that "celestial" marriage persists beyond death. To religiously active Mormon men, therefore, finding the right one may mean the only one. This view of marriage may contribute to a more time-consuming approach to mate selection. Thus it could be stated that the perception of the right one as the only one contributes to marriage delay.

Such a statement does not explain by itself why our respondents took longer to find mates than did their younger Mormon counterparts. Wherever marriage delay is longer, there are probably higher expectations for the prospective spouse. The more expectations attached to the right (only) one likely increase the difficulty of finding that one. Therefore, the higher the expectations for a prospective spouse, the stronger the relationship between the perception of the right one as the "only" one and delay of marriage.

SUMMARY

In summary, the findings of this study suggest the following theoretical propositions:

(1) The greater the perceived value of the attainment of economic security before marriage, the greater the likelihood marriage will be delayed. This relationship is weakened by the perceived value of marriage to the right one.

(2) The greater the perception of risk in intimate relationships, the greater the likelihood that overt activity toward marriage will be decreased. This relationship is weakened by the perception of involvement with the right one (probable spouse).

(3) The greater the perception of risk in intimate relationships, the greater the likelihood that desires to marry will not be reflected in overt activity toward marriage. This relationship is weakened by the perceptive guarantee of the right one.

(4) The higher the expectations of a prospective spouse, the greater the likelihood marriage will be delayed (past the median age).

(5) The greater the expectation of dominance in marriage, the greater the difficulty associated with finding the right one, and hence the likelihood of marriage delay.

(6) The perception of the "right" one as the "only" one contributes to marriage delay. This relationship is strengthened by higher expectations for a prospective spouse.

LIMITATIONS AND RECOMMENDATIONS

The findings of this study are likely applicable only to men from a Church of Jesus Christ of Latter-day Saints (Mormon) population. Because of the small sample size, these findings may have limited generalizability.

It is recommended to future researchers that the major reason given in this study for being single (not having found the right person) could be studied more fully. Specifically, in-depth heterosexual interactional histories could be collected from single men of a given age and compared with the interactional histories of men who married at or near the same age. Special attention could be given to the role that risk-taking behavior and the ideal mate image might play in these interactional histories. The possible differences and similarities may shed light on both why some men remain single and why others marry later.

Since it is probable that having "not found the right person" may also be reported frequently in future studies, it would be useful to probe what respondents mean by that excuse. More specific individual meanings might be important in isolating factors that may contribute to why respondents have not yet been successful in finding spouses.

REFERENCES

Adams, B. A. (1979). Mate selection in the United States: A theoretical summation. In W. R. Burr, R. Hill, F. I. Nye, & I. L. Reiss (Eds.), *Contemporary theories about the family* (Vol. 2). New York: Free Press.

Adams, M. (1976). *Single blessedness: Observations on the single status in married society.* New York: Basic Books.

Bayer, A. E. (1969). Life plans and marriage age: An application of path analysis. *Journal of Marriage and the Family,* 31, 551-558.

Bernard, J. (1972). *The future of marriage.* New York: World.

Bogue, D. J. (1969). *Principles of demography.* New York: John Wiley.

Bradburn, N. M. (1969). *The structure of psychological well-being.* Chicago: Aldine.

Bradburn, N. M., & Caplovitz, D. (1965). *Reports on happiness.* Chicago: Aldine.

Burchinal, L. D., & Chancellor, L. E. (1963). Social status, religious affiliation, and ages at marriage. *Marriage and Family Living,* 25(2), 219-221.

Burr, W. R., Leigh, G. K., Day, R. D., & Constantine, J. (1979). Symbolic interaction and the family. In W. R. Burr, R. Hill, F. I. Nye, & I. L. Reiss (Eds.), *Contemporary theories about the family* (Vol. 2). New York: Free Press.

Cargan, J. (1981). Singles: An examination of the stereotypes. *Family Relations,* 30(3), 377-385.

Carter, H., & Glick, P. C. (1976). *Marriage and divorce: A social and economic study* (rev. ed.). Cambridge, MA: Harvard University Press.

Cherlin, A. (1980). Postponing marriage: The influence of young women's work expectations. *Journal of Marriage and the Family,* 42, 355-365.

Cutright, P. (1970). Income and family events: Getting married. *Journal of Marriage and the Family,* 32, 628-637.

Dahl, P. E. (1971). *Some factors which differ between married and never married males and females who attended 1969 summer school at Brigham Young University in relationship to their families of orientation.* Unpublished doctoral dissertation, Brigham Young University.

Darling, J. (1976). *An interactionist interpretation of bachelorhood and late marriage: The process of entering into, remaining in, and leaving careers of singleness.* Unpublished doctoral dissertation, University of Connecticut.

David, D., & Brannon, R. (1975). *The 49% majority: Readings on the male sex role.* Reading, MA: Addison-Wesley.

Faules, D. F., & Alexander, D. C. (1978). *Communication and social behavior: A symbolic interaction perspective.* Reading, MA: Addison-Wesley.

Glick, P. C. (1975). A demographer looks at American families. *Journal of Marriage and the Family,* 39, 493-504.

Gove, W. R. (1972a). Sex, marital status, and suicide. *Journal of Health and Social Behavior, 13*(2), 204-213.

Gove, W. R. (1972b). The relationship between sex roles, marital status, and mental illness. *Social Forces, 51*, 34-44.

Gove, W. R. (1973). Sex, marital status, and mortality. *American Journal of Sociology, 79*(1), 45-67.

Gurin, G., Veroff, J., & Feld, S. (1960). *Americans view their mental health.* New York: Basic Books.

Hausheer, H., & Moseley, J. O. (1931). A study of the unmarried. *Social Forces, 10*, 394-404.

Havens, E. M. (1973). Women, work, and wedlock: A note on female marital patterns in the United States. *American Journal of Sociology, 78,* 975-981.

Hinkle, B. M. (1949). Spinsters and bachelors. In H. Holland (Ed.), *Why are you single?* New York: Farrar, Straus & Giroux.

Jenson, G. O. (1974). *Antecedents and consequences of nonmarriage in a select Mormon population.* Unpublished doctoral dissertation, Utah State University.

Kelly, K. L. (1977). *Life styles of never married adults.* Unpublished doctoral dissertation, University of Nebraska.

Kirshner, A. M. (1981). Masculinity in American comics. In R. A. Lewis (Ed.), *Men in difficult times.* Englewood Cliffs: NJ: Prentice-Hall.

Knupfer, G., Clark, W., & Room, R. (1966). The mental health of the unmarried. *American Journal of Psychiatry, 122,* 841-851.

Koos, E. L. (1953). *Marriage.* New York: Henry Holt.

Kuhn, M. H. (1948). How mates are sorted. In H. Becker & R. Hill (Eds.), *Family, marriage, and parenthood.* Lexington, MA: D. C. Heath.

Landis, J. T. (1955). *Making the most of marriage.* New York: Appleton-Century-Crofts.

Lasswell, M. E. (1974). Is there a best age to marry? An interpretation. *Family Coordinator, 23,* 237-242.

MacDonald, A. P., Jr. (1967). Birth order effects in marriage and parenthood: Affiliation and socialization. *Journal of Marriage and the Family, 29,* 656-661.

Macklin, E. D. (1980). Nontraditional family forms: A decade of research. *Journal of Marriage and the Family, 42,* 905-922.

Martinson, F. M. (1959). Ego deficiency as a factor in marriage: A male sample. *Marriage and Family Living, 21*(1), 48-52.

Murdoch, P. H. (1969). Birth order and age at marriage. *British Journal of Social and Clinical Psychology, 8*(3), 235-245.

Murstein, B. J. (1967). The relationship of mental health to marital choice and courtship progress. *Journal of Marriage and the Family, 29,* 447-451.

Otto, L. B. (1979). Antecedents and consequences of marital timing. In W. R. Burr, R. Hill, F. I. Nye, & I. L. Reiss (Eds.), *Contemporary theories about the family* (Vol. 1). New York: Free Press.

Popenoe, P. (1953). The old bachelor. *Family Life, 15,* 1-2

Preston, S. H., & Richards, A. T. (1975). The influence of women's work opportunities on marriage rates. *Demography, 12*(2), 209-222.

Rallings, E. M. (1966). Family situations of married and never married males. *Journal of Marriage and the Family, 28,* 485-490.

Rosenwaike, I. (1972). Factors associated with religious and civil marriages. *Demography, 9*(1), 129-141.

Simenauer, J., & Carroll, D. (1982). *Singles: The new Americans.* New York: Simon & Schuster.

Spreitzer, E., & Riley, L. E. (1974). Factors associated with singlehood. *Journal of Marriage and the Family, 36*, 533-542.

Stein, P. J. (1975). Singlehood: An alternative to marriage. *Family Coordinator, 24*, 489-503.

Stone, A. (1949). Celibate facts and fancies. In H. Holland (Ed.), *Why are you single?* New York: Farrar, Straus & Giroux.

Strole, L., Langer, T., Michael, S., Opler, M., & Rennie, T. (1962). *Mental health in the metropolis: The midtown Manhattan study.* New York: McGraw-Hill.

Strauss, A. (1946). The ideal and the chosen mate. *American Journal of Sociology, 42*, 204-210.

Thiesen, N. L., & Cooley, B. B. (1979). The psychological adjustment of the single male adult compared with married males and single and married females, aged 25-34. *Journal of Psychology and Theology, 7*(3), 202-211.

U.S. Bureau of the Census (1981, March). Marital status and living arrangements. In *Current population reports* (Series P-20, No. 372). Washington, DC: Government Printing Office.

Veroff, J., & Feld, S. (1970). *Marriage and work in America.* New York: Van Nostrand-Reinhold.

Warheit, G. J., Holzer, C. E., III, Bell, R. A., & Arey, S. A. (1976). Sex, marital status, and mental health: A reappraisal. *Social Forces, 55*, 459-470.

Willoughby, R. R. (1938). The relationship to emotionality of age, sex, and conjugal condition. *American Journal of Sociology, 43*, 920-931.

3

CHARACTERISTICS OF HUSBANDS' FAMILY WORK AND WIVES' LABOR FORCE INVOLVEMENT

Patrick C. McKenry
Sharon J. Price
Philip B. Gordon
Nancy M. Rudd

The statistical history and demographics of wife's/mother's labor force participation over the last 35 years has been well documented. A 1981 Bureau of Labor Statistics study of the work experience of married women found that 56.5% of all married women had had some work experience during the previous year. Interestingly, among those who had children under 18 years of age, the work experience rate was even higher, 60.7%. And of the women who had children under the age of 6, 55.5% had held jobs (Hacker, 1983).

In regard to the increasing extent of wife/mother participation in the labor force, a rather crucial question is succinctly stated by Hofferth and Moore (1979, p. 112):

> Adding up, we estimate the weekly burden of work in the average household to be between forty and seventy hours. If household work is this time consuming, what happens when a wife goes to work outside the home?

Authors' Note: *Preparation of this manuscript was funded, in part, by the Ohio Agricultural Research and Development Center (H-644), the Ohio State University, and the College of Home Economics, the University of Georgia. This is a revision of a paper originally presented at the Groves Conference on Marriage and the Family, Ocean City, Maryland, June 1-4, 1982.*

Several studies of household work contributions by family members provide strong evidence that wives continue to contribute significantly greater amounts of labor to the maintenance of the household and family than do either their husbands or their children, regardless of the extent of their participation in the labor force (Robinson, 1977; Sanik, 1981; Walker & Woods, 1976). Berger and Wright (1978) note that for men in American society, work outside the home is primary, and all other roles are secondary, whereas for wives family obligations are primary. For women the family role is allowed to intrude into the work role; for men, the work role is allowed to intrude into the family role (Pleck, 1977). As well as being an economic provider, the most a male is commonly expected to do in the home is to assist occasionally with child rearing and light household tasks. All other family responsibilities are "naturally" assigned to the wife/mother. Thus, as Pleck notes, there is a distinct segregation of work and family responsibilities for men in our society. However, Pleck (1979), drawing from a recent study (Quinn & Staines, 1979), has noted that men are beginning to increase their proportion of household tasks, or what he terms "family work," although wives continue to hold the primary responsibility for this work. Scanzoni (1978) also has recently noted a real increase in shared functioning of household tasks; such findings are also reflected by Thornton, Alwin, and Camburn (1983) in their 18-year panel study of women and their children.

Because of the increasing numbers of women entering the labor force and the related real or implied changes in the traditional male role, students of the family and of men's roles within it are beginning to focus on men's performance of housework and child-care tasks (family work). Currently, there is much disagreement about what the data on men's family work actually show. Pleck (1979) notes that if we acknowledge the diversity in men's family experiences, a logical next step in clarifying men's household role performance is to explore what factors appear to lead to greater or lesser involvement by the male in family work. In fact, Condran and Bode (1982) state that there is no consensus on which independent variables most efficiently explain variations in division of labor within the home.

Despite a number of attempts to account for husband's degree of availability for participation in family tasks, few studies have been attempted that describe the process by which aspects of the wife's employment affect his household task performance. As wife/mother employment has become important to women for other than economic reasons, several authors have indicated a relationship between wives' involvement in their employment and several aspects of family role performance. Barnett and Baruch (1979) argue that working outside the home increases a woman's sense of well-being and her sense of being a capable adult, and that these effects may affect family behavior, especially traditional role performance. Nieva and Gutek (1981) and Sobol (1974) stress the need to describe characteristics of wives' employment systematically, as has been done for men, and then to measure the effect on marriage and family life. Sobol specifically contends that as women move into the labor force, their job commitment or involvement, and the factors that affect that involvement, influences relationships and role performance within the home. Burr (1973) uses role theory to propose that as an employed woman's role strain (defined as the inability to comply with all the expectations of two positions) increases, involvement of husbands in household tasks also increases.

REVIEW OF THE LITERATURE

Some research has been conducted on the relationship between selected aspects of wives' work involvement and various husband/father role behaviors. Research examining wives' work involvement and family role performance has focused on the relationship of such measures of work involvement as job satisfaction, reason for working, job commitment, work history, attitudes toward sex roles, and job status as they relate to such dependent measures as family power structure, marital satisfaction, and other general measures in family role performance.

Piotrkowski and Crits-Christoph (1981) stress the importance of wives' job satisfaction in explaining overall family adjustment; they found six measures of wives' job satisfaction positively related to family adjustment and overall home mood. Yet Ridley (1973), in a study of teachers and their husbands, emphasizes the need to distinguish between job satisfaction and job importance. He found that wives' job satisfaction was positively related to marital adjustment only for women highly psychologically invested in their work. Nevill and Damico (1978), looking specifically at family role performance, found that family roles were modified according to the women's perceptions of the importance of their occupations. Scanzoni (1978) speculates that the definitions of obligation and the personal or attitudinal (psychological) importance of both husband's and wife's work performance may ultimately determine the character of household maintenance.

Safilios-Rothschild (1970) was one of the first to introduce the variables of work commitment and role conflict into the analysis of the relationship between wives' employment and various aspects of family structure and dynamics. She noted that wives' work commitment, including lack of ambivalence over work role, was strongly related to differential patterns of family decision making. Sobol (1974), in her review of the literature, also acknowledges the importance of wives' job commitment in altering relationships and role performance within the home.

Three relatively recent publications indicate the importance of wives' work history in determining the impact of their employment on family. Scanzoni (1978) notes that women who have been consistently and highly involved in the labor force over time are able to consider their employment an obligation. Pleck (1977) has contended that women's increased labor force participation throughout their adult lives may well lead to adjustments in normative role functioning. And Condran and Bode (1982) conclude from their findings that as millions of wives enter and remain in the labor force, the family unit will alter its internal functions significantly.

From a more global perspective, Pleck (1977) and Scanzoni (1978) both speculate that as women's sex-role modernity increases, they are increasingly likely to involve men in routine and nonroutine household duties. Studies by Arnott (1972), Gross and Arvey (1977), Richmond (1976), and Perucci, Potter, and Rhoads (1978) validate this direct relationship between wives' sex-role orientation and family task allocation.

Finally, several studies (Bahr, 1972; Blood & Wolfe, 1960; Lupri, 1969) have noted a relationship between the status of wives' employment and increased power in the conjugal relationship, utilizing a resource or exchange perspective. More recently, Scanzoni (1978) has noted an increased rate of husband participation in family work as a result of economic resources obtained from wives' employment; from the findings of their national longitudinal study, Spitze and Waite (1978) suggest that husbands' changing attitudes toward participation in household tasks could be related to the importance of the wife's income.

PURPOSE OF STUDY

As women's labor force participation increases and their ability to carry out traditional tasks declines, researchers have become interested in factors predictive of male participation in these traditionally female tasks. A review of the literature indicates the important role of factors descriptive of wives' work involvement in explaining family role performance. This study was thus an exploratory attempt to investigate the relationship between various characteristics of wives' labor force involvement and husbands' participation in traditionally female home and family tasks, as perceived by both husbands and wives.

METHODOLOGY

DATA COLLECTION

Data were collected from 68 employed women and their husbands who resided in preselected middle-income housing areas in two large metropolitan areas—one in the Southeast (N = 31) and one in the Midwest (N = 37). Households in each of these areas were canvassed and only two-parent families with at least one adolescent child (ages 12-18) living at home were included in this study. (Families at this stage of the life cycle were chosen to ensure the opportunity for a high level of wife/mother involvement in the labor force while still having a significant number of household tasks.) The families were invited to participate in a study of everyday family life, including decision making and task performance. Each family member was given a separate questionnaire and envelope and instructed to complete the question-naire independently. Approximately 75% of all families contacted and meeting these criteria cooperated in the study. Fixed alternative questions were used to collect data relative to the following (the source of the measure is in parentheses):

(1) wife's reason for working (psychic versus economic reasons for working) (Safilios-Rothschild, 1969)

(2) wife's commitment to work (saliency of work role compared to other alternatives) (Safilios-Rothschild, 1970)

(3) wife's role conflict (discrepancy between desire to stay at home and desire to stay in the labor force) (Safilios-Rothschild, 1970)

(4) wife's job satisfaction (expression of satisfaction with various aspects of work role) (Brayfield & Rothe, 1951)

(5) wife's sex-role modernity (liberality of sex-role attitudes) (Osmond & Martin, 1975)

(6) wife's labor force history (number of married years in the labor force)
(7) family size (number of family members currently residing in the household)
(8) wife's occupation (Hollingshead & Redlich, 1958)
(9) education (number of years of formal education)
(10) full-time/part-time employment (full-time employment constituted 35 or more hours per week in the labor force)
(11) husband's participation in family work (degree of participation in traditionally female family tasks—tasks not carried out by husband, tasks shared with another family member, and tasks performed alone by husband) (Price-Bonham & Skeen, 1979)

Subjects

The subjects for this study were intact, white, middle-class (Hollingshead & Redlich, 1958) families with at least one adolescent child living at home. The couples had been married for approximately 19 years and had a mean number of 2.79 children. The mean age of the oldest child was 17.53, whereas the mean age of the youngest child was 12.27. The mean age of the women was 41.08, and the mean age of the men was 43.84.

All but one of the men were employed; all of those employed worked full time. Of the working women, 56% were employed on a full-time basis. The mean education level of the men was approximately 17 years (college completed, some postbachelor education). The mean education level of the women was approximately 15 years (3 years of college). Approximately 80% of the males were employed in white-collar occupations. Approximately 90% of the females were employed in white-collar occupations; approximately 45% of these women were employed in clerical or sales positions.[1]

RESULTS AND DISCUSSION

All possible subsets regression and Pearson product-moment correlation were used to analyze these data. All possible subsets regression performs all possible regression combinations to determine what predictors are significant in the presence of other predictors. All possible subsets regression avoids the difficulties in the interpretation of both stepwise and simultaneous regression when the possibility of multicollinearity exists (Hocking, 1976). It should be noted that in any multivariate procedure a large number of observations relative to the number of variables is critical to the stability of the coefficients and the power of the statistical tests. Because of the large number of regressions performed with all possible subsets regression, this consideration is even more important. Therefore, given the sample size and the number of variables, the results should be interpreted with some caution. The dependent variable (husbands' participation in family work) was regressed on the ten independent variables (measures of wives' work involvement as perceived by wives). Two separate regressions were run—one with wives' responses and one with husbands' responses as the dependent variables—because several studies have indicated that husbands and wives may disagree about who performs various household tasks (Larson, 1974).

Both husbands and wives perceived a rather low level of husband participation in household tasks ($\overline{X}$ = 1.49 and 1.27, respectively, on a three-point participation scale.)[2] This finding is consistent with the bulk of previous research on husbands' household work, as previously noted. Further, the husbands viewed themselves as engaging in family work to a significantly greater degree than did their wives (t = 2.09, p <.05). This finding is also consistent with other research literature (Condran & Bode, 1982); husbands tend to perceive themselves as being more dominant in family life than do their wives. Such differences in perception are thus to be expected, as Safilios-Rothschild (1969, p. 291) concludes that there may be

> two realities, the husband's subjective reality and the wife's subjective reality . . . each spouse perceives "facts" differently according to his own needs, values, attitudes, and beliefs.

These differences in perception by the spouses in this study resulted in two different concepts predictive of husbands' participation in family work. Based on wives' responses, male participation in family work was accounted for largely by the wives' socioeconomic status variables of education and occupation (Table 3.1). (Because education and occupation were highly correlated, r = .71, they did not appear together in a regression equation.) Based on the husbands' responses, wives' commitment to work, job satisfaction, and reason for working were significantly related to husbands' perceived contribution to family work (Table 3.1).

TABLE 3.1
Best Possible Regression with All Predictors[a]

	R^2
Wives' perception of husbands' participation in family work	
education (.46)	.214
occupation (.36)	.131
Husbands' perception of husbands' participation in family work	
commitment to work (.38)	.144
job satisfaction (.29)	.084
reason for working (.29)	.082
reason for working (.29), commitment to work (.38)	.301
reason for working (.29), commitment to work (.38),	
job satisfaction (.29)	.363

a. Significant at $p = .05$, univariate r in parentheses.

The findings with respect to wives suggest that women with higher levels of education or higher-status occupations have more egalitarian values and attribute a greater level of participation in household work to their husbands in order to make "reality" consistent with their values. Indeed, sex-role modernity was significantly ($p < .05$) related to both education ($r = .35$) and occupation ($r = .26$). In contrast, husbands attributed more participation in household work to themselves if their wives enjoyed working and were working for economic reasons. Perhaps these conditions instilled a greater sense of obligation in these husbands.

While these disparate husband-wife perceptions of husband household task performance as a result of wives' work involvement may seem irreconcilable, it should be observed that from the wives' perspective both education and occupation were significantly correlated with both job commitment ($r = .35$, $r = .22$) and sex-role modernity ($r = .35$, $r = .26$). Thus the strong association between the status variables of education and occupation might have masked the effects of psychological predictors of wives' labor force involvement on husband participation in household tasks.

CONCLUSIONS

Some recent research has indicated greater participation of men in household tasks in response to increased female participation in the labor force. Factors related to male household task performance have not been identified clearly. It was the purpose of this exploratory study specifically to assess the relationship between wives' work involvement and perceptions of husbands' household task performance or what is currently termed "family work." The findings provide some support for this relationship from both husbands' and wives' perspectives. Wives perceived husbands' participation in family work as a function of resources that increased their status, whereas husbands perceived their contribution more as a response to the psychological commitment of their wives to employment undertaken primarily out of economic need.

Perhaps of more importance is the very difference in perception of factors related to husbands' family work. The findings of the study, although tentative in nature, thus accentuate the need for dual-spousal perspectives in any investigation of family task performance. Larson (1974) contends that perceptual differences in decision making and task performance reflect varying attempts to articulate the spousal relationship around sex-role expectations, in other words, attempts at an optimum congruity between individual sex-role orientations and the sex-role demands of one's spouse. In this regard, the findings of this study suggest that wives perhaps are more likely to perceive (either rightly or wrongly) male nontraditional role performance when the status or resources of their education and occupation are greater. Husbands, on the other hand, perceive these nontraditional role behaviors as most acceptable when touched by some sense of guilt or obligation. Responses from one spouse surely fail to account adequately for the complexity of family role perception and performance. Instead of dismissing or ignoring such differences, as has so often been the case, researchers and practitioners alike should begin to deal with them. For example, marital adjustment theory and research have long emphasized the importance of understanding techniques married couples use in removing or coping with differences, and family therapy is based on the differing views and responses of family members (Larson, 1974).

Further research in this area is needed to clarify the actual extent of male involvement in family work and to identify other factors related to male participation. Time management studies in which diaries are carefully maintained on actual household participation would clarify inconsistencies in husband-wife perceptions. Also, data on the husband-wife decision-making process would further delineate the differential impact of wives' work involvement on husbands' and wives' perception of family work roles. Finally, further research might profitably identify those areas of family work most and least affected by wives' labor force involvement.

NOTES

1. No statistical differences were found between the two regional samples as a function of these demographic variables or sex-role modernity.

2. On this scale, 3 = husband performs task alone; 2 = husband shares task performance with another family member; and 1 = another family member performs task.

REFERENCES

Arnott, C. C. (1972). Husbands' attitudes and wives' commitment to employment. *Journal of Marriage and the Family, 34,* 673.

Bahr, S. J. (1972). *A methodological study of conjugal power: A replication and extension of Blood and Wolfe.* Unpublished doctoral dissertation, Washington State University.

Barnett, R. C., & Baruch, G. (1979). Career competence and well-being of adult women. In B. Gutek (Ed.), *New directions for education, work and careers: Enhancing women's career development.* San Francisco: Jossey-Bass.

Berger, M., & Wright, L. (1978). Divided allegiance: Men, work and family life. *Counseling Psychologist, 4,* 50-53.

Blood, R. O., & Wolfe, D. M. (1960). *Husbands and wives.* New York: Free Press.

Brayfield, A. H., & Rothe, H. F. (1951). An index of job satisfaction. *Journal of Applied Psychology, 35,* 307-311.

Burr, W. R. (1973). *Theory construction and the sociology of the family.* New York: John Wiley.

Condran, J. G., & Bode, J. G. (1982). Rashomon, working wives, and family division of labor: Middletown, 1980. *Journal of Marriage and the Family, 44,* 421-426.

Gross, R. H., & Arvey, R. D. (1977). Marital satisfaction, job satisfaction, and task distribution in the homemaker job. *Journal of Vocational Behavior, 11,* 1-13.

Hacker, A. (1983). *U/S: A statistical portrait of the American people.* New York: Viking.

Hocking, R. R. (1976). The analysis and selection of variables in linear regression. *Biometrics, 32,* 1-49.

Hofferth, S. L., & Moore, K. A. (1979). Women's employment and marriage. In R. Smith (Ed.), *The subtle revolution: Women at work.* Washington, DC: Urban Institute.

Hollingshead, A. B., & Redlich, F. C. (1958) *Social class and mental illness.* New York: John Wiley.

Larson, L. E. (1974). System and subsystem perception of family roles. *Journal of Marriage and the Family, 36,* 128-138.

Lupri, E. (1969). Contemporary authority patterns in the West German family: A study in cross-national validation. *Journal of Marriage and the Family, 31,* 134-144.

Nevill, D. D., & Damico, S. (1978). The influence of occupational status on role conflict in women. *Journal of Employment Counseling, 15,* 55-61.

Nieva, V. F., & Gutek, B. A. (1981). *Women and work: A psychological perspective.* New York: Praeger.

Osmond, M. W., & Martin, P. Y. (1975). Sex and sexism: A comparison of male and female sex-role attitudes. *Journal of Marriage and the Family, 37,* 744-757.

Perrucci, C. C., Potter, H. R., & Rhoads, D. L. (1978). Determinants of male family role performance. *Psychology of Women Quarterly, 3*, 53-66.

Pleck, J. H. (1977). The work-family role system. *Social Problems, 24*, 417-427.

Pleck, J. H. (1979). Men's family work: Three perspectives and some new data. *Family Coordinator, 28*, 481-488.

Price-Bonham, S., & Skeen, P. (1979). A comparison of black and white fathers with implications for parent education. *Family Coordinator, 28*, 53-59.

Piotrkowski, C. S., & Crits-Christoph, P. (1981). Women's jobs and family adjustment. *Journal of Family Issues, 2*, 126-147.

Quinn, R. P., & Staines, G. L. (1979). *The 1977 quality employment survey.* Ann Arbor: University of Michigan, Institute for Social Research.

Richmond, M. L. (1976). Beyond resource theory: Another look at factors enabling women to affect family interaction. *Journal of Marriage and the Family, 38*, 257-266.

Ridley, C. A. (1973). Exploring the impact of work satisfaction and involvement on marital interaction when both partners are employed. *Journal of Marriage and the Family, 36*, 229-237.

Robinson, J. P. (1977). *How Americans use time: A social psychological analysis of everyday behavior.* New York: Praeger.

Safilios-Rothschild, C. (1969). Family sociology or wives' family sociology: A cross-cultural examination of decision making. *Journal of Marriage and the Family, 31*, 290-301.

Safilios-Rothschild, C. (1970). The influence of the wife's degree of work commitment upon some aspects of family organization and dynamics. *Journal of Marriage and the Family, 32*, 681-691.

Sanik, M. M. (1981). Division of household work: A decade comparison, 1967-1977. *Home Economics Research Journal, 10*, 175-180.

Scanzoni, J. (1978). Sex roles, women's work, and marital conflict: A study of family change. Lexington, MA: D. C. Heath.

Sobol, M. G. (1974). Commitment to work. In L. W. Hoffman & F. I. Nye (Eds.), *Working mothers.* San Francisco: Jossey-Bass.

Spitze, G. D., & Waite, L. J. (1978). Wives' employment: The role of husbands' perceived attitudes. *Journal of Marriage and the Family, 43*, 117-124.

Thornton, A., Alwin, D. F., & Camburn, D. (1983). Causes and consequences of sex-role attitudes and attitude change. *American Sociological Review, 48*, 211-227.

Walker, K. & Woods, M. (1976). *Time use: A measure of household production of family goods and services.* Washington, DC: American Home Economics Association.

4

HUSBANDS' RESPONSIBILITY FOR HOUSEHOLD TASKS IN OLDER MARRIAGES: DOES LIVING SITUATION MAKE A DIFFERENCE?

Timothy H. Brubaker
Linda Ade-Ridder

Husband's participation in household tasks has been the focus of a number of studies within the sex-role literature (Burke & Weir, 1976; Beckman & Houser, 1979; Model, 1981; Yogev, 1981). Generally, it is found that husbands, even husbands in dual-earner households, do not have major responsibility for household tasks. Many wives do not want their husbands to have primary responsibility for household activities. For example, one study indicated that faculty women at a major university did not want their husbands to share household tasks equally (Yogev, 1981). Another recent study of 145 dual-earner women suggested that a traditional division of household labor characterized their marriages (Brubaker & Hennon, 1982).

Attention has been directed toward elderly couples in assessing husbands' participation in household tasks (Keating & Cole, 1980; Brubaker & Hennon, 1982; Keith & Brubaker, 1979; Szinovacz, 1980; Ballweg, 1967). In general, these studies suggested that husbands' participation in household tasks may increase in later life, but the increase is in traditionally masculine activities (taking out trash, car maintenance). Most of these studies have been based on the perceptions of wives and their expectations of husbands. Few have focused on the husband's perceptions of his own responsibility for household tasks. Although it has been estimated that individuals spend at least a quarter of their adult lives in retirement (Torrey, 1982), no analysis has examined the older husband's participation in household tasks when the couple resides in a retirement setting.

This study examines the division of household responsibility of elderly husbands living in a retirement community and in the community at large. The following questions are addressed:

(1) How do older husbands expect to divide the responsibility for household tasks within their marriages?

(2) How do older husbands actually divide the responsibility for household tasks within their marriages?

(3) Do older husbands' expectations and actual division of responsibility for household tasks differ if the couple resides in a retirement community or in the community at large?

Thus this chapter provides an analysis of older husbands' participation in household tasks within marriage.

REVIEW OF THE LITERATURE

Theoretically, it has been argued that a sex-role crossover occurs in later life—that is, men tend to become more feminine in their behavior and women become more masculine. For example, Gutmann (1977, 1975) suggests that men "recapture femininity" that is repressed by the emphasis on instrumental accomplishments in earlier life. Women become more aggressive and independent. Brim (1976) posited that there is a developmental change in later life in which the masculine and feminine definitions are altered. The changes entail the reversal or equalization of sex-role traits so that there is a "normal unisex of later life." Indeed, Minnigrode and Lee (1978) and Cameron (1968, 1976) found that the differences in feminine and masculine definitions of sex roles were less pronounced in older men and women. In fact, Cameron views older men and women as almost neuter in their sex-role orientations. Therefore, if there is any relationship between definitions of femininity and masculinity and couples' involvement in household tasks, older husbands should be less gender specific in their household task participation. Further, the theoretical interpretations suggest that older husbands will be involved in household tasks traditionally assigned to their wives. However, two studies (Puglisi, 1983; Puglisi & Jackson, 1980-1981) suggest that male and female sex roles are differentiated in later life. Thus older men are masculine oriented and do not become neutral or feminine. In any case, there are no conclusive findings or interpretations about the sex-role orientation of older men in later life.

The involvement of older husbands in gender-specific household activities has been discussed in gerontological literature. For example, Sinnott (1977) studied older men and suggested that they become less gender specific and more androgynous than younger men. It has been speculated that older men become more feminine in their sex-role behavior. Others (Donelson, 1977) argue that the decrease in gender-specific behavior positively contributes to the well-being and adaptation of older men. However, there are few empirical data on this topic. Two studies conducted in the 1960s provide some support. Kerckhoff (1966) and Clark and Anderson (1967) found that sharing of household activities was associated with higher morale in older couples. More recently, Keith et al. (1981) examined data from a sample of 1193 men aged 60 years or more. The men represented farmers, blue-collar workers, small businessmen, and salaried and self-employed professionals. Most were employed full time or part time, and 272 were retired. Keith et al. found that involvement in feminine household tasks had little impact on self-esteem.

In another analysis of the same data set, Keith, Powers, and Goudy (1981) found that retired men participated in feminine and masculine household activities more than did older employed men. For these men, involvement in household activities was positively related to well-being. Husbands whose wives were employed engaged in more household tasks than men whose wives did not work. Most of the household involvement by older husbands, regardless of employment status, was in masculine household tasks. When the husbands were involved in feminine household tasks there was a positive relationship with well-being. These studies suggest that older husbands are involved in household activities and that most of the participation is centered on masculine tasks.

Dobson (1983) examined the role expectations and assignment of household tasks of 441 middle-aged and older men and women. She found that role expectations were less gender specific in the older group. Often, assignment of household tasks followed the pattern established during the couples' middle years. That is, husbands who shared household tasks in the middle years continued to share in later years. Husbands who participated in gender-specific tasks appeared to be less gender specific in the later years.

Three other studies provide some conflicting data concerning the involvement of older husbands in household tasks. Brubaker and Hennon (1982) examined data from a sample of 207 wives in dual-earner and dual-retired households. The findings suggest that older husbands do not have responsibility for many household tasks. Further, there is not a great deal of sharing of responsibility. Another finding was that wives in dual-retired households expected their husbands to share more responsibility than they currently were sharing. The dual-earner household wives expected more sharing in retirement, but there was very little sharing of responsibility in their current situation. Thus there is a difference between expectations and the actual patterns of the division of household responsibility in dual-earner and dual-retired marriages.

Keating and Cole (1980) report on the impact of husband's retirement on the role of the housewife. Their sample included 400 retired teachers and their wives. The husbands did not increase their involvement in the feminine household tasks. In fact, it was found that "most couples seemed relatively satisfied to continue their pre-retirement involvement in household chores" (Keating & Cole, 1980, p. 86). However, the wives' workload increased somewhat because they organized their household activities around their husbands. Both the retired husbands and their wives were satisfied with the division of household tasks within their marriages.

Another study focused on the impact of the wife's retirement on marital and household tasks. Szinovacz's (1980) findings supported a continuation of the preretirement divisions of household tasks. Most of the wives stated that there was very little change in their husbands' involvement in household tasks after the wife's retirement. The primary division of tasks was traditional. In the few couples in which the men were involved in feminine household tasks, the wife was not able to participate as a result of illness.

In summary, the studies on older husbands' involvement in household activities are inconclusive and no analysis has compared the different living situations of the older couples. It appears that retirement may not be related to a husband's increased involvement in feminine household tasks, but if he does become involved in these activities his well-being may increase, as the Keith, Dobson, Goudy, and Powers (1981) and Keith, Powers, and Goudy (1981) findings suggest. Given that many retirement communities provide services to perform many of the household tasks typically completed by the husband, does the husband become more involved in feminine household tasks? Do older husbands living in the community become more involved in household tasks? Couples living in independent housing within retirement communities may share more responsibility for household tasks than couples living in the community at large.

SAMPLE

The sample consists of 79 husbands who reside in independent living within a retirement community and 165 husbands who live in the community at large. To obtain the retirement community sample, questionnaires were mailed to all intact married couples residing in a

TABLE 4.1

Selected Characteristics of Husbands Living in a
Retirement Community and Community at Large

	Retirement Community			Community at Large			
	$\overline{X}$	N	SD	$\overline{X}$	N	SD	t Value
Age	75.7	72	6.3	72.4	154	4.7	4.38*
Length of marriage	41.0	72	17.7	43.8	150	10.7	−1.44
Net family income	4.8	68	2.4	5.1	150	2.2	−1.02
Frequency of seeing children	3.5	67	1.0	3.1	149	1.0	2.29**
Health restrictions	2.6	73	.91	2.4	156	.91	1.60
Marital quality	122.0	45	13.8	121.0	110	15.9	.37

*Significant at the .02 level.
**Significant at the .001 level.

large, not-for-profit retirement community. At least one spouse in each couple was over 65 years of age. The community at large sample was derived from the waiting list of the retirement community. The same criteria were used to determine the community sample (N = 165). Table 4.1 presents selected characteristics of the husbands living in the retirement community and those living in the community at large.

MEASURES

Husbands were asked to indicate their ages and the number of years they had been married. They were asked to indicate their family incomes for 1981, using 10 response categories with $4,000 intervals, from less than $4,999 to $45,000 and over (for example, $4,000-$9,999; $10,000-$14,999). The average 1981 family income category for the retirement community men was $15,000-$19,999, and the average for the community at large husbands was the $20,000-$24,999 category. The men were asked how often they saw their children. The response categories included once a day or more, one to six times per week, one to three times per month, and less than once a month. On the average, both groups of men reported seeing their children one to three times a month. However, there is a significant difference between the portion of retirement community men and community at large men who saw their children one to three times a month. A larger group of husbands living in the retirement community saw their children this often. Incidentally, approximately 16% of the retirement community men had no living children, and nearly 7% of the community at large men were childless. In order to determine the men's health conditions we asked them whether their health restricted daily activities. The response categories were never, not usually, occasionally, and most of the time. Husbands living in both the retirement community and the community at large stated that their health usually did not restrict their daily activities.

Marital quality was measured by Spanier's (1976) Dyadic Adjustment scale, which includes 32 items. The only modification to this scale was to change the item "ways of dealing with parents or in-laws" to "ways of dealing with children" so that it was applicable to an older sample. The theoretical range for the marital quality scale is 0 to 15, and the actual range for these husbands was 101 to 131. The mean scores for marital quality were 121.0 for the retirement husbands and 122.0 for the community at large husbands (see Table 4.1). There was no difference between the two groups. Both appear to be relatively satisfied with their marriages.

Responsibility for household tasks was measured by asking who *should* assume major responsibility and who *has* major responsibility for twelve household tasks. The tasks included cooking meals, washing dishes, doing yard work, washing clothes, maintaining the car, writing letters, scheduling family events, getting or earning money, cleaning house, shopping, doing household repairs, and making family decisions. This measure is a modified version of an index of household responsibility used in a number of other studies (Brubaker & Hennon, 1982; Keith & Brubaker, 1977, 1980). Respondents were asked to indicate whether the husband, wife, or both should or does have responsibility for each task. Responses were coded 1 if a respondent indicated a traditional assignment of responsibility, 2 if responsibility is shared, and 3 if the assignment of responsibility is opposite to traditional expectations. For both the expected and current segments of the Division of Responsibility for Household Tasks Index the theoretical range is 12-36.

RESULTS

EXPECTED DIVISION

The expected division of responsibility for household tasks for husbands living in the retirement community and community at large is presented in Table 4.2. A majority of retirement community husbands expected their wives to be responsible for cooking meals and washing clothes. Yard work, car maintenance, earning money, and repairing the house are assigned to husbands. Husbands expect responsibility to be shared equally for washing dishes, writing letters, scheduling family social events, cleaning house, shopping, and making family decisions. Although there are similarities in the expectations of husbands living in the community at large, fewer husbands assign equal responsibility to washing dishes and writing letters. They expect their wives to be responsible for these activities.

CURRENT DIVISION

The current divisions of responsibility for household tasks are presented in Table 4.3. The current division is similar to the expected division. The retirement community husbands stated that their wives have primary responsibility for cooking meals and washing clothes. Husbands were responsible for yard work, car maintenance, earning money, and repairing the house. They shared responsibility for washing dishes, scheduling family social events, cleaning house, shopping, and making family decisions.

It is interesting to note that more than 80% of the retirement husbands expected to be responsible for earning money for the couple, although only 67% stated that they actually were responsible for this task. Some 30% share the breadwinning task with their wives. For the community at large men, 17% expect to share this task, but 25% actually do share it. Apparently there is more sharing of the breadwinner task than these husbands expect.

COMPARISON OF EXPECTED AND CURRENT DIVISIONS

Table 4.4 presents the comparisons of the expected and current divisions of responsibility by residential location. The mean scores for expected responsibility are 17.6 for the retirement community men and 16.8 for the community at large group. There is no significant difference between the scores of the expectations of the retirement community and community at large husbands. However, there is a difference between the retirement and community at large husbands on the current division of household tasks. The means for the current divisions of responsibility

TABLE 4.2
t-Tests of Responsibility for Household Tasks of Husbands
Living in a Retirement Community and Community at Large

	Retirement			Community at Large			
	$\overline{X}$	N	SD	$\overline{X}$	N	SD	t Value
Expected responsibility	17.6	68	2.1	16.8	150	2.1	2.57
Actual responsibility	17.9	59	2.2	16.4	148	2.1	4.38*

*Significant at the .001 level.

were 17.9 for the retirement and 16.4 for the community husbands. Retirement community husbands have a greater tendency to share activities with their wives, or to perform tasks usually assigned to their wives, than community at large husbands.

As might be expected, there is a significant relationship between the expected and current divisions of responsibility for household tasks. The correlation between expected and current divisions for the retirement husbands is .47, and the community husbands' correlation is .75. This indicates that retirement community and community at large men reported current divisions of responsibility that were similar to the divisions they expected. These older husbands actually had responsibility for many household tasks for which they believed they should have responsibility. Their wives also did the tasks for which they (the wives) had responsibility, and the couples shared responsibility when they expected to do so.

RELATIONSHIP WITH OTHER VARIABLES

Because research on the division of household labor suggests that other variables may be associated with expected and current divisions of responsibility, the expected and current divisions were correlated with age, number of years married, level of education, health restrictions, frequency of visits with children, and marital quality. There were no significant relationships between these variables and expected or current divisions of responsibility for the retirement community or community at large husbands. While there may be other variables related to the ways in which these older husbands divide household tasks, none of the variables examined in this study appears to be significantly related.

TABLE 4.3

Percentages of Current Division of Responsibility
for Household Tasks by Husbands Living in a
Retirement Community and Community at Large

	Retirement Community (N = 79)			Community at Large (N = 165)		
Tasks	Husband	Wife	Equal	Husband	Wife	Equal
Cooking meals	5	88	7	–	94	6
Washing dishes	8	38	54	7	58	35
Yard work	72	1	27	82	2	16
Washing clothes	3	83	14	2	90	8
Car maintenance	99	–	1	98	–	2
Writing letters	12	45	43	4	58	38
Family social events	2	27	71	1	32	67
Earning money	67	3	30	74	1	25
Cleaning house	1	46	53	1	58	41
Shopping	11	22	67	5	43	52
House repairs	92	1	7	94	1	5
Family decisions	1	6	92	2	1	97

DISCUSSION AND CONCLUSION

The findings of this study may be summarized as follows: (1) Older husbands living in a retirement community and the community at large expect their wives to be responsible for many of the activities that are generally associated with the wife. (2) Older husbands in a retirement community and in the community at large expect to share two activities equally—washing dishes and cleaning house—which are generally assigned to the wife. (3) For both groups of husbands, the current divisions of household responsibility reflect patterns similar to what they expected. (4) Comparison of the retirement community and community at large husbands indicates that there is no difference between their expectations of responsibility for household tasks. (5) There is a significant difference between the actual divisions of household responsibility. The retirement community men tend to share tasks with their wives, or perform tasks usually assigned to their wives, more than do community at large husbands. (6) Age, number of years married, education, health, contact with children, and marital quality are not related to the divisions of household responsibility.

Two of the questions presented at the beginning of this chapter related to the ways in which older husbands expect and actually divide

TABLE 4.4

Percentages of Expected Division of Responsibility
for Household Tasks by Husbands Living in a
Retirement Community and Community at Large

Tasks	Retirement Community (N = 79)			Community at Large (N = 165)		
	Husband	Wife	Equal	Husband	Wife	Equal
Cooking meals	–	84	16	1	90	9
Washing dishes	3	36	61	3	48	49
Yard work	78	–	23	85	1	14
Washing clothes	3	75	22	1	85	14
Car maintenance	95	1	4	99	–	1
Writing letters	6	32	62	1	62	37
Family social events	–	26	74	–	24	76
Earning money	81	–	19	83	–	17
Cleaning house	–	45	55	2	51	47
Shopping	6	19	75	3	39	58
House repairs	91	–	9	92	1	7
Family decisions	1	–	99	1	–	99

the responsibility for household tasks. Generally, it appears that these husbands tend to follow traditional divisions of responsibility. Husbands are responsible for tasks generally assigned to men and wives are responsible for tasks generally assigned to women. However, there is some sharing of responsibility in the areas of washing the dishes and cleaning the house. Further, these men are doing what they expect to be doing. Unlike the findings in the Brubaker and Hennon (1982) study, in which wives expected more sharing than actually occurred, these husbands reported that they did much of what they expected to do. It may be that the difference is the person being studied. Maybe wives expect more sharing than husbands, and therefore husbands' actual divisions of responsibility tend to correspond to their expectations.

The third question addressed in this study related to the issue of residence. Are there differences between retirement community and community at large husbands? These data suggested that there is little difference between the expected divisions of responsibility of older husbands by residential location. However, the retirement community husbands tend to share more than the community at large husbands. Services provided by the retirement community may have freed the husbands from traditionally masculine responsibilities, and they may have become more involved in sharing or performing traditionally feminine tasks. Although these data are not longitudinal, it would be interesting to know if the community at large husbands will begin sharing activities when they move into the retirement community.

There are a number of issues that are not addressed by these data. An important one relates to the continuity of the divisions of household tasks. Several studies (Dobson, 1983; Brubaker & Hennon, 1982; Szinovacz, 1980) suggest that older wives continue patterns of household responsibilities into later life. Do older husbands continue the patterns they established earlier in their marriages? These data indicate that there may be some differences between retirement community men and community at large husbands in who actually does certain tasks. Did the move to the retirement community encourage different patterns or, for some unknown reason, did the retirees share more responsibility through their marriages? To answer these questions, longitudinal data are needed and an analysis of the impact of living in a retirement community would need to be made.

Another issue to be addressed is the lack of relationships among education, health, and the other variables examined. Usually, more educated persons share more responsibility. Since there was little difference in the education levels of these husbands, this variable will need to be examined with another sample. Similarly, the health conditions were not very restrictive in this sample and the sharing of tasks could not be examined from the perspective of health. Do older husbands do more tasks or share more responsibility as their health or their spouses' health becomes more restrictive? One hopes that future studies will address health and the divisions of household responsibility.

REFERENCES

Ballweg, J. A. (1967). Resolution of conjugal role adjustment after retirement. *Journal of Marriage and the Family, 29,* 277-281.

Beckman, L. J., & Houser, B. B. (1979). The more you have, the more you do: The relationship between wife's employment, sex role attitudes, and household behavior. *Psychology of Women Quarterly, 4,* 160-174.

Brim, O. G., Jr. (1976). Theories of the male midlife crisis. *Counseling Psychologist, 6,* 2-9.

Brubaker, T. H., & Hennon, C. B. (1982). Responsibility for household tasks: Comparing dual earner and dual retired marriages. In M. Szinovacz (Ed.), *Women's retirement: Policy implications of recent research* (pp. 205-219). Beverly Hills, CA: Sage.

Burke, R., & Weir, T. (1976). Relationship of wives' employment status to husband, wife, and pair satisfaction and performance. *Journal of Marriage and the Family, 38,* 279-287.

Cameron, P. (1968). Masculinity/ femininity of the aged. *Journal of Gerontology, 23,* 63-65.

Cameron, P. (1976). Masculinity/femininity of the generations: As self-reported as stereotypically appraised. *International Journal of Aging and Human Development, 7,* 143-151.

Clark, M., & Anderson, B. (1967). *Culture and Aging.* Springfield, IL: Charles C Thomas.

Dobson, C. (1983). Sex-role and marital role expectations. In T. H. Brubaker (Ed.), *Family relationships in later life* (pp. 109-126). Beverly Hills, CA: Sage.

Donelson, E. (1977). Development of sex typed behavior and self-concept. In E. Donelson & J. E. Gullahorn (Eds.), *Women* (pp. 119-139). New York: John Wiley.

Gutmann, D. L. (1975). Parenthood: Key to the comparative psychology of the life cycle. In N. Datan & L. Ginsburg (Eds.), *Developmental psychology: Normative life crisis* (pp. 167-184). New York: Academic.

Gutmann, D. L. (1977). The cross-cultural perspective: Notes toward a comparative psychology of aging. In J. E. Birren & K. W. Schaie (Eds.), *Handbook of the psychology of aging* (pp. 302-326). New York: Van Nostrand Reinhold.

Keating, N., & Cole, P. (1980). What do I do with him 24 hours a day? Changes in the housewife role after retirement. *Gerontologist, 20,* 84-89.

Keith, P. M., & Brubaker, T. H. (1977). Sex-role expectations associated with specific household tasks: Perceived age and employment differences. *Psychological Reports, 41,* 15-18.

Keith, P. M., & Brubaker, T. H. (1979). Male household roles in later life: A look at masculinity and marital relationships. *Family Coordinator, 28,* 497-502.

Keith, P. M., & Brubaker, T. H. (1980). Adolescent perception of household work: Expectations by sex, age and employment situation. *Adolescence, 15,* 171-182.

Keith, P. M., Dobson, C. D., Goudy, W. J., & Powers, E. A. (1981). Older men: Occupation, employment status, household involvement, and well-being. *Journal of Family Issues, 2,* 336-349.

Keith, P. M., Powers, E. A., & Goudy, W. J. (1981). Older men in employed and retired families. *Alternative Lifestyles, 4,* 228-241.

Kerckhoff, A. C. (1966). Family patterns and morale in retirement. In I. M. Simpson & J. C. McKinney (Eds.), *Social aspects of aging* (pp. 173-192). Durham, NC: Duke University Press.

Minnigerode, F. A., & Lee, J. A. (1978). Young adults' perceptions of social sex roles across the life span. *Sex roles, 4,* 563-569.

Model, S. (1981). Housework by husbands: Determinants and implications. *Journal of Family Issues, 2,* 225-237.

Puglisi, J. T. (1983). Self perceived age changes in sex role concept. *International Journal of Aging and Human Development, 12,* 183-191.

Puglisi, J. T. & Jackson, D. W. (1980-1981). Sex role identity and self esteem in adulthood. *International Journal of Aging and Human Development, 12,* 129-138.

Sinnott, J. D. (1977). Sex role consistency, biology, and succesful aging. *Gerontologist, 17,* 459-463.

Spanier, G. B. (1976). Measuring dyadic adjustment: New scales for assessing the quality of marriage and similar dyads. *Journal of Marriage and the Family, 38,* 15-28.

Szinovacz, M. (1980). Female retirement: Effects on spousal roles and marital adjustment. *Journal of Family Issues, 1,* 423-440.

Torrey, B. B. (1982). The lengthening of retirement. In M. W. Riley et al. (Eds.), *Aging from birth to death: Vol. 2. Sociotemporal perspectives* (pp. 181-196). Boulder, CO: Westview.

Yogev, S. (1981). Do professional women have egalitarian marital relationships? *Journal of Marriage and the Family, 43,* 865-871.

5

HUSBANDS' JEALOUSY

Bram Buunk

WHICH IS THE MORE JEALOUS SEX?

There exists considerable disagreement and confusion concerning the question of which sex is the more jealous. In an earlier review of jealousy, Bohm (1960) stated that the disposition to jealousy is generally more pronounced in women. Bohm based his statement largely on Freud's attitude that women are inclined to be more jealous and envious than men, specifically because of penis envy and a greater narcissistic libido. As Bohm pointed out, before Freud, philosopher Immanuel Kant expressed a similar viewpoint when he said, "Men are jealous when in love, women even when not in love." Margaret Mead seemed to agree that women were "the jealous sex," but she emphasized that women were this way because a woman's position has generally been dependent on her husband; by losing him, she would lose the roots of her "social existence."

In contrast, a number of scholars have maintained that men tend to be more jealous than women. In this study on the pathogenesis of morbid jealousy, Vaukhonen (1968) suggests that men become jealous more frequently and with greater intensity than women due to stronger possessive and competitive urges. Symons (1979, p. 240), in his thought-provoking evolutionary perspective on sex differences in sexuality, comes to a similar conclusion: "In cross cultural perspective, there is no doubt that husbands typically are more concerned about their wives' fidelity than wives about their husbands' fidelity." Jealousy is, according

Author's Note: *This chapter has benefited from discussion with Marjan Buunk and the comments and editorial help of Hedy Kleyweg Buunk. It was written when the author was a Fulbright Scholar at the University of California, Los Angeles.*

to Symons, "a more or less obligate response among husbands, but a flexible, facultative response among wives" (p. 245). And Kinsey, Pomeroy, and Martin (1948) note that, on every socioeconomic level, wives rather than husbands are more tolerant of their spouses' extramarital sexual activity. "Husbands are much less inclined to accept the non-marital activities of their wives. It has been so since the dawn of history" (p. 592).

In part, the confusion as to which is the more jealous sex is probably the result of not making a distinction between the experience and the expression of jealousy. There indeed seem to be many more reports on jealousy exhibited by husbands than on jealousy exhibited by wives in anthropological and ethnographic literature (Hupka, 1981). However, this could indicate that male jealousy is more visible because the more powerful position of men gives them more opportunities and social support to express their jealousy in an aggressive, dominant, or violent way. Females may have been as jealous as men, or even more so in many societies, but they may not have been able to express it and act upon it because of their inferior societal position in a given society. As will be detailed later, there exists no evidence to indicate that women experience less jealousy than men when confronted with their spouses' sexual infidelity, but often they may not have seen any other options but to accept and tolerate their husbands' infidelities or even their husbands' other wives. Indeed, in male-dominated societies such as Greece, this was the traditionally prescribed behavior for wives (Safilios-Rothschild, 1969).

A second explanation for the disagreement on the question of which is the more jealous sex is that different observers had different phenomena in mind when they referred to jealousy. For example, some seemed to refer mainly to envy, others to aggressive rivalry, and yet others to concern over a spouse's sexual fidelity. Thus there seem to be different types of jealousy that are very distinct phenomena, and it is quite possible that some of those experiences are more common among men and that others are more prevalent among women.

In this chapter, the characteristics of male jealousy compared to female jealousy will be discussed, taking into account the distinction between the experience and the expression of jealousy, and between different types of jealousy. Some of the experiences discussed here, such as envy and rivalry, would, according to modern definitions of jealousy (for example, see Clanton & Smith, 1977; Bryson, 1976; Buunk, 1982b), not be considered jealousy. However, in daily language these experiences are often refered to as "jealousy." All experiences dealt with here can be said to refer to a negative emotional reaction to the potential, actual, or imagined involvement of the potential, actual, or imagined partner with another person or object.

JEALOUSY AS ENVY

The word "jealousy" is often used to describe the state of *envying* another person for the possession of some attribute. In a society in which males often possess and have more access to such valuable resources as status, power, autonomy, rewarding occupations, and money, it should come as no surprise that housewives, bound to their homes with children, will often envy their husbands more than husbands envy wives. In this sense, women conceivably could be more jealous than men.

Indeed, in her study of working-class marriages, Rubin (1976) found that many more wives than husbands considered their spouses better off and expressed a desire to trade places with their spouses. In a heterogeneous sample of Dutch couples, more women than men found their spouses' work more interesting than their own, believed their spouses had more possibilities for meeting others, and had a greater amount of freedom than they themselves had (Buunk, 1980). Although it is not clear how often these perceptions evoked jealousy, it seems highly likely that more women were jealous of their spouses' lives than the other way around. Hand in hand with this is the complaint expressed by many wives that they are jealous of their husbands' work because of all the attention devoted to it. Thus, in the sense discussed here, women may indeed be considered the more jealous sex. It is quite apparent, however, that this type of jealousy has little if anything to do with the negative emotional response to the spouse's infidelity.

JEALOUSY AS AGGRESSIVE RIVALRY

A completely different phenomenon related to jealousy is *aggressive rivalry* over the other sex. From a cross-cultural perspective it is clear that there exists considerably more violent competition between men over women than between women over men. In ethographic reports, the frequency of male rivalry, quarrels, fighting, and killing over women is consistently apparent (Symons, 1979). Also, in our society, and especially within the lower socioeconomic strata, men will occasionally fight over women. The implicit, or sometimes explicit, sexist assumption behind all such fights is that women do not have the right to choose for themselves with whom they should become involved, but that such a conflict must be determined by a power struggle between men.

Fighting over women is further clearly associated with the traditional image of the masculine male as dominant, tough, and aggressive. This image has been, as Wolfgang (1978) points out, promoted more by females than is often assumed: "In the past, in their own search for identity as females, they have driven the male to highlight differences by encouraging the myth of medieval chivalry; they have sought his strong arms of security, buttressed his aggressivity against other suitors, and passed on this male model to their progeny" (p. 241). Indeed, some women, especially in the lower socioeconomic classes, might find it flattering when men fight courtship battles over them, probably often not realizing that this same aggressive masculine behavior may, once they get married, be directed against them instead of against other males.

EXCLUSIVE SEXUAL ACCESS

The goal of aggressive male rivalry is to obtain the exclusive possession of a woman; once a man has acquired this possession, he will sometimes do everything conceivable to *prevent a violation of* his *exclusive sexual access* to a woman. In most societies, it is men rather than women who are apt to prevent their spouses from becoming sexually involved with others. In this sense, men are clearly the jealous sex; they are more inclined to keep their wives from meeting other men. In Arab societies, women are often extremely restricted in their freedom and forced to avoid any behavior that could arouse the interest of other men. In Western society, many men still resist the idea of their wives taking jobs, not only because it threatens their dominant position as the breadwinner, but also because these husbands are afraid that working outside the home might give their wives too much opportunity to meet other men (seen as potential lovers).

In general, while they themselves often take a large degree of autonomy for granted, many men have difficulty in accepting autonomous behavior on the part of their partners. For example, a study conducted by Buunk and Hupka (1983) covering seven different nations indicated that in all these nations men reacted more negatively than women to independent behavior exhibited by their partners. Reports on abused women testify to the extreme behavior to which some husbands resort in an effort to limit the autonomy of their wives as the result of their insecurity about the mere possibility of their being unfaithful. Martin (1983) describes how one woman was locked up in her bedroom every morning by her husband before he left for work. He took away all her clothes, and just in case she might consider escaping into the street naked, he wired the door handle with electricity.

Men, of course, also use other strategies to prevent any possibility of contact between their wives and other men (such as not giving them any money, accompanying them wherever they go, or doing all the shopping themselves). Several factors make this type of controlling behavior much less likely for females: the still-prevalent norm favoring male dominance, seen especially in the lower socioeconomic class; the greater physical and financial power of most males; and the traditional confinement of the woman to the home. This does not, however, indicate that women are less afraid than men of their spouses being unfaithful. As will be expanded upon later, such jealousy seems to be at least as common among women as among men. What does differ is the way many men react to such fears.

DELUSIONAL AND VIOLENT JEALOUSY

Closely related to the foregoing is what has been described in clinical literature as *delusional jealousy* (Vaukhonen, 1968; Mowat, 1966). In the type of behavior described above, the person acts out of fear that the spouse *may* be unfaithful; the delusionally jealous person acts upon the assumption that the spouse *is* actually unfaithful. The delusionally jealous husband is convinced that his wife is involved with another man and looks for all evidence to back his conviction. Nearly everything can be considered to be proof: independent behavior, lack of sexual interest on the part of the wife, an unfamiliar brand of cigarette in an ashtray, the wife merely being friendly to other men, the wife's daydreaming, or even the vehement denial by the wife that she is unfaithful. According to Gelles (1974), jealousy behavior often takes the form of interrogations, with an aura of Gestapo violence. Gelles describes the case of a woman who had frequently been beaten by her husband, who relentlessly interrogated her: "And he would keep it up [so that] finally you would admit to anything in the world to get him to shut up. He would keep it up for five hours and not let me sleep. I would say 'Yes! Yes! I did, are you glad?' . . . and then he would beat me" (p. 84).

Male jealousy is indeed one of the most important factors associated with wife beating. In a study of 100 court cases involving violence between spouses, Whitehurst (1971) found that in nearly every case the husband accused his wife of being a whore or of having an affair with another man. A recent survey of agencies treating men who batter their wives revealed intense jealousy to be the second most common trait (after alcoholism) of such men (Simpson Feazell, Sanchez Mayers, & Dechesner, 1984). In a study of 150 cases of abused women, Roy (1977) found that, with the exception of arguments over money, jealousy was the most frequently mentioned factor leading to a violent confrontation.

Furthermore, there is some evidence that male jealousy is more likely to lead to murder or attempted murder than is female jealousy. It must be emphasized that of all the murders of one spouse by the other, husbands are nearly as often the victims as wives (Duncan & Duncan, 1978). When men kill, the victims are unlikely to be their wives; when women commit murder, in nearly half of the cases their husbands are the victims (Wolfgang, 1978). But whenever wives are killed by husbands, it is probably more often related to jealousy. In an English study, Mowat (1966) found that 12% of all the murders committed by males were accompanied by delusions of infidelity. As Mowat put it, in absolute numbers, the jealousy murderer is usually male. In another study of male murderers, Faulk (1977) reports a similar percentage of jealousy-related murders. Of the 23 men studied, 3 (13%) had long histories of being unduly suspicious of their wives' fidelity. The husbands were controlling and jealous, but would not leave their wives despite their suspicions.

It must be noted that although violent male jealousy seems to be more severe and frequent in the lower socioeconomic classes, among middle-class men and women the approval of jealousy expressed through violent behavior is by no means absent. In an adult middle-class sample, the majority believed that there are occasions when acting violently in response to a partner's extramarital behavior was justified. In this sample, 12% (all men) believed that a wife should be beaten if she indulges in extramarital sex (Whitehurst, 1971).

SEXUAL INSECURITY AND DESIRE TO CONTROL

The important factors behind the violent expression of jealousy by men—and behind male jealousy in general—are insecurity, especially *sexual insecurity*, and a strong desire to *control* and *dominate* the wife. As Shainess (1977, p. 115), referring to violently jealous husbands, points out: "Here an individual with extremely low self-esteem and high self-hate feels undeserving of his wife, sees most other men as potential thieves of what he values, and yet, is likely to blame and punish the very person he values." In her study of abused women, Roy (1977) found that jealousy was in most cases closely related to sexual problems in the relationship and the husband's doubts of his own virility. Obviously, feeling insecure about his sexual performance, the husband fears his wife will become sexually involved with others and attempts to control her behavior by beating her. In an earlier cited study of 100 court cases involving husbands and wives in litigation over actual violence within a relationship, Whitehurst (1971, p. 686) reports "a strong and pervasive sense of male uncertainty shown either in the inability to control his wife, or what was interpreted as male projection of either real or fantasy life sexual problems."

Other studies confirm the sexual focus and the desire to control and dominate the wife in male jealousy. As will be pointed out later, this does not mean that men will get more jealous per se because of their partners' sexual involvement than women. But in such a situation, men seem more inclined to focus on the sexual aspects of involvement and to try to control the wives in a dominating way, whereas women tend to examine the implications of partners' behavior in regard to the future of the relationship. In a still surprisingly relevant study (given that it was conducted nearly 50 years ago), Gottschalk (1936) found that among men jealousy manifested itself mainly as a shock of feeling either sexually inadequate or sexually repulsive, resulting in a simultaneous and sudden release of rivalry feelings. Basic prerequisites of this shock of displeasure were a certain drive for power and an urge for domination and possession. The women in this study lacked the reaction of sexual rivalry and of injury in regard to the right to sexual possession. The focus of their jealousy was more on the emotional intimacy with the rival (for an English summary of this study, see Bohm, 1960).

More recently, Francis (1977), using a free-association task, found that among men—and not at all among women—sexual involvement with a third person was the most often mentioned situation evoking jealousy. Among women, the partner spending time or talking with a third person turned out to be of major importance. Similarly, a study by Teisman and Mosher (1978) showed that males did experience their jealousy primarily in terms of sexual issues, whereas issues of time and attention evoked females' jealousy. White (1981, p. 23) found a number of differences between the sexes that were, as he put it, generally consistent with the sex-role literature, showing females to be "more relationship centered while males are more concerned with status (sexual or otherwise) and competition and are less relationship-oriented."

STATUS AND SELF-ESTEEM

An important aspect of male jealousy is that, traditionally, the unfaithfulness of the wife lowered the status of the husband within the community, while the erotic escapades of the husband did not affect the wife's status to the same degree. It has even been suggested that some wives have been proud of their husbands' playing around, provided their desire to maintain the marital union remained unimpaired (Bohm, 1960).

This double standard has been described by Safilios-Rothschild (1969) as part of the traditional Greek culture. Unfaithfulness of the husband was not considered to be a crime; it was seen as a normal consequence of the polygamous nature of men and the betrayed wife was socially accepted. In contrast, any unfaithfulness on the part of the wife made the man into a *Keratas*—the worst insult for a man, a sign of weakness and inadequacy. Traditional Greek norms, in fact, gave the man the right to kill his wife as a matter of "honor." It was not socially acceptable for a man to tolerate the infidelity of his wife.

This last pattern may, as Safilios-Rothschild indicates, be disappearing, especially among the better-educated Greeks, but it is still characteristic of many cultures and social groupings (Whitehurst, 1971). Indeed, even recent studies among college students and in the general population show that jealous men more often exhibit strategies to maintain their self-esteem (for example, taking more direct action, confronting the partner of rival), while women are more inclined to employ strategies to improve the relationship or to engage in avoidance, self-blame, and depression (Bryson, 1976; Buunk, 1978, 1982a; Shettel-Neuber & Bryson, 1978; White, 1981; Whitehurst, 1975).

The fact that men undertake more direct action when jealous does not necessarily mean that they are more jealous than women. In many social psychological studies, the differences between the sexes as to the degree of jealousy have been found to be nonexistent (White, 1981; Bringle, 1981). In one study, in fact, it was found that women would become significantly more upset than men when their spouses became sexually involved with others (Buunk, 1978). And Francis (1977, p. 65) found that men were much less often suspicious of their wives' involvement with others than vice versa: "Males repress or deny awareness of potentially jealousy evoking situations, whereas females are unreasonably suspicious of their occurrence." Furthermore, one should not overestimate the differences between the natures of male and of female jealousy. In many studies few sex differences were found and the similarities between the sexes could be greater than the differences. For example, Teismann and Mosher (1978) did not find any differences between the sexes in behaviors to cope with jealousy situations (such as rejecting, coercive, cognitive, reconciling, and appealing acts).

CONCLUSION

Returning to the earlier discussion of which is the more jealous sex, the following conclusions can be drawn: (1) Wives are probably more envious of their husbands' position than vice versa; (2) men engage in aggressive sexual rivalry with much greater frequency; (3) there is no evidence at all that men are plagued more by fears and delusions concerning infidelity of their spouses or become more upset when such infidelity does actually occur; (4) there is, however, some evidence that, when jealous, husbands and boyfriends will focus more on the sexual aspects of their partners' behavior, and wives and girlfriends will focus more on the consequences for the relationship; and (5) it seems likely that, when jealous, men attempt to bolster their self-esteem and to behave in more dominating, controlling, and aggressive ways than women.

A STUDY OF HUSBANDS' JEALOUSY

The remainder of this chapter reports a number of findings on husbands' jealousy (compared to wives' jealousy) that were derived from a larger study on jealousy. Four questions are explored here, all of which are more or less directly related to the previously discussed literature on the differences between male and female jealousy: (1) Do husbands, compared to wives, become more or less emotionally upset when confronted with their spouses' extramarital sexual relationships? (2) Do husbands, compared to wives, focus more on the sexual aspects of the spouse's extramarital involvement? (3) Is husbands' jealousy, compared to wives' jealousy, oriented more to self-esteem and less to relationships? (4) Do husbands express their jealousy differently than wives?

THE SAMPLE

The study was conducted with a focus on the experiences and behaviors of 109 men and 109 women, all of whom had or have a spouse who had had at least one extramarital relationship during the past two years. Most respondents (85%) had themselves also been involved in extramarital relationships. The respondents were selected via advertisements in two Dutch monthly periodicals on human relationships and a weekly political magazine (76%), lectures (18%), or word-of-mouth referrals (6%). A questionnaire was filled out at the subject's home in the presence of a research assistant.

More than half of the respondents (51%) had a high educational level, comparable to at least four years of college. The occupational level was also high, with 79% of the males falling into the two highest of a total of six occupational groups, compared with 15% of the total population. Of the total sample, 78% were between 27 and 46 years old; 15% were older than 46 and 7% were younger than 27. Exactly half of the sample did not belong to any religious denomination. Most couples (68%) had one or more children. Many of the women (42%) were gainfully employed. In comparison with the total population, the attitudes of the respondents concerning sex and women's liberation were liberal. However, they did not differ with a control group in marital satisfaction, self-esteem, or neuroticism. A minority (13%) were not legally married, but cohabiting.

MEASURES RELATED TO EXTRAMARITAL RELATIONSHIP WITH STRONGEST IMPACT

The subjects were asked to remember the extramarital relationship of their spouse that had, according to the respondent, the strongest impact on the marriage. They were then given a questionnaire that contained the following scales concerning their reaction to this occurrence.

Jealousy. This measure consists of a scale of 20 items. All items imply a negative or positive reaction to the partner's most significant extramarital relationship, for example: "I was jealous"; "I found it unpleasant that my spouse enjoyed certain things more with another person than with me"; "I felt bad"; and "I was pleased because it gave me more freedom too" (reverse score). For each item a five-point scale ranging from "did not apply" to "very much applied" was used. The coefficient alpha for this scale is .93.

Attributed need for sexual variety. This scale assessed the degree to which the person thinks the extramarital relationship was triggered by a need for sexual variety. The subject was presented with two statements:

"S/he did it because s/he had a need for sexual variety" and "S/he did it because it was something new." For both items, a five-point scale was used, ranging from "did not apply" to "very much applied." The scores of the two items were summed. The coefficient alpha for this two-item scale is .69.

Decreased sexual satisfaction. This measure consists of two items referring to the degree the sexual satisfaction in the marriage had deteriorated as a result of the extramarital relationship of the spouse. The coefficient alpha of this two-item scale is .60.

Aggression as expression of jealousy. This scale consists of seven items, all of which refer to aggressive behavior against the spouse as a consequence of the subject's jealousy (for instance, "blaming the other" and "acting mean"). For each item a five-point scale ranging from "did not apply" to "very much applied" was used. The coefficient alpha is .82.

Avoidance as expression of jealousy. For this scale, three items were used referring to behaviors aimed at avoiding discussion with the spouse, such as "trying not to talk about it." Again, a five-point scale ranging from "did not apply" to "very much applied" was used. The coefficient alpha is .75.

Measures of person and relationship variables. The subjects were given a separate questionnaire containing the following scales referring to enduring person and relationship characteristics:

- *Self-esteem.* A nine-item scale was used, largely based on Rosenberg's (1965) scale, with a coefficient alpha of .76. Each item had to be rated on a five-point scale, ranging from "completely agree" to "completely disagree."
- *Marital satisfaction.* For this scale, subjects rated how often eight items applied to their relationship on a five-point response scale ranging from "never" to "very often." Items included "I feel happy when I am with my partner"; "My partner irritates me"; and "Things are going well between us." The coefficient alpha is .88.
- *Relationship characteristics.* Subjects were asked to indicate whether they were cohabiting (score 1) or married (score 2), how many children they had (score 1 = none, score 2 = one or two, score 3 = three or four, score 4 = five or more), and how many months they had lived together (whether married or not).

RESULTS

The jealousy scale was correlated with the other measures described above. The results will be described in relation to the four research questions mentioned earlier.

(1) *Do husbands, compared to wives, become more or less emotionally upset when confronted with extramarital relationships on the part of their spouses?* As far as this study is concerned, women, and not men, are the jealous sex. A t-test showed that there was a significant gender difference on the jealousy scale, t(116) = 3.00, p < .01, with women scoring more jealous.

(2) *Do husbands, compared to wives, focus more on the sexual aspects of their spouses' extramarital involvements?* It was expected that if husbands would find the sexual aspects of their spouses' extramarital involvements especially threatening, their jealousy would be more intense the more they thought their partner became involved for reasons of sexual variety. This expectation was confirmed. Among men, the jealousy scale correlated significantly with the scale for attributed need for sexual variety (r = .25, p < .01), while among women the correlation was not significant (r = .12, ns). (For a more elaborate analysis of these and related findings, see Buunk, 1984.) Furthermore, the jealousy scale among men correlated quite highly with the scale measuring decreased sexual satisfaction as a consequence of the spouse's extramarital relationship (r = .40, p < .01), and among women the correlation was low and nonsignificant (r = .13, ns). Obviously, husbands in this study did become especially jealous when they felt the extramarital relationships of their spouses were motivated primarily by a need for sexual variety and had led to deterioration of the marital sexual relationship.

(3) *Is husband jealousy, compared to wife jealousy, more self-esteem and less relationship oriented?* As expected, jealousy among men was significantly and negatively related to self-esteem (r = −.24, p. < 01); among women the correlation was not significant (r = −.12, ns). Thus in this study husbands' jealousy seems more self-esteem oriented than wives' jealousy.

Does that mean that husbands' jealousy is also less relationship oriented? In attempting to answer this question initially, the jealousy scale was correlated with the scale of marital satisfaction. Unexpectedly, the correlation for men was higher than for women (respectively, r = −.42, p < .01 and r = −.19, p < .05). Thus husbands who reacted jealously to their spouses' extramarital involvements tended to be more dissatisfied with their marriages. In another sense, however, male jealousy seems much less relationship oriented than female jealousy. Among women, the jealousy scale was negatively correlated with being married (instead of cohabiting) ($r = -.34$, $p < .01$), with the number of children ($r = -.17$, $p < .05$), and with length of the relationship ($r = -.32$, $p < .01$). Among men, only this last variable was related to jealousy, and much less than among women ($r = -.17$, $p < .05$). Being married ($r = .00$, ns) and number of children ($r = .03$, ns) were not at all correlated with jealousy among men. Thus it seems that women reacted especially strongly when their partners became sexually involved with others while their relationships were not yet well established and committed (for example, when the couple was merely cohabiting and not married, had not been together very long, or did not have children). For men, such factors indicating instability of the relationship hardly seemed to influence their jealousy.

(4) *Do husbands express their jealousy differently than wives?* It has previously been suggested that men express their jealousy with more direct aggression and control than women. On the other hand, some authors (for instance, Clanton & Smith, 1977) have maintained that men tend to deny their jealous feelings and, should they feel them, refrain from showing them. To investigate this issue, the jealousy scale was correlated with the two scales concerning the expression of jealousy. The scale for aggression correlated very highly with the jealousy scale among both men and women (respectively, $r = .82$, $p < .01$ and $r = .77$, $p < .01$). Thus it seems that both men *and* women when experiencing feelings of jealousy tend to behave aggressively toward their spouses.

However, the scale for avoidance as an expression of jealousy did correlate higher with the jealousy scale among men ($r = .38$, $p < .01$) than among women ($r = .22$, $p < .05$). Apparently, men who are jealous often tend to avoid discussion and to hide their feelings, but, in this sample, there is no evidence that husbands react more aggressively than wives.

DISCUSSION AND CONCLUSIONS

The finding that women reacted more jealously than men to their spouses' infidelity is in complete contrast to assertions by, for example, Symons (1979) and Kinsey et al. (1948) that men are more concerned about their wives' infidelity than vice versa. Of course, the present sample is not at all a random sample. It could well be that the relatively nonjealous husbands are overrepresented. But in a study mentioned earlier among a heterogeneous sample of 250 Dutch people, largely consisting of married people from various age and occupational groups with a large variety of levels of sexual permissiveness, women were also found to react more jealously to extramartial behaviors (Buunk, 1978).

These findings also seem to contradict several American studies cited earlier that did not find significant differences between the sexes regarding jealousy (for example, White, 1981; Bringle, 1981). However, these studies were not specifically concerned with the emotional reactions to extramarital sex. Furthermore, they were conducted among college students. Indeed, in a sample of Dutch college students, no significant gender difference in jealousy was found (Buunk, Spapens, Schepens, Koopmans, & Buis, 1981). It is therefore quite possible that, among college students, independent, self-assured women are somewhat overrepresented and that within the general population men indeed become less upset than women when their spouses are unfaithful. In any case, the findings presented here do not give any support to the supposition that men are the more jealous sex.

On the other hand, the sexual focus in male jealousy found in the present study is in line with studies described above showing that men experience and define their jealousy in sexual terms more frequently than do women (Gottschalk, 1936; Francis, 1977; Teismann & Mosher, 1978). This probably reflects the traditional male sex role in the area of sexual behavior. As Gross (1978) has emphasized, sex is perceived as more important and enjoyable for men than for women and sexuality is of the utmost importance in masculine identity. Gross also notes that men tend to isolate sex from other social aspects of life, especially love and affection, and to view sex in terms of goals and success.

Why male sexuality is often experienced in this way is seldom explained satisfactorily. It has been suggested (see Gross, 1978) that isolated sex is a defense against male vulnerability and dependency, and that men often feel hesitant to relate intimately to women because association with them is potentially stigmatizing. From a rather different perspective, Symons (1979) has put forward the challenging explanation that evolution has favored the characteristics of male sexuality described above because men with these features were more likely to have reproductive success. Whatever the reasons, the isolation of sex from love and affection and the emphasis on goals and success in male sexuality make the focus of men on the sexual aspects of their spouses' extramarital involvements quite likely.

The foregoing suggests that sexual competence is an important factor determining husbands' self-esteem. Therefore, it must be emphasized that, although the results presented above seem to confirm a link between male jealousy and male self-esteem, the type of global evaluative self-esteem scale used in these and other studies may not be particularly relevant for sexual jealousy in marital relationships. It could well be that the *self-concept* is a much more important variable in this context. As cognitive consistency theories (see Heider, 1958) would predict, people will attempt to attain a balance in their perception, that is, ensuring that their self-images are supported and validated by important others, such as their spouses. In the case of jealousy, this balance probably gets distorted as the behavior of the spouse is seen as attacking or denying important aspects of the person's self-concept, such as sexual competence, ability to love and care, and other personal qualities. An analysis of what the person considers central to the self, and the degree to which the spouse's behavior is seen as a threat to this, is probably more relevant in the understanding of jealousy than correlating jealousy and self-esteem scales.

In contrast to women, the jealousy of men turned out to be unrelated to factors indicating instability of the relationship. In that sense, male jealousy seems less relationship oriented. However, men who reacted jealously tended to be relatively more dissatisfied with their marriages. There are two processes at work that can probably cause the negative correlation between marital satisfaction and jealousy. First, for men who associate negative affect with their wives and view them in a hostile way, the fact that the wives become involved in extramarital relationships tends to augment already-existing negative feelings. It could be that this process does not occur to the same extent among women because they are often inclined to blame themselves for their husbands' extramarital affairs (Buunk, 1978; Rodgers & Bryson, 1978). The second process would be that the jealousy-evoking events increase the dissatisfaction men feel toward their marital relationships. Perhaps this process is stronger for men because they are less comfortable and less able to deal with strong aversive emotions than are women.

This last process may also be responsible for the finding that jealous husbands do not particularly react aggressively, but tend to avoid interaction with their wives. This finding is in line with a study by Knapp and Whitehurst (1977) on sexually open marriages. Their study indicates that women often complain that their husbands sometimes back away from intense emotional discussion on extramarital involvements by escaping into work, sports, or all-male activities. Indeed, the phenomenon of the emotionally inexpressive male (Balswick & Peek, 1971) has often been discussed. Research has suggested that, in general, men do tend to express their feelings less easily and tend to avoid emotional conflicts in close relationships (for example, Kelley, Cunningham, Grisham, Levevre, Sink, & Yablon, 1978). Thus the present finding on men's avoidance behavior does not seem indicative of male jealousy but of the way many men deal with emotional problems in general.

In conclusion, jealousy is an experience that is probably as painful for men as it is for women, but there is no evidence that husbands are more concerned over their spouses' infidelity than wives. There are even some indications that if one wants to use the label "the jealous sex," the female gender is the best candidate for this label. Not only do women seem to be more emotionally affected than men when their partners are unfaithful—especially in the early phases of the relationship—but they also seem to be more jealous of the lives their spouses are leading in general. Of course, these differences are directly related to the differences between men's and women's social positions and sex-role characteristics. This seems true for most aspects and manifestations of jealousy, such as men's more visible, aggressive, and violent rivalry over women. Men are also probably more concerned with their self-esteem when their wives commit adultery, to the degree to which their sexual competence and their status in the community is threatened by their spouses' behavior. They also seem to react with more control and dominance when jealous. It is, however, not clear if jealous men really do express their feelings more aggressively than jealous women. Quite in contrast, they often do not show their jealousy at all and avoid discussion of it with their wives. More research on male jealousy is necessary. It could well be that, despite some differences, male jealousy resembles female jealousy to a much greater extent than is generally supposed.

REFERENCES

Balswick, J. B., & Peek, C. W. (1971). The inexpressive male: Tragedy of American society. *Family Coordinator, 20*, 363-368.

Bohm, E. (1960). Jealousy. In A. Ellis & A. Arbarbanel (Eds.), *The encyclopedia of sexual behavior* (Vol. 1). New York: Hawthorne.

Bringle, R. G. (1981). Conceptualizing jealousy as a disposition. *Alternative Lifestyles, 4*, 774-796.

Bryson, J. B. (1976). *The nature of sexual jealousy:* An exploratory study. Paper presented at the meeting of the American Psychological Association, San Francisco.

Buunk, B. (1978). Jaloezie 2: Ervaringen van 250 Nederlanders [Jealousy 2: Experiences of 250 Dutch people]. *Intermediair, 14*(12), 43-51.

Bunnk, B. (1980). Sociale vergelijking in liefdesrelaties: Ervaren ongelijkheid en relatie-satisfactie [Social comparison processes in love relationships: The experience of inequity and relational satisfaction]. In J. Rijsman & H.A.M. Wilke (Eds.), *Sociale vergelijkingsprocessen. Theorie en onderzoek.* Deventer, The Netherlands: Van Loghum Slaterus.

Buunk, B. (1982a). Strategies of jealousy: Styles of coping with extramarital involvement of the spouse. *Family Relations, 31,* 13-18.

Buunk, B. (1982b). Anticipated sexual jealousy: Its relationship to self-esteem, dependency, and reciprocity. *Personality and Social Psychology Bulletin, 8,* 310-316.

Buunk, B. (1984). Jealousy as related to attributions for the partner's behavior. *Social Psychology Quarterly, 47,* 107-112.

Buunk, B., & Hupka, R. (1963). *Autonomy and togetherness in close relationships: A study of seven nations.* Paper presented at the meeting of the National Council on Family Relations, St. Paul, October. (ERIC Document Reproduction Service No. ED 243 052)

Buunk, B., Spapens, N., Schepens, J., Koopmans, P., & Buis, M. (1981). *Cross cultureel onderzoek naar relaties 2: Dimensies in de jaloeziebeleving* [Cross-cultural research of relationships 2: Dimensions of jealousy] (Internal Report No. 81-50-11). Nijmegen: Katholieke Universiteit.

Clanton, G., & Smith, L. G. (Eds.). (1977). *Jealousy.* Englewood Cliffs, NJ: Prentice-Hall.

Duncan, J. W., & Duncan, G. M. (1978). Murder in the family. In I. L. Kutash, S. B. Kutash, & L. B. Schlesinger (Eds.), *Violence: Perspectives on murder and aggression.* San Francisco: Jossey-Bass.

Faulk, M. (1977). Men who assault their wives. In M. Roy (Ed.), *Battered women: A psychosociological study of domestic violence.* New York: Van Nostrand Reinhold.

Francis, J. L. (1977). Toward the management of heterosexual jealousy. *Journal of Marriage and Family Counseling, 3,* 61-69.

Gelles, R. J. (1974). *The violent home.* Beverly Hills, CA: Sage.

Gottschalk, H. (1936). *Skinsygens problemer* (Problems of jealousy). Copenhagen: Fremad.

Gross, A. (1978). The male role and heterosexual behavior. *Journal of Social Issues, 34,* 87-107.

Heider, F. (1958). *The psychology of interpersonal relations.* New York: John Wiley.

Hupka, R. B. (1981). Cultural determinants of jealousy. *Alternative Lifestyles, 4,* 310-356.

Kelley, H. H., Grisham, J. A., Lefebvre, L. M., Sink, C. R., & Yablon, G. (1978). Sex differences in comments made during conflict with close heterosexual pairs. *Sex Roles, 4,* 473-492.

Kinsey, A. C., Pomeroy, W. B., & Martin, C. E. (1948). *Sexual behavior in the human male.* Philadelphia: W. B. Saunders.

Knapp, J., & Whitehurst, R. N. (1977). Sexually open marriage and relationships: Issues and prospects. In R. W. Libby & R. N. Whitehurst (Eds.), *Marriage and alternatives.* Glenview, IL: Scott, Foresman.

Martin, D. (1983). *Battered wives.* New York: Simon & Schuster.

Mowat, R. R. (1966). *Morbid jealousy and murder: A psychiatric study of morbidly jealous murderers at Broadmour.* London: Tavistock.

Rodgers, M. A., & Bryson, J. B. (1978). *Self-esteem and relationship maintenance as responses to jealousy.* Paper presented at the meeting of the Western Psychological Association, San Francisco.

Rosenberg, M. (1965). *Society and the adolescent's self image.* Princeton, NJ: Princeton University Press.

Roy, M. (1977). A current survey of 150 cases. In M. Roy (Ed.), *Battered women: A psychosociological study of domestic violence.* New York: Van Nostrand Reinhold.

Rubin, L. B. (1976). *Worlds of pain.* New York: Basic Books.

Safilios-Rothschild, C. (1969). Attitudes of Greek spouses toward marital infidelity. In G. Neubeck (Ed.), *Extramarital relations*. Englewood Cliffs, NJ: Prentice-Hall.

Shainess, N. (1977). In M. Roy (Ed.), *Battered women: A Psychosociological study of domestic violence*. New York: Van Nostrand Reinhold.

Shettel-Neuber, J., & Bryson, J. B. (1978). Physical attractiveness of the "other person" and jealousy. *Personality and Social Psychology Bulletin, 4*, 612-615.

Simpson Feazell, C., Sanchez Mayers, R., & Deschner, J. (1984). Services for men who batter: Implications for programs and policies. *Family Relations, 33*, 217-224.

Symons, D. (1979). *The evolution of human sexuality*. New York & Oxford: Oxford University Press.

Teishmann, M. W., & Mosher, D. L. (1978). Jealous conflicts in dating couples. *Psychological Reports, 42*, 1211-1216.

Vaukhonen, K. (1968). On the pathogenesis of morbid jealousy: With special reference to the personality traits and the interaction between jealous patients and their spouses. *Acta Psychiatrica Scandinavica* (Suppl. 202).

White, G. L. (1981). Some correlates of romantic jealousy. *Journal of Personality, 49*, 129-167.

Whitehurst, R. N. (1971). Violent potential in extramarital sexual responses. *Journal of Marriage and the Family, 33*, 683-691.

Whitehurst, R. N. (1975). Violence in jealous husbands. In L. Gross (Ed.), *Sexual issues in marriage: A contemporary perspective*. New York: Spectrum.

Wolfgang, M. (1978). Violence in the family. In I. L. Kutash, S. B. Kutash, & L. B. Schlesinger (Eds.), *Violence: Perspectives on murder and aggression*. San Francisco: Jossey-Bass.

6

HUSBANDS, LOVERS, AND LONELINESS

Jenny De Jong-Gierveld

HUSBAND AS A PROTECTED STATUS

Most research, the bulk of which originates in North America, has shown a protective effect for marriages on both the physical and the mental well-being of men and women. Married persons on the average are more happy than nonmarried individuals (see, for example, De Jong-Gierveld, 1971, 1984; Gove, 1972). As a consequence, married people are less prone to early mortality and to suicide than nonmarried people (Gove, 1972; Kobrin & Hendershot, 1977; Veenhoven, 1983).

The "protection" idea provides a possible explanation for the relatively high degree of well-being of the married and the relatively low degree of well-being of the nonmarried (Gove & Hughes, 1980; Veenhoven, 1983). It proposes that people need intimate relationships from which they obtain satisfaction in the realms of affection, identity, and care. Thus they would be protected from unhappiness and feelings of loneliness.

To the extent that the bonds of marriage are able to provide such intimacy, married individuals are more likely to be happy and not to be lonely than nonmarried individuals.

Author's Note: *This research was supported by a grant from the Fund for Research into the Social Sciences, which is supported by the National Council on Social Welfare, the Queen Juliana Foundation, and the Ministry of Welfare, Health and Cultural Affairs. I wish to thank Pearl Dykstra and Theo van Tilburg for their help in preparing the manuscript.*

PROTECTION IN MARITAL AND
NONMARITAL PARTNER RELATIONSHIPS

Of course, intimacy can be found in other than marital relationships. In the Netherlands, for example, there has been a recent increase in the number of cohabiting relationships. Data based on a sample of 6660 women revealed that in 1982 approximately 8% of women between the ages of 18 and 37 lived together with male nonmarital partners. The percentage was highest for women who were between 23 and 27 years old—14% (Van de Giessen, 1983). In the present study, we focused on both marriage and nonmarriage partner relationships, provided that the partner is a member of the same family or household. Both kinds of living arrangements can be described as *living with a partner* or *living in families.*

The present investigation proposes a specification of the "protection" idea. In my view, the types of intimate relationships that men and women need in particular are those with marital or nonmarital partner living in the same household. Men who can be provided with affection and attention in the context of their daily activities are better equipped to deal with feelings of fear, unhappiness, and pain than men living without partners, who must rely on others outside the household for comfort and support. A number of recent studies have shown that the incidence of loneliness, suicide, and alcoholism, as indicators of general malaise, is highly dependent on the presence or absence of a partner (De Jong-Gierveld, 1984; Gove et al., 1980).

The aim of this study was to explore further the relationship between experienced loneliness and living arrangement. The *first hypothesis,* which was based on the findings of the previously mentioned studies, was that on the average men and women living with partners will obtain lower loneliness scores than men and women living without partners. Note that loneliness concerns a situation where the number and nature of meaningful, lasting, interpersonal relationships a person has is experienced as inadequate. It is important to distinguish feelings of loneliness from objective isolation. Objective isolation applies to the absence of all those relationships that exhibit a certain degree of durability.

MEN IN FAMILIES

Research findings on the protective effect of the presence of a partner have been scarce until now, and reveal contradictory evidence with respect to gender differences. Gove (1972) concludes from some data on mental illness and psychological well-being that in North America being married is more advantageous for men than for women, while being single is, if anything, more disadvantageous for men than for women. Several studies on loneliness in the Netherlands indicate a similar pattern (De Jong-Gierveld, 1971). However, the differences between married men and women are slight compared to the differences between the married and the nonmarried. Other studies conducted in the Netherlands contradict the previously mentioned findings (De Jong-Gierveld & Dykstra, 1984). They show that the majority of married women report moderate to high levels of general satisfaction, and minimal feelings of loneliness, if any.

In a paper reporting the results of a secondary analysis of existing data sets, Borys, Perlman, and Goldenberg (1982) also conclude that research on gender differences with respect to loneliness has produced inconsistent findings. The authors argue that reported gender differences are not the result of differences in the experience of loneliness. Rather, the finding that men report less intense loneliness feelings should be attributed to men's greater reluctance to report socially undesirable feelings. This brings me to the *second hypothesis:* The intensity of feelings of loneliness expressed will be approximately equal for both men and women living with partners, provided that a research situation has been created in which the respondents (especially the men) feel they can be candid about their loneliness.

POSSIBLE SOURCES OF MEN'S LONELINESS

Next, I wished to examine the factors that can explain reported feelings of loneliness. The central argument of the theory presented here is that to understand loneliness, one must pay specific attention to people's personal interpretations and perceptions of their social networks. In line with this argument, the personal evaluation of the social network is thought to contribute more to loneliness than other objective network characteristics such as the number of reported friends and neighbors. Thus the *third hypothesis* concerned the respondents' evaluations. It predicted that respondents will report more intense feelings of loneliness if they are dissatisfied with their achieved social contacts. The hypothesis applied to the situation of both men and women. In contrast, the *fourth hypothesis* stated that there will be a weak relationship between loneliness feelings and the descriptive characteristics of the social network.

The research literature provides no clues about gender differences within the set of loneliness causes. Wheeler, Reis, and Nezlek (1983) show that the same factors serve to preclude loneliness for both males and females. Nevertheless, according to Chodorow (1978, p. 199), men have different relational needs than women.

> A man achieves his emotional and physical union through the heterosexual bond. . . . [Men] are likely to participate in an intimate heterosexual relationship with the ambivalence created by an intensity which one both wants and fears.

The reason for this fear is located by Chodorow in the fact that men are brought up and grow up rejecting their own emotional needs. In contrast:

> Women have different and more complex relational needs in which an *exclusive* relationship to a man is not enough. . . . In addition, the relation to a man itself has difficulties, . . . due as much to men's problems with intimacy as to outcomes of early childhood relationships. . . . In particular, relationships to men are unlikely to provide for women satisfaction of the relational needs. . . . they are encouraged . . . to look elsewhere for love and emotional gratification. (pp. 199-200; emphasis added)

Rubin (1983, pp. 129-130) states in her report of a series of interviews about friendship with over 200 men and women:

> Even when a woman did name her husband to one or more of these roles [of best friend, most trusted confidant and/or the one they would be most likely to turn to in emotional distress], it was never *exclusively* his, as was most likely to be the case with a man. Most women identified at least one, usually more, trusted friends to whom they could turn in a troubled moment, and they spoke openly and ardently about the importance of these relationships in their lives. (emphasis added)

The last two hypotheses concerned possible gender differences in the type of relational deficits that contribute to loneliness. The *fifth hypothesis* stated that men will be more likely to attribute their experiences of loneliness to a perceived lack of intimacy in the partner relationship than will women. The *sixth hypothesis* predicted that women will be more likely to report dissatisfaction with the social network in general as a cause of loneliness than will men.

METHOD

RESPONDENTS

Data were obtained from a sample of 556 adult men and women (ages 25 to 75). The sample was stratified according to sex and marital status. Names and addresses of the married, nonmarried, divorced, and widowed men and women were selected at random from the population registers of Haarlem, an older city (population approximately 175,000); Purmerend, a rapidly growing commuter city with many high-rise apartment buildings (population about 48,000); and Nieuwkoop (population about 9,000), a village in the "green heart" of Holland. A total of 249 people were registered as living with partners. It is worth mentioning that the sample also included (among others): 143 people living on their own, 70 single mothers, and 18 single fathers. Approximately 30% of the people living with partners proved unavailable or simply refused to be interviewed. All the respondents were interviewed in their own homes. The semistructured interviews lasted from two to three hours.

Social stereotypes dictate that it is unacceptable, especially for males, to express emotional weakness or distress (Borys et al., 1982). Given that lonely men may feel reluctant to talk about their feelings, it is important to provide a research encounter in which the respondents can freely disclose their experiences and conceptions. Therefore, the selection and training of the interviewers received special care. Close attention also was paid to the order in which the questions concerning the central theoretical concepts were presented. The interview involved a progression from less to more personal or intimate inquiries, as the relationship between the participant and the interviewer developed. With the special consideration given to the research situation, I am confident that the respondents were encouraged successfully to be open about their experiences of loneliness. This was demonstrated, for example, by the increasing openness of respondents who had started the interview with a relatively large number of reserved and impersonal answers. Furthermore, a change was observed in the nature of what the respondents conveyed about loneliness. In their answers to the opening question, respondents generally referred to superficial aspects of social isolation; as the interview progressed, personal experiences were related.

QUESTIONNAIRE

Several loneliness measures were utilized in the survey, including a nine-item loneliness deprivation scale that incorporated four items indicating the longing for a very close friend or a confidant, three items assessing emptiness feelings, and two items measuring feelings of abandonment (for further details, see De Jong-Gierveld & Raadschelders, 1982). The deprivation scale yielded a value of .86 for the reliability coefficient α, and a value of .44 for Loevinger's homogeneity coefficient. The loneliness items were alternated with statements indicating a preference for living on one's own to minimize response set.

The other questions in the interview schedule concerned (a) *personality characteristics* such as self-concept and introversion-extroversion; (b) *descriptive characteristics of the social network* such as the frequency of contact and the sexes and ages of friend, family, colleague, and neighbor contacts; (c) the *subjective evaluation of the social network*, that is, the degree of satisfaction with the achieved relationships in general, the degree of intimacy in the relationships, the desire for improvement of the relationships; and (b) *background variables* such as age, living and housing arrangements, employment, and daily working activities.

RESULTS

THE PRESENCE OF MEN'S FEELINGS OF LONELINESS

The findings with respect to the respondents' feelings of loneliness revealed a striking difference between men living with partners and men living without partners. Table 6.1 shows that men living with partners were significantly less lonely than men not living with partners, $p < .001$. This observation held for the female respondents as well. Females living with partners were significantly less lonely than females not living with partners, $p < .001$. Thus the data provided ample support for hypothesis 1.

Note that the rest of this chapter concerns the situation of men and women with partners only. With respect to hypothesis 2, Table 6.1 indicates a marginal difference in lonely feelings between men and women living with partners. As predicted, the differences were not significant.

TABLE 6.1
Mean Loneliness Scores on the Loneliness-Deprivation Scale
(range 0.00-9.00)

	Males[a]	(n)	Females[b]	(n)	Gender Difference Test[c]
In families living with					
a partner (total)	.52	(136)	.61	(113)	
married	.48	(80)	.69	(85)	−1.38
nonmarried, divorced, widowed	.59	(36)	.36	(28)	1.21
Living alone (total)	3.37	(56)	2.63	(87)	
nonmarried	2.42	(12)	2.16	(32)	.31
divorced	3.81	(21)	2.67	(15)	1.28
widowed	3.48	(23)	3.00	(40)	.74

a. Means of men living in families differ significantly from means of men living alone: $t(72.71) = -7.91, p < .001$, two-tailed test.
b. Means of women living in families differ significantly from means of women living alone: $t(106.95) = -7.24, p < .001$, two-tailed test.
c. Student's t-test; none of the means differed significantly at $p < .05$.

LONELINESS AND THE SUBJECTIVE EVALUATION OF THE SOCIAL NETWORK

Table 6.2 presents the correlations between the intensity of lonely feelings and a number of variables indicating the respondents' subjective evaluations of their social networks. The overall evaluations of the social networks are presented in the top section of Table 6.2. These measures assess the dissatisfaction with relationships in general and an explicit wish for new (or better) relationships.

Significant correlations between loneliness and the overall evaluations of the social network were found for both men and women. The more specific evaluative measures are presented in the middle and bottom sections of Table 6.2. For men, feelings of loneliness were related to low intimacy ratings of their most important relationship, and to the absence of close contacts in the neighborhood. For women, there was a significant correlation between feelings of loneliness and agreement with the statement that people in the neighborhood are not friendly. Thus the results confirmed hypothesis 3: Loneliness is significantly related to the subjective evaluation of achieved social relationships.

TABLE 6.2

**Correlations Between Loneliness and the Subjective
Evaluation of Respondents' Social Networks**

	Men in Families (n = 136)	Women in Families (n = 113)	Gender Difference Test[a]
Dissatisfaction with relationships in general	.17**	.48**	<.01
Desire for new relationships	.14*	.35**	n.s.
Intimacy score of most important relationship	−.28**	−.00	<.01
Desire for improved confidant relationship	.11	−.09	n.s.
Agreement with statement, "People in this neighborhood are not friendly."	.08	.16*	n.s.
Agreement with statement, "I do not have any good contacts in this neighborhood."	.27**	.07	n.s.

NOTE: n.s. = not significant.
a. Fischer's z-test.
$*p < .10$; $**p < .05$.

LONELINESS AND THE DESCRIPTIVE CHARACTERISTICS OF THE SOCIAL NETWORK

The findings on the relationship between loneliness and a number of descriptive characteristics of the social networks of the respondents are presented in Table 6.3. For men in families, the frequency of contacts with neighbors and, to a lesser extent, the number of individuals mentioned with whom they have the closest ties were negatively correlated with loneliness. No effects were revealed for the number of relationships with family members, colleagues, or acquaintances. Furthermore, inspection of Table 6.3 shows that for women in families, the frequency of contacts with neightbors was also negatively correlated with loneliness. The other variables did not yield significant correlations for the female respondents.

A comparison of Table 6.3 with Table 6.2 indicates that the subjective evaluation of the social network was more closely related to loneliness than were its objective characteristics. The findings showed that hypothesis 3 and hypothesis 4 could not be rejected: For men and women living with partners the perception of the quality and quantity of their social networks was a more important factor in the experience of loneliness than other characteristics such as the number of friends and the frequency of contacts.

TABLE 6.3
Correlations Between Loneliness and the Descriptive
Characteristics of Respondents' Social Networks

	Men in Families (n = 136)	Women in Families (n = 113)	Gender Difference Test[a]
Number of relationships	−.15*	.00	n.s.
Number of relationships with friends	−.14*	−.04	n.s.
Number of family relationships	.01	−.03	n.s.
Number of relationships with neighbors or colleagues	.06	.06	n.s.
Frequency of contacts with neighbors	−.33**	−.17*	n.s.

NOTE: n.s. = not significant.
a. Fischer's z-test.
*$p < .01$; **$p < .05$.

GENDER DIFFERENCES IN THE TYPES OF RELATIONAL DEFICITS CONTRIBUTING TO LONELINESS

The results of Fischer's z-test of the correlation coefficients, which are presented in the far right columns of Tables 6.2 and 6.3, indicated possible gender differences in the types of relational deficits that contribute to loneliness. A number of striking differences between males and females living with partners can be observed. For men the correlation between loneliness and the intimacy rating of their most important relationship was significantly higher than for women ($p < .01$). This led to the conclusion that the loneliness of men in families was largely and exclusively dependent on the evaluation of their relationship with only one person: their confidant, usually the spouse or partner. Thus the data provided evidence for hypothesis 5.

With respect to hypothesis 6, loneliness among women in families did not appear to be related to a perceived lack of intimacy in the partner relationship. Rather, experiences of loneliness appeared to be related primarily to the women's subjective evaluation of a broader range of contacts with others; that is, their dissatisfaction with their social networks in general. The correlation between loneliness and the overall evaluation measure "dissatisfaction with relationships in general" was significantly higher for women than for men ($p < .01$).

DISCUSSION

The present study showed that for men and women living with partners, the mean loneliness scores were low in comparison with those of single men and women. The results also revealed that there were no differences in the likelihood that men and women living in family situations will become lonely. The absence of a significant gender difference in the incidence of loneliness is in line with previous research (Borys et al., 1982; Wheeler, Reis, & Nezlek, 1983). To control for the possibility that differences in the findings between men and women could be attributed to a greater reluctance on the part of the men to be open about their experiences of loneliness, special care was taken to provide a research encounter in which the respondents could disclose their feelings freely.

As predicted, the severity of lonely feelings of these adults was shown to be related primarily to the subjective evaluation of their social networks. The greatest effects were found for the variables measuring the dissatisfaction with relationships in general and the desire for new or improved contacts. These subjective factors were more influential than other more objective social network characteristics such as the number or frequency of contacts. The latter observation is consistent with the findings of Wheeler et al. (1983).

Finally, an important gender effect was found. The loneliness of male respondents was strongly associated with the perceived quality of only one relationship, namely, that with the female confidant/partner. In contrast, the loneliness of female respondents was strongly associated with the subjective evaluation of their network in general. These findings fit in with the notion that men, socialized to be emotionally independent, are generally hesitant to enter into emotionally demanding relationships, except the one sexually and emotionally intimate bond with a live-in partner (Chodorow, 1978; Rubin, 1983).

At this point where this important relationship fails, men will acknowledge intense feelings of loneliness. Little is known about what happens after this primary relationship ends, through either death of the partner or divorce. Research findings have shown that about 60% of these men report feelings of loneliness (De Jong-Gierveld, 1984). More knowledge is required about the factors that determine whether or not men without partners will become lonely. I will be addressing precisely this issue in a coming research project.

REFERENCES

Borys, S., Perlman, D., & Goldenberg, S. (1982, May). *Gender differences in loneliness.* Paper presented at the meeting of the Midwestern Psychological Association, Minneapolis.

Chodorow, N. (1978). *The reproduction of mothering.* Berkeley: University of California Press.

De Jong-Gierveld, J. (1971). Social isolation and the image of the unmarried. *Sociologia Neerlandica, 7,* 1-14.

De Jong-Gierveld, J. (1984). *Eenzaamheid* [Loneliness]. Deventer: Van Loghum Slaterus.

De Jong-Gierveld, J., & Dykstra, P. (1984, April). *Task demands and experienced problems for women in different life circumstances.* Paper prepared for the Second International Interdisciplinary Congress on Women, Groningen, The Netherlands.

De Jong-Gierveld, J. & Raadschelders, J. (1982). Types of loneliness. In L. A. Peplau & D. Perlman (Eds.), *Loneliness: A sourcebook of current theory, research and therapy* (pp. 105-119) New York: John Wiley.

Gove, W. R. (1972). Sex, marital status and suicide. *Journal of Health and Social Behavior, 13*(2), 204-213.

Gove, W. R., & Hughes, M. (1980). Reexamining the ecological fallacy: A study in which aggregate data are critical in investigating the pathological effects of living alone. *Social Forces, 57,* 1157-1177.

Kobrin, F., & Hendershot, G. (1977). Do family ties reduce mortality? Evidence from the US, 1966-68. *Journal of Marriage and the Family, 39,* 737-747.

Rubin, L. B. (1983). *Intimate strangers: Men and women together.* New York: Harper & Row.

Van de Giessen, G. J. (1983). Onderzoek gezinsvorming 1982: Voorburg/Heerlen: CBS. *Maandstatistiek van de bevolking, 31,* 4-5.

Veenhoven, R. (1983). The growing impact of marriage. *Social Indicators Research, 12,* 49-63.

Wheeler, L., Reis, H., & Nezlek, J. (1983). Loneliness, social interaction and sex roles. *Journal of Personality and Social Psychology, 4,* 943-953.

PART II

Men as Fathers

Since 1976, when Michael Lamb described fathers as "forgotten
contributors to child development," the paternal role has received a
great deal of attention from theorists and researchers. Although
research on the mother's role still dominates the literature, the
contribution and involvement of fathers has now been well
documented. It is clear, however, that there is still much we do not
know about fathers.

At this point in the history of the study of fathers we can see a
number of trends. First, the majority of studies on fathers have
focused on fathers' involvement with infants and preschoolers.
Second, the use of white, middle-class subjects predominates in the
literature. Third, most theory and research on fathers focuses on the
father-child relationship outside of any broader familial context. We
believe that this section on fathers, although brief, will help to fill in
some of the gaps in the field. We especially want to emphasize the
importance of seeing the various dimensions of fatherhood in a
setting that includes other aspects of men's familial roles.

One of the least appreciated and least understood aspects of
fathering is the involvement of the would-be father in childbearing
decisions. Most of us assume that men are not interested in these
issues. As Baber and Dreyer point out in Chapter 7, even researchers
have given little attention to the male role in the decision to parent or
not to parent. They conclude that there is a great deal of ambivalence
on the part of many males. Their thoughtful discussion reminds us
that, as with women, there is great variance in men's interest and

desire to parent. Therefore we should not replace the traditional assumptions with new stereotypes too quickly.

In Chapter 8, Michael Lamb, Joseph Pleck, and James Levine sound a similar warning against replacing traditional concepts of the father's role with new stereotypes. They argue that it is misguided to see increased paternal involvement as a panacea. Rather, they suggest that *increased options* for fathers and mothers may be a more reasonable goal. This article represents a cutting edge of work on paternal involvement with children, because it stems from their mutual work on the Fatherhood Project, a major ongoing investigation of many aspects of the father role.

One of the aspects of fatherhood that has been overlooked by many researchers is the father role played in various ethnic groups. There are little or no data available on fathers in many of the ethnic groups that make up our pluralistic society. This is especially true of the Black father.

In Chapters 9 and 10, Michael Conner and John McAdoo, respectively, provide new insights into the Black father. It is interesting to see the similar findings from these two studies, given that Connor's sample is composed of predominantly working-class men, while McAdoo's sample is mostly from the middle class. Connor and McAdoo both argue that not only has the Black father been overlooked, but he has been the victim of extremely negative stereotypes. Connor provides the argument that, contrary to some oversimplified viewpoints, Black fathers *are* interested, involved, and present in the majority of Black families. McAdoo also finds that Black fathers have a highly nurturant attitude toward their children. He adds yet another dimension by looking at nurturance and restrictiveness by Black fathers and the reciprocal effects of these variables upon their children's behavior and ethnic identity.

In Chapter 11, Shirley Hanson provides a thorough review of the literature on the single-father family. Hanson finds that, although the increase in single-parent families has been dramatic in the past twenty years, little is known about the impact of single fathers on children. Hanson concludes that "the majority of single fathers appear to be supportive and nurturing parents to children, irrespective of social class, historical experiences with their own fathers, or even the circumstances through which they receive custody."

In the final chapter of this section, Draughn and Waggenspack point out that most of what we know about fathers and their children is about fathers and *sons;* these authors urge increased investigation of fathers' interactions with their daughters. For their own part they found very low correlations between fathers' and daughters' perceptions of the support fathers had given their daughters. As little research has compared these perceptions directly, they suggest that such comparison could provide new insights not only into father-daughter interaction, but into father-son interaction as well.

7

DELAYED CHILDBEARING: MEN'S THINKING ABOUT THE FERTILITY DECISION

Kristine M. Baber
Albert S. Dreyer

The research on delayed childbearing and childlessness has generally focused on the women involved and how their educational and career goals and their desires to fulfill themselves in nontraditional ways affect the timing of their first child. Little attention has been given to the partners of these women, their contribution to the decision-making process, and their readiness for parenthood. With the exception of a study by May (1982), men's readiness for fathering has been unresearched in spite of a recent burgeoning interest in fatherhood in general. Even studies such as that by Feldman, Nash, and Aschenbrenner (1983) that focus on the "antecedents of fathering" have not investigated this variable. A man's readiness or unreadiness for the parental role may well affect not only his future development, but the pregnancy and parental adjustment of his spouse and the father-child relationship as well. This is, therefore, a subject worthy of investigation, particularly in a sample of delayed childbearers, among whom one would expect readiness for parenting to be quite high.

This study, as part of a longitudinal project on delayed childbearing, explores readiness for parenting in a sample of 34 men who, along with their wives, were either expecting their first child or were voluntarily child free. The larger study investigated various psychosocial and personality factors in childbearing decisions that differentiated couples choosing to become parents after age 30 and those remaining child free.[1] The focus of the current report is on the two groups of men and their thinking about fertility decisions and fatherhood.

SAMPLE CHARACTERISTICS

The demographic characteristics of the two groups, expectant and child free, were remarkably similar. There was no significant difference between the two groups in regard to age, the number of years the partners had known each other, years married, income or educational levels, religious affiliation, or the importance of religion in their lives.

Both groups of men were in their middle thirties. Their spouses were in their early thirties. No participant in the study had ever been a parent by this or a previous relationship. The child-free individuals had to be so by choice. Individuals with histories of infertility problems were not considered for participation. Both groups of couples had known each other for about ten years; both groups of couples had been married about seven years.

The men in this study were well educated. A large majority of the men (and their spouses) had advanced degrees of some type. All of the men but one, who was a graduate student, were employed at the time of the study, mainly in professional, managerial, or executive positions. A large majority of both groups of men said that religion plays little or no role in their lives.

PROCEDURE

Data were collected through in-depth semistructured interviews and five paper and pencil questionnaires. An attempt was made to interview all expectant participants in the last trimester of the pregnancy, generally in the seventh month. Interviews were conducted individually, generally in the participants' homes, by two trained female interviewers, to allow each individual to express his or her own thinking on the subject whether it was in agreement or disagreement with the partner's. All interviews were tape recorded. Interview questions focusing on the men's thinking about becoming fathers, the decision-making process regarding childbearing, the marital relationship, and career importance were content analyzed and coded. Percentage agreement between the coders ranged from .74 to 100% for the variables used in this study.

OTHER INSTRUMENTS

Each participant completed a one-page demographic questionnaire that provided basic information on age, sex, education, occupation, income, marital history, family of origin, religiosity, and pet ownership.

An instrument referred to as the PIE and used by Cowan, Cowan, Coie, and Coie (1978) with expectant couples as a measure of identity was employed for similar purposes in this study. Each individual was given a page with a circle four inches in diameter on it and was asked to divide up the pie to show all the different parts that make up the total self. To code the PIE diagrams, the parts were divided into categories— individually oriented, relationship oriented, and career oriented—and the percentage of the PIE represented by each category of parts was determined.

An abbreviated version of the Jackson (1974) Personality Research Form was used to measure personality factors suggested by the literature as potential mediators of the childbearing decision. The seven eight-item scales used were Achievement, Impulsivity, Autonomy, Dominance, Nurturance, Succorance, and Social Desirability scale.

In addition, an instrument developed by Miller (1980) was used to investigate participants' orientations to female roles. More detailed information on this instrument is available in Baber (1983).

FINDINGS

The first-time fathers in May's (1982) study identified three factors important to a sense of readiness for the parental role: stability in the couple relationship, relative financial security, and a sense of closure to the childless period of their lives. The first two criteria could easily be seen to have been met by the men in this sample. The child-free men have known their partners for an average of 10.94 years and the expectant men for 9.67 years, and 80% of them describe their marriages in very positive terms. A total of 59% of the child-free men and 71% of the expectant men have individual annual incomes of over $20,000, and most indicate a sense of financial stability they had not known earlier in their adult lives.

The third criterion, then, might be seen to be the most critical in exploring the readiness of these men to move into the fathering role. All of the men in this study have been child free throughout their adult lives and, almost without exception, spoke of the freedom and spontaneity of that lifestyle. Now, however, they are being faced with decisions about childbearing as their wives face both real and perceived limits to their childbearing years. Because it is the female who feels this biological press more directly, it is not surprising that the men reported that it was usually the women who would raise the issue for discussion and who pushed for resolution one way or another. This more intense interest on the part of the women in making a commitment to either having a child or remaining child free underscores the need to examine the men's readiness for closure to the child-free period of their lives.

Fundamental factors influencing a movement toward closure to the child-free period in a man's life are the intention ever to have a child and the degree to which a child is wanted. The interviews with the child-free men indicated that they were, indeed, child-free by choice and only one man indicated that he and his wife had ever tried to conceive. The expectant men were asked whether the pregnancy was planned or not, and each interview was coded to reflect the intendedness and wantedness of the pregnancy and the expected child. All but three of the men indicated that the pregnancy was fully planned. In two cases, the child was wanted even though the timing was not exactly as planned; in only one case, the expectant father indicated that he would have preferred that the pregnancy had not occurred.

To quantify wantedness of a child scores, each man was asked to place himself on a scale from 0 to 10 in regard to how much he wanted a child (0 = do not want a child at all; 10 = want a child very much). As might be predicted, the expectant men had significantly higher mean wantedness scores (M = 8.34) than did the child-free men (M = 4.94), $t(32)$ = +4.38, p = .001. These scores are particularly interesting when one inspects the pattern of means of the husbands and wives in each group. The expectant women have a somewhat higher mean score (M = 8.95) than do the expectant men, and the child-free women have a lower mean wantedness scores (M = 8.34) than did the child-free men (M = 4.94), t that for both groups, it is the woman's preference that prevails.

There are at least two possible explanations for this and they are not necessarily mutually exclusive. One is that these women are, in fact, more influential than their spouses in the area of childbearing decisions, whether the decision is to have a child or not. Both husband and wife interviews were coded by independent coders to determine which partner was most influential in the decision-making process—the husband, the wife, whether it was a mutual decision, or whether it could not be determined. A 2×4 chi-square analysis indicated that there were no significant differences between the groups across influence categories. The wives were perceived by the coders to be the most influential in 42% of the child-free cases and 49% of the expectant. The husband was most influential in only 8% of the expectant cases, compared with 27% of the child-free. Of the cases in each group, 8% could not be coded. In the remaining cases, neither spouse was seen to be more influential than the other.

The second explanation may be that some of the husbands do not care as much as their wives, one way or another, and therefore their wives appear to be more influential. The child-free males' mean wantedness score, unencumbered by the effects of cognitive dissonance engendered by the pregnancy itself, lends support to this explanation. On a scale of 0 to 10 it is difficult to get much closer to the middle of the scale than have the child-free men.

All interviews were coded to reflect the participants' perceptions of who felt more strongly about the fertility decision—the husband, the wife, or both having similar feelings. In 41% of the cases in each group, the women were perceived to feel more strongly about the decision. In the child-free group, 30% of the husbands were perceived to feel more strongly, while in the expectant group, only 16% did. Mutuality of feeling was perceived in 43% of the expectant and 22% of the child free. (This variable could not be coded for 3 of the child-free interviews.)

These findings suggest that the women, particularly the expectant women, may be as influential as they are because they do feel more strongly about the fertility decision. An exploration of the men's responses to various questions about childbearing decisions reveals considerable ambivalence about having a child; this is particularly true among the expectant men.

[Expectant father, age 36]: I have never really thought that children were that important in my life. It's something that if we had one, fine. If we didn't have one, it didn't bother me either. It didn't bother me, the thought of never having a child.

[Expectant father, age 33]: I don't think when we decided to have a child we made a conscious decision—at least on my part it was not a conscious decision.... If it hadn't happened, I would still be just as happy, or just the same person. I wouldn't say my life revolves around having a child, a baby.

[Expectant father, age 40 (talking about discussion with wife)]: My expectation is that your career would suffer more than mine and if you are willing to do that, then I would like to have a child. If you are not willing to do that, then it is okay with me. I'd be perfectly happy not to have a child, I could go either way. But at this point, I'm not willing to sacrifice part of my career to have a child.

[Expectant father, age 33]: I never felt the need to perpetuate my name, continue the family line. I never thought about it that much. Work is more important to me.... Frankly, I am still torn between my work and this. I have a decision to make about my career. I am going for tenure and this is a critical year for me. I am trying to get a lot of my work done so that I will have more time once the baby is born.

The conflict between careers and childrearing was a theme underlying the ambivalence of many of the expectant men. Though careers were important to both groups of men, it was found that the expectant rated their careers as more important in relationship to their other life goals and activities than did the child free. On a scale of 1 to 7, with 7 being most important, the expectant men had a mean score of 6.08 and the child-free men, 5.18, $t(32) = -2.38$, $p = .02$. The expectant men were also significantly more likely to define themselves as achievement oriented than were the child free, $t(32) = -2.25$, $p = .03$. Although some of the expectant men did feel increased financial pressure due to the impending birth, the importance of their careers seemed separate from this. In fact, when participants were asked why their work was important to them, both expectant men and expectant women were significantly less likely than the child free to indicate that it was for financial reasons, $\chi^2(1, 68) = 10.24$, $p = .001$.

The fact that these men perceive a conflict between their careers and childbearing is somewhat revolutionary in itself and reflects what Fein (1978) refers to as the "emergent perspective" on fathering. This is based on the belief that men are psychologically able to participate in a full range of parenting activities, and also that fathering is beneficial to all members of the family system—the child and the mother, as well as the father himself. This perspective is manifested in our society in a whole new set of expectations about men and their roles in pregnancy, childbirth, and child rearing. In this older, well-educated group of men, both child free and expectant, it was assumed that if and when they became fathers they would be active, involved, and nurturing. Yet these men had no clear role models for combining participatory parenting with other aspects of their lives. There is no well-defined set of goals, attitudes, and behaviors for these men to assume. As a result, they are forced to construct new fathering roles. Turner (1962) calls this "role-making," a term that refers to a dynamic, process-oriented conception of roles and how they develop. The content of many of the roles in our society is increasingly the result of improvisation (Aldous, 1978), and this is particularly true for these delayed childbearing men. Whereas with traditional sex-role preferences one is spared the necessity of making decisions about most of one's actions because the norms are so clear (Scanzoni & Fox, 1980), role-making continually demands decisions and innovations, and this process may not be comfortable.

[Expectant father, age 32]: I wasn't ready and she was. I felt like I was being pressured into something I didn't want.

One expectant father expresses conflict about changes he anticipates in more psychological terms:

[Expectant father, age 34]: I don't know what it will be like. . . . The strongest thing I see it being is an antithesis to my ego which will cause that ego to make adjustments . . . and somewhere in the back of me something says that's probably a good idea, although on the face of it, the ego obviously doesn't think it's a good idea.

But change and innovation, role-making, is not totally new to these men, as this same expectant father suggests as he talks about other changes the baby will bring about.

It will be outwardly different but I don't see anything substantively different. There will still be tensions and areas to work on and deal with and they will revolve around the child, no doubt, whereas now they revolve around cleaning the house.

One of the most striking differences between the child-free and expectant men in the study was the autonomy and individual orientation of those who chose to have no children. On the Autonomy scale of the Personality Research Form, the child-free had significantly higher scores than did their expectant counterparts, t (31) = 2.18, p = .04. According to Jackson (1976), autonomous individuals are more likely to resist confinements or restrictions of any kind. They enjoy being unattached, free, and not tied to people, places, or obligations. In graphically depicting their sense of self, the child-free men also defined 32% of their PIE diagrams in terms of individual roles and activities, compared to only 18% for the expectant men. The thinking of the child-free men about having a child reflects this individual orientation.

[Child-free man, age 33]: There have been so many other things that I have wanted to do with my life that have been more important.

[Child-free man, age 40]: I have no desire whatsoever to reproduce, but I keep myself open continuously to reevaluation on that. . . . Our lifestyle revolves a lot around continuing personal growth and an environment that allows spontaneity and promotes spontaneity.

[Child-free man, age 31]: I have one life as far as I know. Do I really want to devote such a huge chunk of it to just caring for this needy other when things could just be so much easier without having a child. It's like I am split in two.

Another type of ambivalence is evident in the thinking of the child-free men and this has to do with the relativity of the childbearing decision. One of the men explains that "having a child is a very situational kind of thing. It's not a sort of absolute decision. It's totally related to how everything else is going." It may be this sense of relativity that helps account for the fact that only two of the child-free men have chosen to be sterilized, the others preferring to keep their options open. And even though they have chosen not to have children in their current relationships, many of them do not preclude exercising this option in the future.

[Child-free man, age 31]: I have a strong feeling that if I were not involved in a relationship now, I would not be thinking of children in that I know I can have a child several decades from now with another woman if I so desire. If I were alone, I would have the freedom to feel that and then the issue of children would be temporarily shelved because I wouldn't have to answer to anyone. I feel pressured and cornered in a predicament where the years are ticking away, the childbearing years, and I have to make a decision and I don't feel as though I'm ready to have children.

[Child-free man, age 40]: I could imagine myself at 60. If L. were gone and I had a relationship with someone else, I could conceive of having a child even that late in life.

This sense of ambivalence about making a decision to have or not have a child, then, was found in both the child-free and the expectant men's thinking, though it assumes different forms in each. Not all of the men in either group are ambivalent, of course, but what is striking is this pervasive lack of readiness for a full commitment to either parenthood or a child-free lifestyle.

DISCUSSION

Although the finding of men's ambivalence about becoming fathers is not in itself unusual, the information provided by exploration into men's thinking about the meaning of parenthood in their lives is important for a number of reasons. Most obviously it adds to the growing body of conceptual and empirical knowledge about men's transition to parenthood. Perhaps most important, in this regard, it will act as a healthy corrective to researchers, educators, and practitioners who would move too quickly to replace traditional and now outdated assumptions about men's desire and ability to parent with new stereotypes. While there is a movement toward increased participation by fathers in all aspects of the childbearing and -rearing processes, this study suggests that, just as with women, there is great variance in men's interest and desire to parent. We would reiterate Harrison's (1978, p. 366) warning that "until we have a new paradigm securely in place, all claims to 'new knowledge' about what it means to be male or female in modern society should be treated with much more than the usual dose of skepticism."

The ambivalence of the men in this study may also help to explain some of the anomalies in the findings of other transition to parenthood studies. For example, in a sample of fathers with very young infants, Cordell, Parke, and Sawin (1980) found that fathers with less than full-time work loads, either because they had taken time off from work after the child's birth or because they were unemployed, were less willing to assume infant care responsibilities than were fathers with full-time work loads. Perhaps the readiness of men to parent needs to be investigated further as an intervening variable.

While attention has been focused on the effects of men's involvement in their wives' pregnancies and parental adjustment (Entwisle & Doering, 1981; Grossman, Eichler, & Winiskoff, 1980; Shereshefsky & Yarrow, 1973) and on the child's growth and development (Clarke-Stewart, 1978; Belsky, 1980), no systematic investigation has been done of the role of fathering in a man's individual development. Future research should consider the developmental implications of having to construct the father role when men approach it with different degrees of readiness.

NOTE

1. The larger study also included six women whose husbands declined to participate.

REFERENCES

Aldous, J. (1978). *Family careers: Developmental changes in families*. New York: John Wiley.

Baber, K. M. (1983). *Delayed childbearing: the psychosocial aspects of the decision-making process*. Unpublished doctoral dissertation, University of Connecticut, Storrs.

Belsky, J. A. (1980). A family analysis of parental influence on infant exploratory competence. In F. Pedersen (Ed.), *The father-infant relationship: Observational studies in a family context* (pp. 87-110). New York: Praeger.

Clarke-Stewart, K. A. (1978). And daddy makes three: The father's impact on mother and young child. *Child Development, 49,* 466-478.

Cordell, A. S., Parke, R. D., and Sawin, D. B. (1980). Fathers' views on fatherhood with special reference to infancy. *Family Relations, 29,* 331-338.

Cowan, C. P., Cowan, P. A., Coie, L., & Coie, J. D. (1978). Becoming a family: The impact of a first child on the couple's relationship. In W. B. Miller & L. F. Newman (Eds.), *The first child and family formation* (pp. 296-324). Chapel Hill, NC: Carolina Population Center.

Entwisle, D. R., & Doering, S. G. (1981). *The first birth: A family turning point*. Baltimore: Johns Hopkins University Press.

Fein, R. A. (1978). Research on fathering: Social policy and an emergent perspective. *Journal of Social Issues, 34,* 324-336.

Feldman, S. S., Nash, S. C., & Aschenbrenner, B. G. (1983). Antecedents of fathering. *Child Development, 54,* 1628-1636.

Grossman, F. K., Eichler, L. S., & Winickoff, S. A. (1980). *Pregnancy, birth, and parenthood*. San Francisco: Jossey-Bass.

Harrison, J. B. (1978). Men's roles and men's lives. *Signs, 4,* 324-336.

Jackson, D. N. (1974). *Personality Research Form Manual*. Port Huron, MI: Research Psychologists Press.

May, K. A. (1982). Factors contributing to first time fathers' readiness for fatherhood. *Family Relations, 31,* 353-362

Miller, W. B. (1980). *The psychology of reproduction*. Unpublished manuscript, American Institutes for Research, Palo Alto, CA.

Scanzoni, J., & Fox, G. L. (1980). Sex roles, family and society: The seventies and beyond. *Journal of Marriage and the Family, 42,* 743-758.

Shereshefsky, P. M., & Yarrow, L. J. (1973). *Psychological aspects of a first pregnancy and early post-natal adaptation*. New York: Raven.

Turner, R. H. (1962). Role-taking: Process vs. conformity. In A. Rose (Ed.), *Human behavior and social process*. Boston: Houghton Mifflin.

8

EFFECTS OF INCREASED PATERNAL INVOLVEMENT ON CHILDREN IN TWO-PARENT FAMILIES

Michael E. Lamb
Joseph H. Pleck
James A. Levine

In the aftermath of the women's movement, there has been much speculation about the effects of changing female roles on the roles assumed by their male partners and coworkers. Since *Kramer vs. Kramer*, much of the attention in the country has focused on presumed increases in the degree of paternal participation in child care. Fathers have indeed become more involved in at least some aspects of child care in the last two decades (Lamb, Pleck, Charnov, & Levine, in press), although the changes have been much smaller than is generally realized. Nevertheless, these secular changes in the levels of paternal participation have raised questions about the effects of increased paternal involvement on child development. Although some have expressed concern about negative effects on child development, the majority of professional and lay commentators have welcomed these changes with loud claims concerning the positive effects they are likely to have. We take issue with both positions is this chapter, arguing that the available empirical evidence does not support these claims, and that there is no theoretical reason to expect either to be true. To be sure, paternal involvement and the attitudes/values associated with it *can* have positive consequences when it is in accord with the desires of both parents. However, consequences are likely to be either mixed or

Authors' Note: *The work reported here was supported in part by the Fatherhood Project, chiefly funded by the Ford, Levi Strauss, and Ittleson Foundations, as well as by the Rockefeller Family Fund. This chapter is adapted from a longer report by Lamb, Pleck, and Levine (1985). Used by permission of Plenum Publishing Corp.*

negative when either or both parents view increased paternal involvement as an unfortunate circumstance that flies in the face of their values and better judgment.

Because of this, we think it is misguided to see increased paternal involvement as a universally desirable goal. Instead, we believe that attempts should be made to increase the options available to fathers and mothers, so that those who want to be more involved in their children's lives can become so. The evidence reviewed in this chapter, we submit, supports this argument. Children tend to do best when their parents are able to organize their lives and responsibilities in accordance with their own values and preferences, rather than in accord with a rigid, socially determined pattern. While there is evidence that fathers do have significant effect—both positive and negative—on their children's development, none of the evidence reviewed in this chapter suggests that increased paternal involvement *necessarily* has beneficial consequences for children. Instead, it seems that paternal involvement can have positive consequences when it is the arrangement of choice for the family concerned. The goal of this chapter is to review the evidence supporting this conclusion.

Unfortunately, the effects of increased paternal participation were not researched until recently, and thus much of the chapter is concerned with the effects of traditional fathers on child development. Most of these studies, like most studies concerned with increased paternal involvement, have considered effects on sex-stereotyped attitudes and interests, intellectual development and school performance, moral development, and general psychosocial adjustment. In this chapter, two sorts of studies are described. First, there are those studies in which characteristics of paternal behavior are related to measures of the children's development. Unfortunately, paternal involvement is seldom assessed, so these studies tell us little about the correlates of substantial increases in the extent of paternal involvement. However, they demonstrate that even traditionally uninvolved fathers can have a significant influence—for good and for ill—on their children's development.

The second type of study involves comparing children in traditional families with those in which fathers are unusually involved in home and child care. In these studies, the question is not whether fathers have an influence; it is whether increased paternal involvement has an effect. The latter question is more important to us, and so more emphasis will be placed on studies of this sort. Unfortunately, such studies are still rare and are marred by methodological flaws that weaken their interpretability. The most important such problem is that no one has yet studied families from before the adoption of nontraditional family roles. Thus we cannot determine whether paternal involvement per se, rather than associated family characteristics such as maternal employment and attitudes regarding male and female roles, influences the family members. Without such studies, we cannot explain any observed differences between traditional and nontraditional families.

PATERNAL INFLUENCES IN TWO-PARENT FAMILIES

Over the last few decades, there have been many studies designed to determine how fathers in traditional families affect the development of their children. Many of the early studies explored paternal influences by comparing children whose fathers were absent with those whose fathers were present on the assumption that the differences between these two groups of children represented the fathers' influence in two-parent families. With the realization that father-present and father-absent families differed in many other ways (for example, economically and socially), researchers turned their attention from studies of father absence to studies focused on father-child interaction and paternal influences in two-parent families. With a few recent exceptions, all of these studies were focused on traditional families in which fathers were primarily responsible for breadwinning, while mothers were not employed and were primarily responsible for home and child care. For the reasons articulated earlier, our review is necessarily brief; more comprehensive and detailed reviews are provided in two recent volumes (Lamb, 1981e; Adams, Milner, & Schrepf, 1984).

INFANCY

Do infants form attachments to their fathers? Students of infancy have long emphasized the importance of attachment, which is believed to develop in the middle of the first year of life. Attachments by definition involve trustful, focused relationships to specific people; they are marked by preferences in contact seeking, separation protest, greeting, and the desire to be held (Ainsworth, 1973; Bowlby, 1969; Lamb, 1974, 1977b).

Research on father-infant relationships has been undertaken only in the last two decades because it has long been assumed that infants were capable of forming attachments only to their mothers. The first suggestion that this might be untrue came from two studies in which mothers were asked about their infants' responses to separation from and reunion with various people. Many of the mothers in Schaffer and Emerson's (1964) study reported that their infants began to cry when separated from specific people at around 6-8 months of age. Such "separation protest" occurred most reliably when the babies were separated briefly from their mothers, but in many cases similar reactions occurred following separation from grandparents, sitters, and fathers. By 18 months of age, about three-quarters of the infants reportedly cried when separated from their fathers, indicating that at least this proportion had formed attachments to their fathers as well as to their mothers. Similarly, most mothers told Pedersen and Robson (1969) that their 8- to 9-month-old infants responded with happy excitement when their fathers returned home at the end of the work day.

Concerned about the possibility of bias affecting mothers' reports, researchers in the 1970s began actually observing infants, mothers, and fathers both in their homes and in structured experimental settings. A variety of measures, including separation protest, greeting responses, and bids for contact, proximity, and comfort, indicated that infants typically formed attachments to both of their parents at about the same time—that is, at around 6-8 months of age (Belsky, 1978; Kotelchuck, 1976; Lamb, 1976b, 1977b, 1979). There were usually preferences, however, with infants turning to their mothers especially when they were distressed and had the choice between their two parents (Lamb, 1976a, 1976d).

What about the quality of infant-father attachments? Infants form attachments to their parents when their experiences have led them to trust the accessibility and reliability of the adult concerned (Lamb, 1981a, 1981b). Because parents vary in their responsiveness and interactional styles, infants develop rather different sorts of expectations of their parents. This means not only that there are various types of parent-infant relationships depending on the quality of prior infant-parent interaction, but also that the same infant may form differentially secure relationships with its mother and father (Grossmann, Grossmann, Huber, & Wartner, 1981; Lamb, 1978; Lamb, Hwang, Frodi, & Frodi, 1982; Main & Weston, 1981; Sagi et al., in press). This issue is important because the type of relationship infants form with their parents may have formative or predictive significance (Lamb, Thompson, Gardner, Charnov, & Estes, 1984). At least in stable, middle-class contexts, infants who are "securely attached" to their mothers appear to be more cooperative and sociable with unfamiliar adults and peers, while also being more curious, persistent, and enthusiastic in challenging task-like situations (Arend, Gove, & Sroufe, 1979; Main & Weston, 1981; Matas, Arend, & Sroufe, 1978; Pastor, 1980; Sagi, Lamb, & Gardner, n.d.; Thompson & Lamb, 1982).

Although few studies have considered the issue, it is known that the security of the father-infant attachment can have formative significance as well. In traditional families, the relationships with mothers—the primary caretakers—are probably most significant, but the nature of the infant-father attachments may also have an independent influence (Main & Weston, 1981). Main and Weston found that infants who were securely attached to both parents showed the greatest interest in unfamiliar adults. Next came those who were securely attached only to their (primary caretaking) mothers, then those securely attached only to their (relatively uninvolved) fathers, and finally those who were securely attached to neither parent. This leads us to expect that the relative importance of the infant-father relationships would increase in relation to the degree of paternal involvement. However, this was not found in a Swedish study involving families in which paternal involvement varied across a wide range (Lamb et al., 1982). The degree to which fathers were involved was unrelated to the degree of influence they had. Perhaps this was because the Swedish fathers, although highly involved in child care, rarely engaged in the types of playful interactions that usually increase the salience of father-child relationships.

These findings, along with other results obtained in this longitudinal study, confirm that the relationship between the amount of involvement and the degree of influence on the child is not straightforward. Many researchers—particularly those concerned with the effects of day care or maternal employment—have stressed that the quality of interaction is more important than the quantity. In the Swedish longitudinal study, the degree of paternal involvement appeared to have no effect on the infants' preferences; most infants preferred their mothers regardless of variations in paternal involvement. Noting that these Swedish fathers were not noted for their playfulness in the way American fathers are (Lamb, 1976c, 1981c), Lamb and his colleagues (1983) suggested that paternal playfulness may play an important role in increasing the salience of father-child interactions, even when they are temporally limited. Thus playful, uninvolved American fathers appear more affectively salient to their infants than less playful but substantially more involved Swedish fathers. If correct, this makes it considerably more difficult to assess the effects of increased paternal involvement than it would have been if degree of involvement was the only relevant variable. Overall, however, it seems reasonable to expect that increased paternal involvement has some effect on infant preferences, even though this has yet to be demonstrated empirically.

Does the husband-wife relationship affect the father-infant relationship? Examinations of parental preferences and of the security of infant adult attachments and their influence on the children's later behavior exemplify concerns about *direct* parental influences. Recently, however, researchers have come to recognize that parents may also have indirect influences on their children's development (for instance, Belsky, 1981; Parke, Power, & Gottman, 1979). Thus, for example, mothers and fathers are more nurturant and responsive toward their infants when the interaction between the two parents is warm and positive (Pedersen, Anderson, & Cain, 1980). Likewise, the supportiveness of husbands and friends affects maternal satisfaction with parenthood and thus, presumably, the quality of mothers' behavior toward their infants (Frodi, Lamb, Frodi, Hwang, Forsstrom, & Corry, 1981; Owen, Chase-Lansdale, & Lamb, 1982). What this means is that when we are exploring the effects of increased paternal involvement on infant or child development, we have to consider also the effects of the father's involvement on the mother, since her satisfaction or dissatisfaction is likely to influence the quality of her maternal behavior and thus, indirectly, the child's development. In other words, increased paternal involvement may have adverse consequences if the mother prefers that her spouse not be highly involved. Desirable effects are only likely when both parents feel that paternal involvement is itself desirable. Elsewhere, we review the effects of paternal involvement on mothers and fathers, and thus examine more closely whether and in what circumstances the direct effects on children are likely to be either positive or negative (Lamb, Pleck, & Levine, 1985).

OLDER CHILDREN

Although both direct and indirect effects surely remain important as children grow older, most of the research on parental influences has been focused on direct influences—more particularly, on the ways in which parents shape their children's behavior by the discriminating application of rewards and punishments and by providing models of socially approved behavior for their children to emulate. In the paragraphs that follow, we briefly review the available evidence, focusing on the five aspects of child development regarding which paternal influences have been implicated most frequently.

Do "masculine" fathers have masculine children and does increased paternal involvement affect children's sex-role development? From infancy onward parents (especially fathers) are particularly attentive (and thus salient) to children of the same sex (Lamb, 1977a, 1981d; Parke & Sawin, 1977). This may facilitate the acquisition of gender identity, which seems to occur in the first two to three years of life (Money & Ehrhardt, 1972). "Gender identity" involves both the intellectual knowledge of one's gender and the awareness that it is fixed, as well as psychological satisfaction with one's gender. Important as this appears to be, however, we know little about the origins of gender identity. Instead, most researchers have studied "gender role"—the extent to which the individual's interests and attitudes resemble those that are specified by society to be appropriate for persons of the individual's gender—and the degree of sex typing. Thus we face an ironic situation in which reseachers have studied an aspect of development that may be of little importance, while failing to study the related construct that indeed appears important.

Probably because they are more concerned about "appropriately" sex-typed behavior than mothers are (Bronfenbrenner, 1961; Goodenough, 1957; Sears, Maccoby, & Levin, 1957; Tasch, 1955), fathers emit reinforcements and punishments for sex-typed behavior more consistently than mothers do (Langlois & Downs, 1980). On average, boys whose fathers are absent or uninvolved tend to have either more or less stereotypically masculine attitudes and interests than those whose fathers are psychologically and physically present (see Biller, 1974 and 1981, for reviews). Most boys whose fathers are absent develop normal sex roles, however, underscoring the fact that sex-role development is multiply- and over-determined. Contrary to the initial predictions of social learning theorists, it is not the case that "masculine" fathers have "masculine" sons (for example, Mussen & Rutherford, 1963; Payne & Mussen, 1956). Significant correlations between paternal and filial "masculinity" tend to occur only when the father is also warm: Indeed, nurturance is more reliably related to the masculinity of sons' attitudes and interests than the fathers' "masculinity" is (Mussen & Rutherford, 1963; Payne & Mussen, 1956; Sears et al., 1957). Girls whose fathers have "masculine" interests and attitudes tend to have more stereotypically "feminine" interests (Heilbrun, 1965; Johnson, 1963; Mussen & Rutherford, 1963; Sears, Rau, & Alpert, 1965), presumably because these fathers complement and encourage their daughters' femininity. Both boys and girls develop less traditionally sex-stereotyped self-perceptions and attitudes about male and female roles when their mothers work outside the home (see Hoffman, 1974, and Lamb, 1982b, for reviews) and when their fathers are highly involved in child care (Baruch & Barnett, 1979; Radin, 1978; Radin & Sagi, 1982). Both of these effects are probably attributable to the fact that these parents provide less traditional models for their children to emulate. Sagi (1982) found no effects of increased paternal involvement on the sex roles of boys in his study of Israeli children; perhaps, he suggested, because of a ceiling effect.

We also have major reservations about the meaning of "masculinity" and "femininity" in these studies. To most people, terms such as "masculinity" and "femininity" imply an integrally important aspect of the individual's identity and adjustment. Operationally, however, the terms probably mean much less than this. "Masculinity" and femininity" are typically assessed by determining how closely the individual's attitudes, interests, and self descriptors match those that are stereotypically masculine or feminine. For example, one popular measure, the Bem (1974) Sex Role Inventory, asks people to indicate on scales of 1 to 7, how timid (female), dominant (male), aggressive (male), or shy (female) they are. Their self ratings on 60 such adjectives are then summed to give a total masculinity score and a total femininity score. Obviously, we then have to wonder whether a very aggressive and dominant male should be considered well-adjusted just because he is "highly masculine."

For researchers working with children, meanwhile, the "It" scale has long been popular (Brown, 1956, 1957). This test requires that children choose activities and clothes for an ambiguously drawn figure (It); the more stereotypically "masculine" things chosen (trousers, guns, vehicles), the higher the individual's assessed "masculinity"; the more stereotypically "feminine" things (dolls, dresses, long hair), the higher the individual's assessed "femininity." Again, there is no reason to believe that this tells us anything at all about the individual's intrinsic identity or adjustment.

Overall, these popular tests probably tell us nothing at all about the individual's identity and personality adjustment; they tell us only about the attitudes or interests the person wishes to acknowledge. This fact has two major implications for the interpretation of research. First, when we rely on standard sex-role inventories we learn something only about acknowledged attitudes or interests in sex-stereotyped issues, rather than about personality adjustment. Second, it means that hypotheses about the effects of paternal involvement or father-child relationships on personality adjustment (as manifested by the individual's intrinsic masculinity or femininity) have not really been tested yet, so we cannot consider them either proven or disproven. In addition, Pleck (1981) has recently shown that these inventories may not tap coherent dimensions of masculinity or femininity at all. Thus the extent to which individuals perceive themselves to be shy, for example, may be independent of the extent to which they consider themselves sympathetic or gullible, although self-ratings on all three are usually combined to yield a "femininity" score.

Of course, sex-role acquisition is not only affected by parental behavior. From the preschool years through adulthood, significant influences are exerted also by peers (Fagot, 1977; Fagot & Patterson, 1969; Lamb, Easterbrooks, & Holden, 1980; Lamb & Roopnarine, 1979; Nash & Feldman, 1981), teachers (Dweck, 1978; Fagot, 1977; Serbin, Tonick, & Sternglanz, 1977), and the media. Most of these socializing agents have a similarly traditionalizing effect, making it difficult to appraise the relative importance of each. Further, controversy about the meaning of sex-role measures of masculinity and femininity severely limits interpretations of research in this area (Pleck, 1981), as does evidence that there is little continuity in sex-role adherence since sex roles continue to change across the life span in response to changing role demands (Nash & Feldman, 1981). In other words, whether or not children and/or fathers are sex typed may well be of no great consequence.

Do fathers affect achievement and achievement motivation and does increased paternal involvement enhance these effects? Appropriate responsiveness to infant signals and needs appears to foster the development of a sense of personal efficacy, which is a basic component of achievement motivation (Lamb, 1981a). Other studies show that parents who provide stimulation that is developmentally appropriate and plentiful have more cognitively competent children (see Stevenson & Lamb, 1981, for a review). High achievement motivation develops in boys when parents are warm, not controlling, and encourage independence (Radin, 1976, 1981; Rosen & D'Andrade, 1959; Winterbottom, 1958). Girls benefit when they receive less unconditional nurturance than they usually receive (Barnett & Baruch, 1978; Radin, 1976, 1981). In traditional families (when fathers are primary breadwinners and are the instrumental leaders of their families), the models fathers provide are especially important. Warm encouragement from fathers may be important to many highly achieving women, since there are few female role models for them to emulate (Barnett & Baruch, 1978; Lamb, Owen, & Chase-Lansdale, 1979).

Children whose fathers are absent tend to perform more poorly at school than children from two-parent families (Radin, 1981; Shinn,

1978), but these effects are much more consistent in lower-class than in middle-class families (Radin, 1981). Perhaps this is because single mothers in lower-class families are subject to more severe economic and socioemotional stresses, which affect their ability to guide and stimulate their children. Interestingly, Blanchard and Biller (1971) reported that qualitatively similar effects occurred when fathers were nominally present but were uninvolved with their sons. By contrast, children with highly involved (relative to other traditional men), nurturant fathers tend to be more cognitively competent and to manifest the internal locus of control which is one aspect of higher achievement motivation (Radin, 1978, 1982; Sagi, 1982). The effects of increased paternal involvement on intellectual performance may reflect fathers' traditional association with achievement and occupational advancement, or it could reflect the benefits of having extensive stimulation from two highly involved and relatively competent parents instead of only one.

Recently, conceptualizations of achievement motivation have been influenced by attribution theory (Dweck, 1978; Weiner, 1974), which proposed that individuals can attribute their successes or failures to either controllable or uncontrollable (external) factors and to either effort or ability. Achievement motivation is enhanced when others attribute the child's success to his or her effort and failures to his or her lack of effort; by virtue of their attributions, the child is encouraged to attribute responsibility similarly. By contrast, achievement motivation is squelched when failures are attributed to a lack of ability and success to the easiness of the task. Although most researchers have studied the ways in which teachers affect the development of attributional styles (Dweck, 1978), it is likely that parents are also influential. A recent study by Parsons, Adler, and Kaczala (1982) did in fact show that parents' attitudes and beliefs about their children's mathematics aptitude were more influential in shaping their children's self-concepts and expectations than were the children's past performances.

Do fathers influence the moral development of their children and do more involved fathers have stronger effects? Psychologists who study moral development are concerned about the ability to distinguish right from wrong, the tendency to behave in a socially approved way, and the tendency to feel guilty when one disobeys social norms. In recent years, unfortunately, the ascendance of Kohlberg's cognitive developmental theory of moral development (Kohlberg, 1969) has provoked a focus on general developmental trends, and so less attention has been paid to the origins of individual differences. Furthermore, to the extent that he has explicitly considered environmental influences, Kohlberg has emphasized interactions with peers rather than parents.

A comprehensive review of research on the determinants of moral development a decade and a half ago concluded that parental disciplinary style was indeed influential (Hoffman, 1970). Hoffman suggested that children develop internalized controls ("consciences") most readily when their parents discipline through induction, and least when their parents employ a power-assertive strategy. Induction involves encouraging children to consider the implications of their behavior (notably, their disobedience) for other people. Although some studies show that boys whose fathers are absent display less moral internalization and are more likely to become delinquent than boys whose fathers are present, the preponderance of the evidence indicates that mothers have a much greater influence on moral development than fathers do (Hoffman, 1981). Presumably, this is because mothers spend much more time with their children, especially in the early years. Relative paternal and maternal influences would be expected to increase in accordance with their relative involvement or availability, but this has not yet been directly tested. However, Sagi (1982) found that highly involved fathers had children who were more empathic. If Hoffman (1976) is correct in believing that empathy plays a crucial role in moral development, then Sagi's findings suggest that paternal influences on moral development may increase when fathers are more involved in child care.

Does paternal involvement affect psychological adjustment? Most of the research on this topic has been concerned with the antecedents of psychological maladjustment. Many studies show that children whose parents are divorced or whose fathers are absent are more likely to manifest signs of psychological maladjustment (see Biller, 1981, for a review) but the mode of influence is unclear. Large-scale epidemiological studies (for instance, Rutter, 1973, 1979) show that marital hostility and discord—rather than the father absence which may follow—are among the most reliable causes of psychological maladjustment.

In one of the few studies concerned with parental influences on psychological adjustment, Baumrind (1971, 1975) reported that "instrumentally competent" children (those who are friendly, independent, and assertive with peers and compliantly nonintrusive with adults) are likely to have authoritative parents—that is, parents who provide firm and articulately reasoned guidance for their children. Both authoritarian parents (those who fail to provide any rationale for their instructions) and permissive parents (those who fail to provide adequate guidance) have less instrumentally competent children. Similar effects seem to hold for both mothers and fathers, but we know nothing about the effects of increased paternal involvement.

SUMMARY

It is clear that parents influence their children both by the way they behave toward their children and by the way they interact with one another. Direct and indirect parental influences on the development of sex roles, morality, social competence, effectance, achievement, and psychological adjustment have been demonstrated, although we can for the most part only speculate about the processes of influence because they have been inadequately explored.

In the past, developmental psychologists emphasized maternal influences, and considered fathers only to the extent that they were believed to provide masculine models for their sons to emulate. This emphasis on the parents' sex roles was probably misguided. Of course, in cases where the parent's sex role is important (say, in the development of sex differences and sex roles), mothers and fathers appear to affect their children differently, but in the main, they influence their children in similar ways. In some areas (like sex role development), fathers may exert a disproportionate influence, either because they are especially concerned about the issue, or because their relative novelty increases their salience in the eyes of their children. In other respects (for instance, the predictive validity of early attachments, or moral development), mothers are more influential. However, in these cases the mothers' greater importance is probably due to their greater accessibility and involvement. Consequently, the relative importance of the fathers' influence may increase as their relative involvement in child rearing increases. Furthermore, the quality of the marital relationship and other indirectly mediated effects may be much more influential than was once believed (Parke et al., 1979).

However, there is no evidence that in any of these aspects of development, the father's role is *necessary*. In his absence, development usually proceeds quite normally, because development is multiply determined. The implication is that while increased paternal involvement may increase the magnitude of paternal influence, it does not have effects on children sufficient to justify a conclusion that increased paternal involvement would be beneficial to all children.

✓ Obviously, more research is needed before we fully understand the effects of increased paternal involvement. Based on the available evidence, however, we can discount popular fears that the personal adjustment and gender identity of children will be seriously disturbed if their fathers assume an extensive role in child care.

At this stage, however, we need to wonder whether the "effects" of increased paternal participation can really be attributed directly and simply to the differences in paternal involvement rather than to any other differences between the families (Lamb, 1982a). Families in which fathers share in or take primary responsibility for child care differ in many ways other than the level of paternal involvement (Russell, 1982, 1983). According to Russell, differences in parental attitudes and values antedate, rather than succeed, differences in paternal involvement. Consequently, in the absence of longitudinal evidence showing changes in the children's behavior in reaction to changes in the fathers' level of involvement, we really cannot conclude that paternal involvement is the only important dimension of difference. Instead, Russell's findings underscore our belief that children benefit when their parents are able to divide parental responsibilities in accordance with their individual preferences and values.

CONCLUSION

The evidence reviewed in this chapter is sketchy, inconclusive, and at times contradictory. Attempts to assess the effects of increased paternal involvement on children are hampered by the fact that all available data are derived from comparisons of children whose fathers are and are not currently involved: We do not know whether paternal involvement "caused" the differences between the groups of children, or whether some other factor may be more crucial. Until we have longitudinal studies, in which changes in child behavior and personality are tracked in relation to changes in paternal involvement, we really cannot say what the effects on children are. It is interesting, however, that the available studies, flawed as they are, all show no adverse effects on child development, and that some suggest positive effects on intellectual performance, achievement motivation, and self-confidence as well as more flexible attitudes toward male and female roles.

REFERENCES

Adams, P. L., Milner, J. R., & Schrepf, N. A. (1984). *Fatherless children.* New York: John Wiley.

Ainsworth, M.D.S. (1973). The development of infant-mother attachment. In B. M. Caldwell & H. N. Ricciuti (Eds.), *Review of child development research* (Vol. 3). Chicago: University of Chicago Press.

Arend, R., Gove, F. L., & Sroufe, L. A. (1979). Continuity of individual adaptation from infancy to kindergarten: A predictive study of ego-resiliency and curiosity in preschoolers. *Child Development, 50,* 950-959.

Barnett, R. C., & Baruch, G. K. (1978). *The competent women: Perspectives on development.* New York: Irvington.

Baruch, G. K., & Barnett, R. C. (1979). *Fathers' participation in the care of their preschool children.* Unpublished manuscript, Wellesley College.

Baumrind, D. (1971). Current patterns of parental authority. *Developmental Psychology Monographs, 1* (whole no. 2).

Baumrind, D. (1975). *Early socialization and the discipline controversy.* Morristown, NJ: General Learning Press.

Belsky, J. (1979). Mother-father-infant interaction: A naturalistic observational study. *Developmental Psychology, 15,* 601-607.

Belsky, J. (1981). Early human experience: A family perspective. *Developmental Psychology, 17,* 3-23.

Bem, S. L. (1974). The measurement of psychological androgyny. *Journal of Clinical and Consulting Psychology, 42,* 155-162.

Biller, H. B. (1974). *Paternal deprivation: Family, school, sexuality and society.* Lexington, MA: D. C. Heath.

Biller, H. B. (1981). Father absence, divorce, and personality development. In M. E. Lamb (Ed.), *The role of the father in child development* (rev. ed.). New York: John Wiley.

Blanchard, R. W., & Biller, H. B. (1971). Father availability and academic performance among third grade boys. *Developmental Psychology, 4,* 301-305.

Bowlby, J. (1969). *Attachment and loss: Vol. 1. Attachment.* New York: Basic Books.

Bronfenbrenner, U. (1961). The changing American child. *Journal of Social Issues, 17,* 6-18.

Brown, D. G. (1956). Sex role preference in young children. *Psychological Monographs, 70,* 1-19.

Brown, D. G. (1957). Masculinity-femininity development in children. *Journal of Consulting Psychology, 21,* 197-203.

Dweck, C. S. (1978). Achievement. In M. E. Lamb (Ed.), *Social and personality development.* New York: Holt, Rinehart & Winston.

Fagot, B. I. (1977). Consequences of moderate cross-gender behavior in preschool children. *Child Development, 48,* 902-907.

Fagot, B. I., & Patterson, G. R. (1969). An in vivo analysis of reinforcing contingencies for sex-role behavior in the preschool child. *Developmental Psychology, 1,* 563-568.

Frodi, A. M., Lamb, M. E., Frodi, M., Hwang, C. -P., Forsstrom, B., & Corry, T. (1981). Stability and change in parental attitudes following an infant's birth into traditional and nontraditional Swedish families. *Scandinavian Journal of Psychology.*

Goodenough, E. W. (1957). Interest in persons as an aspect of sex differences in the early years. *Genetic Psychology Monographs, 55,* 287-323.

Grossmann, K. E., Grossmann, K., Huber, F., & Wartner, U. (1981). German children's behavior towards their mothers at 12 months and their fathers at 18 months in Ainsworth's Strange Situation. *International Journal of Behavioral Development, 4,* 157-181.

Heilbrun, A. B. (1965). An empirical test of the modeling theory of sex-role learning. *Child Development, 36,* 789-799.

Hoffman, L. W. (1974). Effects of maternal employment on the child: A review of the research. *Developmental Psychology, 10,* 204-228.

Hoffman, M. L. (1970). Moral development. In P. H. Mussen (Ed.), *Carmichael's manual of child psychology* (Vol. 2, 3rd ed.). New York: John Wiley.

Hoffman, M. L. (1976). Empathy, role-taking, guilt and the development of altruistic motives. In T. Likona (Ed.), *Moral development: Current theory and research.* New York: Holt, Rinehart & Winston.

Hoffman, M. L. (1981). The role of the father in moral internalization. In M. E. Lamb (Ed.), *The role of the father in child development* (rev. ed.). New York: John Wiley.

Johnson, M. M. (1963). Sex role learning in the nuclear family. *Child Development, 34,* 315-333.

Kohlberg, L. (1969). Stage and sequence: The cognitive-developmental approach to socialization. In D. A. Goslin (Ed.), *Handbook of socialization theory and research.* Chicago: Rand McNally.

Kotelchuck, M. (1976). The infant's relationship to the father: Experimental evidence. In M. E. Lamb (Ed.), *The role of the father in child development.* New York: John Wiley.

Lamb, M. E. (1974). A defense of the concept of attachment. *Human Development, 17,* 376-385.

Lamb, M. E. (1976a). Effects of stress and cohort on mother- and father-infant interaction. *Developmental Psychology, 12,* 435-443.

Lamb, M. E. (1976b). Interactions between eight-month-old children and their fathers and mothers. In M. E. Lamb (Ed.), *The role of the father in child development.* New York: John Wiley.

Lamb, M. E. (1976c). The role of the father: An overview. In M. E. Lamb (Ed.), *The role of the father in child development.* New York: John Wiley.

Lamb, M. E. (1976d). Twelve-month-olds and their parents: Interaction in a laboratory playroom. *Developmental Psychology, 12,* 237-244.

Lamb, M. E. (1977a). The development of mother-infant and father-infant attachments in the second year of life. *Developmental Psychology, 13,* 637-648.

Lamb, M. E. (1977b). Father-infant and mother-infant interaction in the first year of life. *Child Development, 48,* 167-181.

Lamb, M. E. (1978). Qualitative aspects of mother- and father-infant attachments. *Infant Behavior and Development, 1,* 265-275.

Lamb, M. E. (1979). Separation and reunion behavior as criteria of attachment to mothers and fathers. *Early Human Development, 3/4,* 329-339.

Lamb, M. E. (1981a). Developing trust and perceived effectance in infancy. In L. P. Lipsitt (Ed.), *Advances in infancy research* (Vol. 1). Norwood, NJ: Ablex.

Lamb, M. E. (1981b). The development of social expectations in the first year of life. In M. E. Lamb & L. R. Sherrod (Eds.), *Infant social cognition: Empirical and theoretical considerations.* Hillsdale, NJ: Lawrence Erlbaum.

Lamb, M. E. (1981c). The development of father-infant relationships. In M. E. Lamb (Ed.), *The role of the father in child development* (rev. ed.). New York: John Wiley.

Lamb, M. E. (1981d). Fathers and child development: An integrative overview. In M. E. Lamb (Ed.), *The role of the father in child development* (rev. ed.). New York: John Wiley.

Lamb, M. E. (Ed.) (1981e). *The role of the father in child development* (rev. ed.). New York: John Wiley.

Lamb, M. E. (1982a). Generalization and inferences about causality in research on nontraditional families: Some cautions. *Merrill-Palmer Quarterly, 28,* 157-161.

Lamb, M. E. (1982b). Maternal employment and child development: A review. In M. E. Lamb (Ed.), *Nontraditional families: Parenting and child development* (pp. 45-69). Hillsdale, NJ: Lawrence Erlbaum.

Lamb, M. E., Easterbrooks, M. A., & Holden, G. W. (1980). Reinforcement and punishment among preschoolers: Characteristics, effects, and correlates. *Child Development, 51,* 1230-1236.

Lamb, M. E., Frodi, M., Hwang, C.-P., & Frodi, A. M. (1983). Effects of paternal involvement on infant preferences for mothers and fathers. *Child Development, 54,* 450-458.

Lamb, M. E., Hwang, C.-P., Frodi, A. M., & Frodi, M. (1982). Security of mother- and father-infant attachment and its relation to sociability with strangers in traditional and nontraditional Swedish families. *Infant Behavior and Development, 5,* 355-367.

Lamb, M. E., Owen, M. T., & Chase-Lansdale, L. (1979). The father-daughter relationship: Past, present and future. In C. B. Kopp & M. Kirkpatrick (Eds.), *Becoming female: Perspectives on development.* New York: Plenum.

Lamb, M. E., Pleck, J. H., Charnov, E. L., & Levine, J. A. (in press). A biosocial perspective on paternal behavior and involvement. In J. B. Lancaster, A. Rossi, J. Altmann, & L. R. Sherrod (Eds.), *Parenting across the lifespan: Biosocial perspectives.* Chicago: Aldine.

Lamb, M. E., Pleck, J. H., & Levine, J. A. (1985). The role of the father in child development: The effects of increased paternal involvement. In B. B. Lahey & A. E. Kazdin (Ed.), *Advances in clinical child psychology* (Vol. 8). New York: Plenum.

Lamb, M. E., & Roopnarine, J. L. (1979). Peer influences on sex-role development in preschoolers. *Child Development, 50,* 1219-1222.

Lamb, M. E., Thompson, R. A., Gardner, W., Charnov, E. L., & Estes, D. (1984). Security of infantile attachment: Its study and biological interpretation. *Behavioral and Brain Sciences, 7,* 127-147.

Main, M. B., & Weston, D. R. (1981). Security of attachment to mother and father: Related to conflict behavior and the readiness to establish new relationships. *Child Development, 52,* 932-940.

Matas, L., Arend, R. A., & Sroufe, L. A. (1978). Continuity of adaptation in the second year: The relationship between quality of attachment and later competence. *Child Development, 49,* 547-556.

Money, J., & Ehrhardt, H. A. (1972). *Man and woman, boy and girl.* Baltimore: Johns Hopkins University Press.

Mussen, P. H., & Rutherford, E. (1963). Parent-child relation and parental personality in relation to young children's sex-role preferences. *Child Development, 34,* 589-607.

Nash, S. C., & Feldman, S. S. (1981). Sex role and sex-related attributions: Constancy or change across the family life cycle? In M. E. Lamb & A. L. Brown (Eds.), *Advances in developmental psychology* (Vol. 1). Hillsdale, NJ: Lawrence Erlbaum.

Owen, M. T., Chase-Lansdale, P. L., & Lamb, M. E. (1982). *Mothers' and fathers' attitudes, maternal employment, and the security of infant-parent attachment.* Unpublished manuscript.

Parke, R. D., Power, T. G., & Gottman, J. (1979). Conceptualizing and quantifying influence patterns in the family triad. In M. E. Lamb, S. J. Suomi, & G. R. Stephenson (Eds.), *Social interaction analysis: Methodological issues.* Madison: University of Wisconsin Press.

Parke, R. D., & Sawin, D. B. (1977, March). *The family in early infancy: Social interactional and attitudinal analyses.* Paper presented to the Society for Research in Child Development, New Orleans.

Parsons, J. E., Adler, T. F., & Kaczala, C. M. (1982). Socialization of achievement attitudes and beliefs: Parental influences. *Child Development, 53,* 310-321.

Pastor, D. L. (1980, April). *The quality of mother-infant attachment and its relationship to toddlers' initial sociability with peers.* Paper presented at the International Conference on Infant Studies, New Haven, CT.

Payne, D. E., & Mussen, P. H. (1956). Parent-child relations and father identification among adolescent boys. *Journal of Abnormal and Social Psychology, 52,* 358-362.

Pedersen, F. A., Anderson, B., & Cain, R. (1980). Parent-infant and husband-wife interactions observed at age 5 months. In F. A. Pedersen (Ed.), *The father-infant relationship: Observational studies in the family setting.* New York: Praeger.

Pedersen, F. A., & Robson, K. S. (1969). Father participation in infancy. *American Journal of Orthopsychiatry, 39,* 466-472.

Pleck, J. H. (1981). *The myth of masculinity.* Cambridge: MIT Press.

Radin, N. (1976). The role of the father in cognitive, academic and intellectual development. In M. E. Lamb (Ed.), *The role of the father in child development.* New York: John Wiley.

Radin, N. (1978, September). *Childrearing fathers in intact families with preschoolers.* Paper presented at the meeting of the American Psychological Association, Toronto.

Radin, N. (1981). The role of the father in cognitive, academic, and intellectual development. In M. E. Lamb (Ed.), *The role of the father in child development* (rev. ed.). New York: John Wiley.

Radin, N. (1982). Primary caregiving and role-sharing fathers. In M. E. Lamb (Ed.), *Nontraditional families: Parenting and child development.* Hillsdale, NJ: Lawrence Erlbaum.

Radin, N., & Sagi, A. (1983). Childrearing fathers in intact families in Israel and the U.S.A. *Merrill-Palmer Quarterly.*

Rosen, B. C., & D'Andrade, R. (1959). The psychosocial origins of achievement motivation. *Sociometry, 22,* 185-218.

Russell, G. (1982). Shared-caregiving families: An Australian study. In M. E. Lamb (Ed.), *Nontraditional families: Parenting and child development.* Hillsdale, NJ: Lawrence Erlbaum.

Russell, G. (1983). *The changing role of fathers?* St. Lucia, Queensland: University of Queensland Press.

Rutter, M. (1973). Why are London children so disturbed? *Proceedings of the Royal Society of Medicine, 66,* 1221-1225.

Rutter, M. (1979). Maternal deprivation, 1972-1978: New findings, new concepts, new approaches. *Child Development, 50,* 283-305.

Sagi, A. (1982). Antecedents and consequences of various degrees of paternal involvement in child rearing: The Israeli project. In M. E. Lamb (Ed.), *Nontraditional families: Parenting and child development.* Hillsdale, NJ: Lawrence Erlbaum.

Sagi, A., Lamb, M. E., & Gardner, W. (n.d.). *Security of attachment and stranger sociability among infants on Israeli kibbutzim.* Unpublished manuscript.

Sagi, A., Lamb, M. E., Lewkowicz, K., Shoham, R., Dvir, R., & Estes, D. (in press). Security of infant-mother, -father, and -metapelet attachments among kibbutz-reared Israeli children. In I. Bretherton & E. Waters (Eds.), Growing points in attachment theory and research [Special issue]. *Monographs of the Society for Research in Child Development.*

Schaffer, H. R., & Emerson, P. E. (1964). The development of social attachments in infancy. *Monographs of the Society for Research in Child Development, 29* (Serial No. 94).

Sears, R. R., Maccoby, E. E., & Levin, H. (1957). *Patterns of child rearing.* Evanston, IL: Row Peterson.

Sears, R. R., Rau, L., & Alpert, R. (1965). *Identification and child rearing.* Stanford, CA: Stanford University Press.

Serbin, L. A., Tonick, L. J., & Sternglanz, S. H. (1977). Shaping cooperative cross-sex play. *Child Development, 48,* 924-929.

Shinn, M. (1978). Father absence and children's cognitive development. *Psychological Bulletin, 85,* 295-324.

Stevenson, M. B., & Lamb, M. E. (1981). The effects of social experience and social style on cognitive competence and performance. In M. E. Lamb & L. R. Sherrod (Eds.), *Infant social cognition: Empirical and theoretical considerations.* Hillsdale, NJ: Lawrence Erlbaum.

Tasch, R. J. (1955). Interpersonal perceptions of fathers and mothers. *Journal of Genetic Psychology, 87,* 59-65.

Thompson, R. A., & Lamb, M. E. (1982). Quality of attachment and stranger sociability in infancy. *Developmental Psychology.*

Weiner, B. (1974). *Achievement motivation and attribution theory.* Morristown, NJ: General Learning Press.

Winterbottom, M. (1958). The relation of need for achievement in learning experiences to independence and mastery. In J. Atkinson (Ed.), *Motives in fantasy, action and society.* New York: Van Nostrand.

9

SOME PARENTING ATTITUDES OF YOUNG BLACK FATHERS

Michael E. Connor

A review of the parenting literature suggests that while moms continue to be the primary focus of attention, attempts are being made to understand the impact fathers, stepfathers, and surrogate fathers have on children and family life (Fein, 1970; Green, 1976; Lamb, 1981; Lynn, 1974; Parke, 1981; Pleck, 1981; Rapoport et al., 1980). These researchers primarily discuss the middle-class Anglo family, with little attention given to Blacks or other ethnic minority families. Unfortunately, the emphasis that is directed toward Black fathers usually relates to absenteeism or other perceived deficits (Hetherington et al., 1975; Lamb, 1981; Lynn, 1974), including the following: family disorganization (the matriarchy, the unstable family, juvenile delinquency, illegitimacy); low aspirations/low self-esteem; sensory deprivation (or overstimulation); unemployment or underemployment; educational handicaps; alcohol and drug abuse; genetic inferiority—in short, pathology. Petras (1975), in an otherwise serious and scholarly book, deals with Black males from a "humorous" perspective. It appears that nothing positive happens within the Black family, or with Black fathers.

Years ago, Billingsley (1970) noted that the majority of Black families include men, most of whom are married to their original wives and are employed full time, but are unable to pull themselves from the confines of poverty. Social scientists ignore these facts and deal with Black families in one of four manners: Social scientists focus on the lowest income group among Blacks; they ignore Black families totally; they view the Black poor family that is experiencing problems as the "causal nexus" for difficulties experienced in the wider society; or they ignore the majority of stable Black families (Billingsley, 1970). Unfortunately, the consequences of these approaches leave the serious student with many doubts and concerns as to what is known about the Black family in general and the Black father in particular. It seems reasonable and important not merely to study what Black families do not do, but what they *do*.

We do know that a disproportionate number of *low-income* Black families are headed by women and that this number has grown from 28% in 1970 to 40% in 1980 (Glick, 1981). However, the fact remains that a majority of Black families have always had mothers *and* fathers present. Perhaps serious scholarship might be directed toward this population. It seems reasonable that the Black family's survival under suppression, ridicule, prejudice, and discrimination indicates a hidden strength—a strength of togetherness, of unity, of caring, of involvement, of continuing under extreme conditions, and of adapting. It is this strength to which this chapter is addressed.

According to Pinkney (1969), Billingsley (1970), and Diggs (1973), the nuclear Black family is headed by a father *and* mother, both in the original marriage, with their offspring residing with them. Somehow this fact does not get transmitted in much of the social science literature. The Black father plays a very important and positive role in his family; however, this issue has yet to be adequately addressed.

The purpose of this research is to gather some data about the young Black father in relation to these four points:

(1) his perceptions of his role as father
(2) his perceptions of other Black men's role as fathers
(3) his perceptions of Black males' role as mate
(4) his perceptions regarding male-female child-rearing differences

It is hypothesized that Black men perceive themselves and other Black men as involved, adequate fathers and mates; that they believe in treating their children equally; and that they share child-rearing responsibilities with their mates.

METHOD

Questionnaire. A two-page self-report questionnaire was developed to elicit both demographic information and information on attitudes Black fathers have toward their children, mates, and other Black fathers.

A group of 16 students (Es: 8 males and 8 females) in a junior-level psychology course taught by the author were trained to administer the questionnaire. Each E was given 30 questionnaires and told to complete them themselves.

Training consisted of making E familiar with the questionnaire, having E practice recording while another was talking, and teaching E how to approach a prospective subject. The Es introduced themselves to S, read an introductory statement, and requested permission for participation. E then read the questions to S and recorded the responses verbatim. Each "session" lasted 18 to 45 minutes, depending on the length of response, how quickly S responded, and how fast E was able to write. Those questionnaires that were not answered completely were omitted from the data analysis. The results are based on 136 completed questionnaires

Subjects. The Black males included in this sample are from a Southern California urban area and were found in a variety of settings. The only place Es were told not to question Black men was on any college or university campus.

"The man on the street" was the targeted subject. Settings where subjects were questioned included barber shops, churches, work sites, shopping centers, parks, department of public social service offices waiting rooms, and "on the street."

RESULTS

(A) Demography (see Table 9.1):
  (1) Most of the males sampled were between 20 and 39 years old (86%).
  (2) The vast majority of those sampled were married (77%) and have been married between one and ten years (71%).
  (3) Approximately two-thirds of the sample have one or two children (66%); 84% were reared in an urban area; most (81%) came from larger families than they now have (at least three siblings).
  (4) Some 75% are Baptist; 89% are laborers (most skilled); a large number have a high school (33%) or better education (59%), approximately two-thirds have spouses who work, and a majority (61%) have an income less than $12,000. Educationally, the sampled population has progressed beyond their own fathers, as 87% of their dads had high school or less education. A majority had mothers who worked (59%).
(B) Responses to questions (see Table 9.2):
  (1) About 42% thought a woman's place was at home, 21% thought she should be working, and 37% thought it should be her choice.

(2) Two-thirds shared disciplining of children with their wives—usually using corporal punishment. Over half of the males felt the father was the "boss" at home, while 38% indicated a sharing attitude. Their mothers had been their primary discipliner, also using corporal punishment.

(3) The men felt that education and obtaining the "good life" were the major goals for their children (82%) and they thought their mates shared these goals (84%).

(4) Regarding roles, Black males report positive influences on both their mates (66%) and their children (74%); they want to offer guidance, leadership, support and understanding. However, when asked about the needs of other Black fathers in relation to their mates, a surprising 63% felt there is a need for change or were undecided. Usually they suggested that couples need to "get along better." A large number (66%) were also undecided or reported a need to change the Black father role with their children. They felt Black men should spend more time with their children, listen more, or offer more guidance.

(5) Most fathers reported spending positive leisure time with their children (93%) with the vast majority (94%) allowing the child to have a say in these activities.

(6) Finally, Black fathers were about equally divided regarding the treatment of male and female children. Those who felt that children should be treated differently based on gender were harsher, rougher, and more physical with male children, apparently wanting to teach them dominance or prepare them for dealing with a cruel, harsh, racist world outside. A few felt that male children should be shown more love and should be trained to be more respectful of women.

DISCUSSION

The primary purpose of this research was to attempt to get a feeling for how Black males who are fathers feel about themselves as fathers and as mates, and how they feel about other Black fathers. A review of the literature indicated an absence of relevant empirical data about Black men who are fathers. Therefore, a two-page questionnaire was developed to sample the expressed attitudes of this population.

It was suggested that Black men would report they were actively involved with their children and with their mates; that they perceived other Black men as also being so involved; and that they treated their children equally. These notions were generally supported; however, subjects tended to perceive other Black men as lacking in their

TABLE 9.1

Demographic Data (percentages)

Age	
20-29	42
30-39	44
40-49	14
Marital status	
married	77
divorced/separated	19
never married	4
Years married	
1-5	39
6-10	32
11-15	20
16 or more	9
Number of children	
1	31
2	35
3	19
4	10
5	3
6 or more	2
Number of siblings respondent had as a child	
1	8
2	11
3	17
4	26
5	15
6 or more	27
Area in which respondent was reared	
rural	16
urban	84
Religion	
Baptist	72
other	28
Education of respondent	
less than high school	8
high school graduate	33
1-3 years college	33
college graduate	12
graduate/professional school	14
Education of respondents' fathers	
less than high school	59
high school graduate	28
1-3 years college	4
college graduate	3
graduate/professional school	6
Occupation	
skilled laborer	72
unskilled laborer	17
professional	11
Annual income	
under $6,000	12
$6,000-$9,000	22

(continued)

TABLE 9.1 Continued

$9,000-$12,000	27
more than $12,000	39
Wife who works	
yes	62
no	34
not married	4
Mother who worked	
yes	59
no	41

relationships with both children and mates. Subjects tended to report that Black men should learn to get along better with their families. One possible explanation for this "I'm okay, you're not" attitude is that perhaps Black men have accepted the stereotype put forth by social scientists in the past. This is most alarming. Social scientists must begin to exercise reasonable caution in the perpetuation of such a negative (and inaccurate) viewpoint. Further, Black men must begin to understand and question such notions.

In no way is the present study intended to be negative toward Black mothers. Certainly social scientists have previously and continue currently to treat Black females from a "deficit" perspective to the point that the serious scholar must wonder what, if anything, is known about her. The Black men in this study seem to be cognizant of Black women's positive impact on them and their children. Additionally, the current study would be strengthened if Black females were asked similar questions about Black fathers to determine the degree of correlation with the fathers' responses.

There are several limitations in this study. First, the problems with any self-report methodology, including problems of validity and reliability, are obvious. However, this study represents but a beginning; additional research can use more elaborate procedures. Further, it is recognized that caution must be exercised in generalizing these findings—Southern California is not representative of the entire nation. The sample population tended to be young, educated beyond high school, stable, and with intact small families (one or two children). It is certainly possible that these findings are indicative of the attitudes and behaviors of Black fathers from similar backgrounds across the nation. However, additional data are needed from this population prior to drawing any such conclusion.

Second, the author's perceptions represent a limitation. It is felt that as much can be learned from research that focuses on positives as from research that focuses on negatives. At some point social scientists might

TABLE 9.2
Questionnaire Responses (percentages)

A woman's place is	
at home	42
working	21
her choice	37
Who disciplines your children?	
father	23
mother	12
both	65
Who disciplined you as a child?	
father	24
mother	45
both	31
Means of discipline you use	
physical	15
verbal	20
withhold reinforcement	31
physical and verbal	34
Means your adults used	
physical	54
verbal	11
withhold reinforcement	12
physical and verbal	23
Your goals for your children	
education	36
good life	46
children set own goals	14
stay out of trouble	4
Mate's goals for children	
education	44
good life	40
children set own goals	13
stay out of trouble	3
Who is "boss" in your household?	
father	57
mother	5
share	38
In general, how do you characterize Black men's roles in relationship to their mates?	
mutual understanding/support	59
guidance/leadership	7
poor interaction	25
same as whites	9
Does the Black man need to change his relationship with his mate?	
yes	62
no	37
undecided	1
If yes, how should he change? (most frequent responses)	
offer more understanding	
improve communication	
show more respect	
In general, how do you characterize Black men's roles in relation to their children?	
mutual understanding/support	41
love/leadership	33

(continued)

TABLE 9.2 Continued

poor interaction	16
same as whites	10
Does the Black man need to change his relationship with his children?	
yes	64
no	34
undecided	2
If yes, how should he change? (most frequent responses)	
spend more time with them	
offer more guidance	
listen to them more	
How do you spend your leisure time with your children?	
recreation	74
education	15
discipline	1
"everything"	4
no leisure time	6
Do your children have a "say" in these activities?	
yes	94
no	6
Regarding Black children, should males be treated differently from females?	
yes	52
no	46
undecided	2
If yes, in what ways should they be treated differently? (most frequent response)	
teach males greater responsibility	
teach respect for Black women	
teach identity and freedom to males	
teach male dominance	
treat males rougher	
show boys more love than shown in the past	

seriously attempt to focus on successful persons (fathers, mothers, readers, children, happy persons, and the like) to determine how and why they're doing what they're doing. Perhaps information might be gleaned that can be used to help others become happy, satisfied, successful, and so on. Thus, while an attempt is made to be objective and the data are represented as gathered, no effort was made to focus on perceived deficits, which are often presented in the literature. That is, the researcher was not interested in asking negative questions or questions that reinforced negative stereotypes (absenteeism, marginality, matriarchies, and so on). There are serious flaws in those studies that do focus on stereotypes, and ethical concerns should be raised about those who seem to have the need to perpetuate negative images. This in no way implies that there may be no validity in these negative notions. However, one must begin to question these notions when they are presented as the norm in the face of obvious contradictions.

Third, much of the literature reviewed is dated. However, it is currently the only research available. As other Black social scientists have indicated, there is a need for further research on Black fathers (McAdoo, 1981). Ideally, this research should take its direction from in-culture researchers. Possible areas of scientific endeavor include the following: longitudinal studies about Black father-infant interaction; the long-term effects of prepared childbirth on the child, the mother, and the father; attitudes and values of those Blacks who are successful fathers; impact of father involvement on child development (moral, social, intellectual, and so on); Black fathers and daughters; Black fathers and sons; programs for young Black fathers; and shared parenting among Black couples.

Summarizing, these data suggest that many Black men prefer to be and are involved with their children and their mates in a meaningful way. They see themselves in a positive light and they tend to share child-rearing responsibilities with their wives. In short, they tend to be "democratic" at home. As Diggs (1973) suggested years ago, Black families have been both intact and democratic traditionally but were usually ignored or misrepresented. The time is ripe for us to begin to study what Blacks *are* doing rather than what it is assumed they aren't doing; to limit meaningless comparisons with vague, superficial, biased criteria; and to question the motives of those who focus on deficits, reinforce stereotypes, or perpetuate negative orientations in relation to minorities in the United States.

REFERENCES

Billingsley, A. (1970). Black families and white social science. *Journal of Social Issues, 26*(3), 127-142.

Diggs, I. (1973, October). Today's Black family. *Encore.*

Fein, R. A. (1970). Research on fathering: Social policy and an emergent perspective. *Journal of Social Issues, 34*(1), 122-135.

Glick, P. C. (1981). A demographic picture of Black families. In H. P. McAdoo (Ed.), *Black families.* Beverly Hills, CA: Sage.

Green, M. (1976). *Fathering.* New York: McGraw-Hill.

Heatherington, E. M., & Parke, R. D. (1975). *Child psychology: A contemporary viewpoint.* New York: McGraw-Hill.

Lamb, M. (1981). *The role of fathers in child development.* New York: John Wiley.

Lynn, D. B. (1974). *The father: His role in child development.* Monterey, CA: Brooks/Cole.

McAdoo, J. L. (1981). Involvement of fathers in the socialization of Black children. In H. P. McAdoo (Ed.), *Black families.* Beverly Hills, CA: Sage.

McAdoo, J. L. (1981). Black fathers and child interactions. In L. E. Gary (Ed.), *Black men.* Beverly Hills, CA: Sage.

Parke, R. D. (1981). *Fathers*. Cambridge, MA: Harvard University Press.

Petras, J. W. (1975). *Sex male, gender masculine: Readings in male sexuality*. Sherman Oaks, CA: Alfred.

Pinkney, A. (1969). *Black Americans*. Englewood Cliffs, NJ: Prentice-Hall.

Pleck, J. H. (1981, September). Prisoners of manliness. *Psychology Today*.

Rapoport, R. et al. (1980). *Fathers, mothers, and society*. New York: Vintage.

10

BLACK FATHERS' RELATIONSHIPS WITH THEIR PRESCHOOL CHILDREN AND THE CHILDREN'S DEVELOPMENT OF ETHNIC IDENTITY

John Lewis McAdoo

This chapter explores the relationship between Black father-child interaction patterns and the preschool child's ethnic identity, including the father's attitude toward and involvement in the child-rearing process. The symbolic interaction theory (Mead, 1934) suggests that a Black child develops identity through interactions with significant others in the social environment, but very few studies on the differential effects of paternal nurturance and paternal control in a child's development of a positive racial identity have been made.

RACIAL IDENTITY

Proshansky and Newton (1968) note that there are two interrelated processes involved in the Black child's development of ethnic or racial identity. The first is racial identification. Racial identification may be defined as the Black child's development of attitudes, feelings, and beliefs about him- or herself as a result of awareness of skin color differences within his or her social environment. These attitudes, feelings, and beliefs may be positive or negative. Clark (1952) and Goodman (1952) have found that Black children became aware of and could make accurate racial distinctions as early as the age of 3.

Early studies on racial attitudes of Black children have consistently found that Black children have negative racial attitudes (Williams & Roberson, 1967; Williams & Edwards, 1969; Williams, Boswell, & Best,

1975). Black researchers (McAdoo, 1970, Hraba & Grant, 1970; H. McAdoo, 1974) have reported more positive racial attitudes in Black children. Their findings suggest that when we control for race and sex of the examiner, the racial attitudes of Black children do not appear any different from the racial attitudes of children of other ethnic groups.

The second process identified by Proshansky and Newton is racial evaluation. This process may be defined as the Black child's development of an attitude toward or preference for his or her own ethnic group. The Black child's group identity or preference may be positive or negative, and it is seen as being more affected by the negative attitudes toward the child's ethnic group by the larger society. Early racial preference studies have consistently found that Black children reject their ethnic identity (Clark & Clark, 1939, 1950; Goodman, 1952; Moreland, 1966).

Other studies have found Black children to be more positive in their racial preferences (Hraba & Grant, 1970; Harris & Baum, 1971; Gregor & McPherson, 1968; Winnick & Taylor, 1977). Bank (1976) reanalyzed the data from the major racial preference studies and found that only 6% of the Black children rejected their ethnic identity. The majority of the children (69%) in these studies did not accept or reject their ethnic identity.

The findings of studies related to ethnic identity appear to be, at best, mixed. There are some Black preschool children who have a negative racial self-identification or self-concept, although most do not. The literature indicates that there are a number of Black children who reject their racial group membership. Finally, some preschool Black children may reject their racial identity and their racial group membership. While we can never underestimate the influence of the racial prejudice of the dominant society on a child's rejection of his or her ethnic identity (Proshansky & Newton, 1968), the parents' role in controlling this negative influence needs to be examined.

FATHER-CHILD INTERACTION

As noted elsewhere (McAdoo, 1979), the observation of father-child relationship patterns in a natural environment (within their own homes) is a relatively new phenomenon for social science researchers. The two most studied patterns of father-child interactions are nurturance and restrictiveness. "Nurturance" is defined as the expression of warmth and positive feelings toward the behaviors and attitudes of the child. "Restrictiveness" is the expression of negative feelings and rejection of the attitudes and behaviors of the child expressed within the father-child relationship.

Radin (1972, 1975) and Baumrind (1971) have suggested that maternal warmth (nurturance) facilitates the child's identification with the mother. Radin (1972) and McAdoo (1979) have similarly suggested that paternal nurturance facilitates the male child's identification with the father. Identification with either parent should lead the child to incorporate into his or her own identity those ideas, attitudes, beliefs, and feelings about the child expressed by the parents. Nurturant fathers verbally communicate their positive acceptance of the child's attitudes, behaviors, and beliefs. They may also communicate nonverbally their positive feelings toward the child by hugging and other behavior that tells about their acceptance of the child as a person (McAdoo, 1979).

Parental control is another dimension of father-child relationship patterns that is deemed important to the development of the child's ethnic identity. Parental control is operationalized by most researchers (Baumrind, 1971; Radin, 1972; McAdoo, 1979) as an insistence by the parents that the child follow directions and adhere to family rules they feel are important. Control and nurturance, when used in balance, are felt to assist in optimally developing socially competent children. Balanced control is used by the Black father in a manner that suggests to the child that the father loves the child, but will not accept negative behaviors.

Restrictiveness is seen as the pattern of control most often used by authoritarian parents (Baumrind, 1971). In this type of parent-child relationship pattern, fathers are seen as restrictive, aloof, rather cold, and unfeeling. This pattern represents the authoritarian father's negative feelings toward his child and often restricts facilitation of positive communications and identification between the child and the father (Radin, 1972). Further restrictiveness may not only lead to decreased identification with the father, but may also have negative consequences in the formation of the child's ethnic identity.

Bing (1963) found a positive relationship between authoritarian fathers and the academic achievement level of their daughters. Honig (1980) notes that more often than not paternal nurturance has also been found to be related to the child's high achievement in school.

Parent-child relationship studies have traditionally observed the impact of the parent on the child's activities, development, and behavior (Bing, 1963; Radin, 1972, 1975; Baumrind, 1971; Bell, 1968). Several authors (Bell, 1968; Buss, 1981; Osofsky & O'Connell, 1972), however, have indicated a need to study the child's influence on the parent-child interaction patterns also. Building on the work of Bell (1968), Osofsky and O'Connell (1972) found significant changes in parental behaviors as a result of the influences of their children. Fathers were found to be more positively reinforcing of their children when the children behaved in a dependent, as opposed to an independent, manner. Buss (1981) found that children who were more active in the interview situation forced parents to utilize more control strategies in that situation.

In summary, very little is known about the relationship of paternal nurturance and restrictiveness and the development of ethnic identity in Black children. This study examines paternal nurturance and restrictiveness separately and attempts to determine the degree to which there is a relationship between these two variables and the child's ethnic identity. Further, this investigation will explore the role of the Black child and his or her influence on these patterns of nurturance and restrictiveness.

METHODOLOGY

The subjects were 40 middle-income Black fathers; their children ranged in age from 4 to 6. Both parents in the subjects' families were employed. The study sample lived in a planned community in the Baltimore-Washington metropolitan area. They were randomly selected from a pool of Black fathers who volunteered to take part in the study. All of the fathers were middle class, with 46% employed in upper-middle-income occupations. The others (54%) were in lower-middle-income occupations. More than 80% of these fathers were born into the working class and achieved middle-class status. Over 80% of these fathers had college degrees, and 40% of them had graduate or professional degrees. There were 20 boys and 20 girls in this study.

The fathers were asked to respond to a series of questions related to their perceived involvement in the child-rearing practices within their family. Questions were related to decision making, time spent with children, rewards, and expectations of child behavior. In addition, the Radin (1972) paternal observation scale was employed by trained interviewers/observers to determine the types of interaction patterns that occurred between a father and his child. Finally, the child was asked to respond to a series of questions related to the child's ethnic identity.

The paternal observational scale was designed to measure the types of verbal communication patterns between a father and his child concerning a behavior, attitude, or event that had meaning to both of them. The two major types of verbal interaction patterns observed were nurturance and restrictiveness (Radin, 1972).

The father and his child were observed on two occasions for two hours in their own home. The first occasion provided the observer an opportunity to become acquainted with the father and child, while at the same time allowing him to collect background data on the family. The second occasion allowed the interviewer to collect a series of parental attitudinal questions and, at the same time, observe the verbal communication patterns between the father and his child. The length of the inverview was designed to encourage natural interchange between the father and his child.

Two weeks after the observations the child was interviewed. A series of scales related to ethnic identity (Williams & Edwards, 1969) and racial identification and preference (Clark, 1952) were administered to the child. The interviewers and verbal coders were trained over a three-week period using role-playing and videotape methods. They were selected on the basis of achieving a reliability of .85 or better in coding.

The major questions of this study were as follows:

(1) How do the black fathers in this sample perceive their roles and responsibilities in child rearing?
(2) To what degree do they participate in child-rearing activities?
(3) What type of relationship patterns predominate in the father-child relationships?
(4) What are the relationships between the father's patterns of interaction and the child's ethnic identity?
(5) How does the child feel about his or her ethnic identity?

RESULTS

CHILD-REARING PRACTICES

Of the fathers in this study, 71% reported that they shared the major child-rearing decision making with their wives. Some of the fathers (11%) reported that they made all of the decisions, and 18% of the fathers reported that their wives made all the major child-rearing decisions.

In response to questions related to activities between father and child, almost 50% (19) of the fathers reported that they spent two or more hours a day with their child. A total of 18% of the fathers reported that they spent between one and two hours a day, and another 18% of the fathers reported that they did spend some time with their children, but not every day. Of all the fathers, 15% reported spending more than two hours a day playing with their children.

In response to questions related to the fathers' expectations of and control over their children's behavior, 55% of the fathers said that their children should obey their commands immediately. Another 23% of the fathers agreed that it was important for their children to obey their commands, but felt that the children need not respond right away. The remaining 22% of the fathers did not feel that they could commit themselves on this question and responded that their expectations and their children's responses depended on the situation. The fathers of boys responded in the same manner as the fathers of girls.

Of the fathers, 53% reported that they would not accept any disorderly behavior from their preschool children. Some of the fathers (21%) admitted that their preschool children would not be punished for some unacceptable behavior. A few fathers (26%) reported being more flexible and allowing their children a great deal of leeway in expressing themselves in a disorderly manner. Half of the fathers (50%) reported having some minor problems with their children's show of temper. Only 15% of the fathers reported having more than occasional and minor problems with their children's inability to control their tempers. The rest of the fathers (35%) claimed that their children presented them with no temper control problems. There were no sex of child differences in the fathers' responses to the questions related to their children's disorderly behavior and show of temper.

In response to questions related to their own and their spouses' firmness in dealing with their children's behavior, over half (51%) of the fathers reported that they and their wives were moderately strict with their children. Almost 20% of the fathers claimed that they and their wives were very strict in their handling of their children's behavior. About 30% of the fathers felt that they and their wives were not strict at all in dealing with their children's attitude and behavior. No sex of child differences in the fathers' responses to the question of perceived strictness were observed.

The majority of the fathers (50%) reported sharing equally with their wives in the disciplining of their children. A third of the fathers noted that they alone provided the discipline when their children needed disciplining. The mothers were expected to do the disciplining by 18% of the fathers. Regardless of who was designated as the discipliner in the family, over two-thirds of the fathers claimed that they and their wives were in agreement as to the type of discipline their children should receive. There were no sex of child differences noted in the fathers' reponses on this subject.

More than 80% of the fathers reported that they were rearing their children differently than they were reared. They noted that they were less strict than their fathers. The children's needs were placed before their own. Fathers of boys and fathers of girls were similar in their responses to these questions.

PARENT-CHILD RELATIONSHIPS

Three-fourths of the fathers in this study were found to be verbally nurturant, warm, and loving in their relationships and interaction with their children. One-fourth of the fathers in this study were restrictive in their attempts to control their children's behavior. Almost one-third of the children (30%) initiated the interaction with their fathers. Fathers of sons were as nurturant or restrictive toward their sons as fathers of daughters were to their children. No significant sex differences were observed in the racial attitudes and racial preference scores of the children in this sample (see Table 10.1).

Table 10.2 represents a summary of the relationship between types of verbal interaction and ethnic identity scores for the fathers and children in this sample. Fathers who were found to be significantly nurturant, warm, and loving toward their children exhibited significantly less restrictive and controlling behaviors ($p < .001$). Nurturant fathers had children who were significantly more content to sit and not become involved in the interview situation. Fathers who were significantly more restrictive and controlling were significantly more likely to have active children ($p < .001$) who made demands upon their time and would need more controlling behavior from the father. No significant differences in the amount of verbal interaction between father and child were observed.

Restrictive fathers had children who were significantly more positive in their racial attitudes ($p < .05$) and their racial preferences ($p < .05$), but the greater the amount of child-initiated interactions between the restrictive father and his child, the less positive the children felt about their ethnic identity. Children who were found to be positive in their racial self-concept were also found to be significantly more positive in their racial preferences ($p < .001$) (see Table 10.2).

TABLE 10.1

Means, Standard Deviations and t-Test of Nurturing and Restrictive Fathers, Child Initiates, Racial Attitudes, and Racial Preferences of Children[a]

	N	X	SD	df	t
Nurturing fathers					
daughter	20	.747	.22	35.6	−.29
sons	20	.765	.17		
total	40	.756			
Restrictive fathers					
daughters	20	.254	.22	36.7	−.02
sons	20	.255	.19		
total	40	.254			
Initiating child					
daughters	20	.313	.20	37.6	.16
sons	20	.302	.22		
total	40	.307			
Racial attitudes					
daughters	20	12.1	6.8	36.3	.08
sons	20	11.9	8.2		
total					
Racial preferences					
daughters	20	4.3	3.1	37.5	−.63
sons	20	5.1	3.5		
total	40				

a. Scores by sex for total sample.

SUMMARY

The middle-income Black fathers in this study did not appear to be different from middle-income fathers of other ethnic groups in their child-rearing attitudes and expectations for their children. They presented a picture of being moderately strict with their children. Our observations indicated that the majority of these fathers were warm and loving toward their children. Many of these fathers reported having to pick their children up from nursery school and were more involved with the children than fathers of nonworking wives.

These fathers appeared to be more flexible in their child-rearing behavior. This may be because 90% of them reported being upwardly mobile from working class to middle class in this generation. The combination of educational achievement and occupational status re-

TABLE 10.2
Intercorrelations Among Verbal Interactions,
Racial Attitudes, and Racial Preference Scores[a]

Nurturance				
Restrictiveness	−960*			
Child initiates	−633*	571*		
Racial attitudes	−.235	.262*	.134	
Racial preferences	.225	.271*	−.306*	−653*

a. Total sample.
*$p < .05$.

quirements, along with wives who were also upwardly mobile and working, may have helped the fathers to develop different attitudes and behaviors toward their children.

The findings in this study suggest that a positive relationship existed between the observed restrictiveness of Black fathers and their preschool children's racial attitudes and racial preferences. It is possible that these fathers may not be as restrictive with their children in their everyday relationships as they were in their interview relationships. The father's behavior may be explained by his inability to respond effectively to the unusual amount of child-initiated interaction during the interview. The children's racial self-identity and their preference for their own ethnic group are viewed as stable and relatively robust attitudes that do not fluctuate situationally.

The preschool children of these restrictive fathers appear to have the same characteristics as very active preschool children in other studies (Bell, 1968; Osofsky & O'Connell, 1972; Buss, 1981). These children were more active during the interview sessions and made frequent requests for attention from their fathers. When their fathers ignored their behavior or failed to satisfy their needs completely, the behavior of the children increased until their fathers asserted their control in a more restrictive fashion.

Children of nurturant fathers were observed to be less active in the interview situation. They were content to sit quietly and play with their toys. When they did make demands, their fathers were more likely to interrupt the interview and respond completely to their expressed needs. No relationship was found between the fathers' patterns of nurturance and their children's racial self-identities and racial preferences. The differences in racial attitudes and racial preferences of the children in the two types of father-child relationship patterns may be explained better in future studies that include and assess the mother's interaction styles.

The Black children as a group appeared to have a positive racial identity and a positive ethnic group identity. Unlike children in previous studies (Clark, 1952; Williams, 1967), these children seemed to prefer their own ethnic group and to accept the ethnicity of others. Parental nurturance and economic stability may be the most likely explanation of the differences between the children in this sample and samples drawn by Clark (1952) and others (Williams & Edwards, 1969). An equally likely explanation may be found in the criticism of forced-choice types of racial identity studies (Brand, Ruiz, & Padilla, 1974) that question whether acceptance of being Black means the rejection of other ethnic identities and vice versa.

We have found the Black fathers in this study to be actively concerned and involved in the socialization of their children. They were warm, loving, and nurturant in their interaction patterns. The data from this study suggest that we may need to utilize a multimethod multitrait research model to evaluate the role the Black father plays in the identity formation of his preschool children. Such a design would need to be more longitudinal in character.

The study has focused on Black fathers in economically stable families in order to provide a more balanced view of the role they play in the socialization of their children. There is a need to develop a more longitudinal observation model in which the interactions of the total family are observed. Future studies may also attempt to explore the effects of technological advances in reducing time and energy spent in household tasks on the role fathers play in the family. Finally, there is a need to develop studies related to some of the societal influences, educational attainment, employment and employment stress, and kin and friendship relations that influence the degree to which a Black father is able to participate actively in the development of ethnic identity in his children.

REFERENCES

Asher, S., & Allen. (1969). A racial preference and social comparison process. *Journal of Social Issues, 25*(1), 157-166.

Bank, W. C. (1976). White preference in Blacks: A paradigm in search of phenomenon. *Psychological Bulletin, 83*, 1179-1186.

Baumrind, D. (1971). Current patterns of parental authority. *Developmental Psychology Monographs, 4*(1, p. 2).

Baumrind, D. (1973). Authoritarian vs. authoritative parental control. In S. Scarr-Salapatek & P. Salapatek (Eds.), *Socialization*. Columbus, OH: Merrill.

today, exhibit the potential that all men have for a more involved, caring, primary relationship with children.

NOTES

1. Masnik and Bane's (1980, p. 58) report on the American family from 1960 to 1990 projects that there will be an increase of almost 7 million male-headed households (approximately one-third of all new households). This will bring the share of all households headed by single, widowed, divorced, separated, or spouse-absent males to 15%, which is twice the 1960 level.

2. Kerlinger (1973, pp. 378-394) states that social science research is not always in a position to control historical variables. Nevertheless, ex post facto research is a valid approach to determining associations.

3. Post hoc analyses performed with the numbers of boys versus girls living with single custodial fathers was statistically significant ($\chi^2 = p < .01$). That is, fathers were more likely to have boys living with them and this occurrence was more than one could expect by chance.

REFERENCES

Ambert, A. M. (1982). Differences in children's behavior toward custodial mothers and custodial fathers. *Journal of Marriage and the Family, 44,* 73-85.

Bartz, K. W., & Witcher, W. C. (1978). When father gets custody. *Children Today, 7,* 2-6.

Benedek, T. (1970). Fatherhood and providing. In A. E. James & T. Benedek (Eds.), *Parenthood: Its psychology and psychopathology.* Boston: Little, Brown.

Besner, A. (1968). Economic deprivation and family patterns. In M. B. Sussman (Ed.), *Sourcebook in marriage and the family.* Boston: Houghton Mifflin.

Biller, H. B. (1971). *Father, child and sex roles.* Lexington, MA: D. C. Heath.

Bowlby, J. (1972). *Child care and the growth of love.* Harmondsworth, England: Penguin.

Bozett, F. W., & Hanson, S.M.H. (Eds.). (1985). Perspectives of fatherhood [Special issue]. *American Behavioral Scientist, 28*(6).

Bronfenbrenner, U. (1961). The changing American child: A speculative analysis. *Journal of Social Issues, 17*(1), 6-18.

Cath, S. H., Gurwitt, A. R., & Ross, J. M. (Eds.). (1982). *Father and child: Developmental and clinical perspectives.* Boston: Little, Brown.

Chang, P., & Deinard, A. (1982). Single father caretakers: Demographic characteristics and adjustment process. *American Journal of Orthopsychiatry, 52,* 236-243.

Defrain, J., & Eirick, R. (1981). Coping as divorced parents: A comparative study of fathers and mothers. *Family Relations, 30,* 265-274.

Devereaux, E., Bronfenbrenner, U., & Rodgers, R. (1969). Child rearing in England and the United States: A cross-national comparison. *Journal of Marriage and the Family, 31,* 257-270.

Ellis, G. J., Thomas, D. L., & Rollins, B. C. (1976). Measuring parental support: The interrelationship of three measures. *Journal of Marriage and the Family, 38*, 257-270.

Freeberg, N. E., & Payne, D. T. (1967). Parental influence on cognitive development in early childhood: A review. *Child Development, 38*, 65-87.

Gasser, R. D., & Taylor, C. M. (1976). Role adjustment of single fathers with dependent children. *Family Coordinator, 25*, 397-401.

Gaylin, W. (1976). *Caring.* New York: Knopf.

George, V., & Wilding, P. (1972). *Motherless families.* London: Routledge & Kegan Paul.

Gersick, K. (1979). Fathers by choice: Divorced men who receive custody of their children. In G. Levinger & O. Moles (Eds.), *Divorce and separation.* New York: Basic Books.

Greene, R. S. (1977). *Atypical parenting: Custodial single fathers.* Unpublished doctoral dissertation, University of Maryland.

Grief, G. L. (1982). Dads raising kids. *Single Parent, 25*, 19-23.

Grief, G. L. (1985). *Single fathers.* Lexington, MA: D. C. Heath.

Hanson, S.M.H. (1980). Characteristics of single custodial fathers and the parent-child relationship (Doctoral dissertation, University of Washington, 1979). *Dissertation Abstracts, 40*(12), 6438A.

Hanson, S.M.H. (1981). Single custodial fathers and the parent-child relationship. *Nursing Research, 30*, 202-204.

Hanson, S.M.H. (1985a). Single fathers with custody: A synthesis of the literature. In B. Schlesinger (Ed.), *The one-parent family.* Toronto: University of Toronto Press.

Hanson, S.M.H. (1985b). Fatherhood: Contextual variations. *American Behavioral Scientist, 28*(6).

Hanson, S.M.H. (in press). Father-child relationships beyond *Kramer vs. Kramer. Marriage and Family Review.*

Hanson, S.M.H., & Bozett, F. W. (in press). Fatherhood: A library. *Marriage and Family Review.*

Hanson, S.M.H., & Bozett, F. W. (Eds.). (1985). *Dimensions of fatherhood.* Beverly Hills, CA: Sage.

Heilbrun, A. (1964). Parental model attributes, nurturant reinforcement, and consistency of behavior in adolescents. *Child Development, 35*, 151-167.

Hollingshead, A. B. (1968). Social class and the family. In M. B. Sussman (Ed.), *Sourcebook in marriage and the family.* Boston: Houghton Mifflin.

Hollingshead, A. B. (1975). *Four factor index of social status.* New Haven, CT: Yale University Press.

Kerlinger, F. N. (1973). *Foundations of behavioral research.* New York: Holt, Rinehart & Winston.

Keshet, H. F., & Rosenthal, K. M. (1978). Fathering after marital separation. *Social Work, 23*, 11-18.

Keshet, H. F., & Rosenthal, K. M. (1978). Single-parent fathers: A new study. *Children Today, 7*, 13-17.

Kohn, M. L. (1967). Social class and parent-child relationships: An interpretation. In G. R. Medinnus (Ed.), *Readings in the psychology of parent-child relations.* New York: John Wiley.

Lamb, M. E. (Ed.). (1981). *The role of the father in child development.* New York: John Wiley.

Lewis, K. (1978). Single-father families: Who they are and how they fare. *Child Welfare, 57*, 643-651.

Lewis, R. A., & Pleck, J. H. (Eds.). (1979). Men's roles in the family [Special issue]. *Family Coordinator, 28*(4), 429-462.

Masnick, G., & Bane, M. J. (1980). *The nation's families: 1960-1990.* Cambridge, MA: MIT and Harvard University, Joint Center for Urban Studies.

McCandless, B. R., & Evans, E. D. (1973). *Children and youth: Psychosocial development.* Hinsdale, IL: Dryden.

McFadden, M. (1974). *Bachelor fatherhood: How to raise and enjoy your children as a single parent.* New York: Charter Communications.

McKinley, D. G. (1964). *Social class and family life.* New York: Free Press.

Mendes, H. A. (1976). Single fatherhood. *Social Work, 21,* 308-312.

Mendes, H. A. (1976). Single fathers. *Family Coordinator, 25,* 438-444.

Nye, F. I. (1969). Adolescent-parent adjustment: Socio-economic level as a variable. In M. A. Strauss (Ed.), *Family analysis.* Chicago: Rand McNally.

Orthner, D., Brown, T., & Ferguson, D. (1976). Single fatherhood: An emerging family life style. *Family Coordinator, 25,* 429-437.

Orthner, D. K., & Lewis, K. (1979). Evidence of single-father competence in child rearing. *Family Law Quarterly, 13,* 27-47.

Pearson, J., Munson, P., & Thoennes, N. (1982). Legal change and child custody awards. *Journal of Family Issues, 8,* 5-24.

Rapoport, R., Rapoport, R., & Strelitz, Z. (1977). *Fathers, mothers and society: Towards new alliances.* New York: Basic Books.

Reiss, I. (1980). *The family system in America.* New York: Holt, Rinehart & Winston.

Rosen, B. C. (1967). Social class and the child's perception of the parent. In G. R. Medinnus (Ed.), *Readings in the psychology of parent-child relations.* New York: John Wiley.

Rosenthal, K. M., & Keshet, H. (1981). *Fathers without partners.* Totowa, NJ: Rowan & Littlefield.

Santrock, J. W., & Warshak, R. (1979). Father custody and social development in boys and girls. *Journal of Social Issues, 35,* 112-125.

Shaefer, E. S. (1965). Children's reports of parental behavior: An inventory. *Child Development, 36,* 413-424.

Schlesinger, B. (1984). *The one-parent family: Perspectives and annotated bibliography* (5th ed.). Toronto: University of Toronto Press.

Siegelman, M. (1965). Evaluation of Bronfenbrenner's questionnaire for children concerning parental behavior. *Child Development, 36,* 163-174.

Smith, R. M., & Smith, C. W. (1981). Child-rearing and single-parent fathers. *Family Relations, 30,* 411-417.

U.S. Bureau of the Census. (1982). Marital status and living arrangements: March 1981. In *Current population reports* (Series P-20, No. 372). Washington, DC: Government Printing Office.

U.S. National Center for Health Statistics. (1983). *Monthly vital statistics report* (Vol. 32, No. 3, Supplement). Washington, DC: Government Printing Office.

Victor, I., & Winkler, W. A. (1977). *Fathers and custody.* New York: Hawthorn.

Walters, J. (Ed.). (1976). Fatherhood [Special issue]. *Family Coordinator, 25*(4).

Washington Chapters of U.S. Divorce Reform. (1978). *What you always wanted to know about divorce but were afraid to ask: A guide to divorce for the man (or woman) seeking child custody in a divorce or who wishes to have a joint custody arrangement.* Auburn, WA: Author.

12

FATHERS' SUPPORTIVENESS: PERCEPTIONS OF FATHERS AND COLLEGE DAUGHTERS

Peggy S. Draughn
Mary L. Waggenspack

Over the past two decades, research relating to the parent-child relationship has focused on the mother-child relationship. Considerable attention has been devoted to the mothering role, because the sole responsibility of child rearing was presumably in the mother's hands (Kopp & Kirkpatrick, 1979). Until the past decade, little systematic research concentrated on the paternal role.

> The past decade was one in which father-child relationships were emphasized, and the conclusion reached is that fathers are more nurturant than many would have believed a decade ago. The importance of the father in the parent-child relationship no longer can be ignored. (Walters & Walters, 1980, p. 819)

Recent literature supported the importance attributed to the father role, but there appeared to be an unequal emphasis on father-son relationships. Lamb, Owen, and Chase-Lansdale (1979) contend that

> fathers have, for the most part, regarded their daughters as the responsibilities of their wives. To the extent that they take an interest in their daughter's development, their concern has been with the attainment and maintenance of conformity to traditional sex role. (Kopp & Kirkpatrick, 1978, p. 89)

Fathers have an "enormously important" role to play in the socialization of their daughters (Lamb et al., 1979). Limited evidence suggests that the failure to fulfill this role may be detrimental to the daughter's development (Johnson, 1963; Biller & Weiss, 1970; Fish & Biller, 1973).

Drastic changes are ocurring in women's lives (Huber, 1973; Lynn, 1979; Safilios-Rothschild, 1977; Reuther, 1977). Social and cultural standards that once dictated that women's sole responsibility was care of home and children are now in a state of flux (Heer & Grossbard-Sheetman, 1981). Sex-role definitions are changing. Today's woman is confused about her role in life and receives very little direction or encouragement. This is particularly the case with the women now in college.

The study reported here examines the fathering role for young, adult daughters enrolled in college. Specifically, it compares general supportiveness of daughters by fathers as perceived by both daughters and their fathers. Effects of structural variables of occupational status and marital status of fathers and class level of daughters are analyzed.

PRIOR RESEARCH

SEX-ROLE ORIENTATION AND IDENTIFICATION

The overwhelming majority of studies conducted on father-daughter relationships concern the father's influence on the sex-role orientation of his female offspring (Deaux, 1976; Weitz, 1977). The mass confusion over cultural roles for both men and women in America today justifies the sex-role orientation of children as a contemporary concern.

Until recently, sex-role research oversimplified the assumption that boys are similar to their fathers and girls are similar to their mothers. A summary of previous studies found most to emphasize the importance of imitation and identification, but little support for same-sex modeling (Maccoby & Jacklin, 1974). Other studies (Heilbrun, 1976; Lynn, 1976; Leupton, 1980) offer partial support for the parental-modeling theory. Lynn (1976) finds support only when referring to specific traits. Hamilton (1977) contends that male and female parents respond differentially by the sex of the child and that normal daughters may acquire some of their characteristics through imitation of the fathers' characteristics.

Another emerging area that may contribute to children's identifying with same- or opposite-sex parents is the theory of "social power of parental identification" (McDonald, 1977). This theory contrasts sex-role theories of identification in that it argues that offspring will identify with the parent perceived to have more power.

High school seniors usually perceive equal influence from each parent (Leupton, 1980). When influenced by only one parent, it is usually the same-sex parent, with girls less likely to make cross-sex choices than boys. Structural forces affect youth in that they tend to perceive the higher-status parent as more powerful and thus more influential. Perceived influence is more closely related to the father's external status than to the mother's. Leupton (1980) found support for the proposition that the father is the more important determiner of sex-role patterns in his children, in spite of the recent changing sex roles and emphasis on the rights of women; in other words, maternal influence has not increased but decreased slightly in the past decade.

Smith (1981), utilizing the theory of social power, found that late adolescents experienced conflict with their parents in several areas, but as they approached adulthood, they appeared to be influenced by both parents in many important ways. In McDonald's (1977, 1980) examination of the relationship between parental power and adolescents' identification with their parents, he found equal strength in both male and female identification with their fathers. Females more than males had a slight tendency to identify with their mothers, but, for the most part, both sexes reported stronger relationships with their fathers than with their mothers. Several factors appear to influence the father-daughter relationship. The following discussion identifies some of the variables.

FATHER ABSENCE

The absence of the father in a household due to separation or divorce appears to have a negative effect on daughters. Hetherington (1972) found that the effect of father absence usually appeared during adolescence and those females from fatherless homes experienced difficulties in relating to males. Blanchard and Biller (1971) studied the effects of psychological absence (occurring when men spend little time with their children because of professional or attitudinal reasons) on young male children. Effects of psychological absence were similar to the effects of physical absence of fathers on the intellectual achievement of young male children. Less is known about the effects of psychological absence on female children. The nature of the father-child relationship must be determined in order to understand the effect father absence has on children (Lamb, 1979).

DAUGHTER'S PERCEPTION OF PARENTAL SUPPORT

General supportiveness is defined as "that interaction characterized by nurturance, warmth, approval, and other positive sentiments from the parent to the child" (Ellis, Thomas, & Rollins, 1976, p. 713). Thomas, Gecas, Weigert, and Rooney (1974, p. 10) define support as the "quality of interaction which is perceived by the investee (self) as the significant others establish a positive affective relationship with him." Thomas et al. (1974, p. 11) claim that supportive parents usually endorse their children's attempt to create an "effect upon the environment" and simultaneously communicate that they are available if their children need them. They discovered a strong relationship between parental support and adolescent self-esteem, concluding that

> parental support has a substantial and consistent influence on adolescent self-esteem. Children raised by emotionally supportive parents develop high self-esteem; they conceive of themselves as happy, active, good and confident individuals. (pp. 61-62)

Armentrout and Burger (1972) and Thomas and his colleagues (1974) found that mothers were more accepting than fathers and females received support from both parents more often than males. Stinnett, Farris, and Walters (1974) discovered different parental effects on offspring according to the sex of the child. Girls perceived their mothers as the more influential parent. They reported more positive and supportive relationships with parents and received more praise during their childhood than did boys.

The previous studies indicate that at least to the end of the adolescent years, females view their mothers as the more accepting (Armentrout and Burger, 1972; Thomas et al., 1974) and the more influential parent (Stinnett, Farris, & Walters, 1974). Lederer (1964) asserts that a father and a mother stand for two different modes of loving. Mother loves her children for what they are, for merely existing. This love is blind, unconditional, giving, loyal, and complete. Mother will love even if her child proves to be a failure. Father loves his children for what they can do. This love is demanding, conditional on performance, and establishes value. It is something to be proud of and reassured by; it cannot be taken for granted (Lederer, 1964).

PARENTS' PERCEPTION OF SUPPORT

Gilbert, Hanson, and Davis (1982) found only slight differences between both parents' views of major parental responsibilities. Mothers held similar standards in regard to child rearing for both male and female children, and fathers viewed their parental responsibilities differently according to the sex of the child. The parental role responsibility relating to the development of skills and attitudes for effectively dealing with the real world were viewed more often by fathers as their duty to instill in the male children but not in the female child. They also concluded that fathers felt more responsibility toward the male child than toward the female child.

FATHERS' INFLUENCE ON COLLEGE DAUGHTERS

Social and career goals. Goldberg and Shiflett (1981) found career and social goals were important to both sexes. Men chose carrying out parental wishes and economic success as important, whereas women hoped to obtain challenging work coupled with feelings of accomplishment.

Socioeconomic status of fathers. McBroom's (1981) analysis of perceived childhood relationships and socioeconomic status of fathers indicated that neither social class alone nor perceived childhood relationships with mothers had significant bearing on sex-role orientations of university women. Women reporting good childhood relationships with their fathers were more likely to have traditional sex-role views. Comparisons by social class indicated that the lower the socioeconomic status, the more traditional the sex-role views. Women reporting poor relationships with fathers during childhood rejected traditional views, regardless of social class (McBroom, 1981). McBroom concludes that fathers are an important source of role influence for college women, particularly when childhood relationships are good. He implies that men in lower social positions have traditional views of women and that higher social class men hold nontraditional views.

Personal adjustment. Fish and Biller (1973) discovered that high degrees of paternal nurturance and paternal involvement during childhood seemed to facilitate the college female's personal adjustment. Women reporting negative self-perceptions received a high degree of paternal rejection.

Autonomy. Fathers appear to influence their daughters' development by enhancing or discouraging autonomy (Lazoff, 1974). Autonomous women, defined by Lazoff as those not restricting themselves to the traditional roles of wife and mother, sought challenging jobs tapping their intellect and "service-giving resources." Their fathers were dynamic, ambitious, and brilliant, married to admiring and supportive wives. They reported a father-daughter relationship characterized by deep emotional involvement. These women identified with mothers who provided traditional role models.

Lazoff (1974) identifies other groups as "supercompetents" and least autonomous. Both groups of women reported childhood relationships with aloof, demanding, or uninvolved fathers and weak, submissive mothers. These women experienced intellectual success but had conflict in interpersonal relationships.

Mothers alone do not serve as role models for their children. Fish and Biller (1973), Lazoff (1974), and McBroom (1981) present evidence that fathers do provide a source of influence that could encourage or deter the healthy development of their college daughters. According to Lynn (1979, p. 126), "College women who feel close to their fathers tend to view themselves as in control of events, rather than simply at the mercy of the capriciousness of others or of the environment."

Previous studies have focused most often on the effects of earlier childhood experiences and parental relationships as they affected the daughter. Most of these studies have been concerned with the mother-daughter relationship. Virtually nothing appears in the literature concerning fathers and their daughters during the launching years in terms of the young woman's assumption of adult roles. Females in college are emancipating themselves from their families and their childhoods. Fathers' support at this time may be crucial to the daughters' well-being.

This investigation attempts to examine the father-daughter relationship. The specific purpose is to explore the association of fathers' and daughters' perceptions of fathers' supportiveness of daughters. It is limited to fathers and their daughters who are enrolled in college.

PROCEDURE

INSTRUMENTATION

A section of the instrument designed for this study included 11 items from the long form of the Cornell Parent Behavior Inventory developed by Urie Bronfenbrenner (1964). These items were taken from the fourth version of Bronfenbrenner's 30-item long form. The Cornell Parent Behavior Inventory measures children's perceptions of child rearing along 12 dimensions: nurturance, physical punishment, achievement demands, retribution, principled discipline, deprivation of privileges, protectiveness, praise, predictability of standards (combining two factors—prescription of responsibility and consistency), rejection, indulgence, and instrumental companionship (Rodgers, 1966). Ellis, Thomas, and Rollins (1976) report an internal consistency reliability range of alpha = .85 to .92 for this instrument. The researchers conclude that the scale has adequate internal consistency reliability and is a valid measure of general parental support.

For the purpose of this study, items from the nurturance factor and the praise factor were selected for identifying fathers' general supportiveness. One question was added under nurturance to better ascertain the university women's perception of this aspect of support.

An additional 37 items were included to further explore daughters' and fathers' perceptions of unique aspects of the college daughter-father relationship. These items measured dimensions of the father-daughter relationship identified as autonomy enhancement, verbal approval, and nurturant companionship. Two versions of the instrument were developed. The father's version was a self-assessment of supportiveness as a father and the daughter's version allowed daughters to assess supportiveness of fathers. Each version measured 5 dimensions of the father-daughter relationship. The 35 items employed in this measurement were designed for a 5-point, forced-choice scale, ranging from very often (4) to never (0). Thus, the higher the score, the more supportive the father.

SAMPLE

The sample for this study was composed of fathers and their daughters: single, white, university students between the ages of 18 and

23 enrolled at a large southern state university, in the fall semester of 1982. Women students were randomly selected and stratified according to class level: freshman, sophomore, junior, and senior. The names of selected students' fathers were obtained from university records. Questionnaires were mailed to 70 freshmen, 60 sophomores, 58 juniors, 69 seniors, and the fathers of these women. Oversampling of freshmen was necessary due to the high dropout rate and of the senior class because of possible graduation before the survey reached them. Responses were received from 23 freshman, 32 sophomores, 31 juniors, and 52 seniors. A total of 277 usable responses, including 110 father-daughter pairs, were received. Additional responses were received from 28 fathers and 29 daughters. Total responses from fathers were 138 and from daughters 139. Only responses from father-daughter pairs will be reported in this paper.

The final sample included 17 fathers classified as blue-collar workers, 91 white-collar workers, and 2 retired. The majority (101) were married to the mothers of their daughters and 9 were divorced. Fathers' ages ranged from 40 to 70, with most under 60. Most of the fathers had at least four years of college. Only 26 had not attended college. Incomes ranged from $10,000 to $40,000 and above, with 50% in the latter category. Religious preference was almost equally divided between Protestant and Catholic. Two were Jewish and three agnostic.

DATA ANALYSIS AND RESULTS

Responses to items from questionnaires were grouped under 5 factors as predetermined in the development of the instrument. Names of factors and item groupings were as follows: nurturance, items, 1, 2, and 29; praise, items 8 and 9; autonomy enhancement, items 3, 14, 15, 16, 17, and 18; verbal approval, items 19 and 21; and nurturant companionship, items 23-28, 30, 31, and 35. Response levels were never (0); hardly ever (1); sometimes (2); fairly often (3); and very often (4).

Scores for each factor were determined by summing the response levels in each item grouping and were labeled by the appropriate factor name. Father supportiveness was determined by summing the five factor scores. Separate scores were determined for fathers and daughters for father supportiveness and for each of the five factors.

The mean perceived father supportiveness score and the means of each of the five factors were calculated for fathers and daughters. A score of zero on the five-point Likert scale represented the least favorable perception of father's support and a score of four constituted the most favorable perception of father's support. When items in general supportiveness were omitted, average scores were used in the analysis.

Scores for father supportiveness as perceived by fathers ranged from a minimum of 2.00 (sometimes) to a maximum of 3.95 (fairly often to very often) for father-daughter pairs with a mean score of 3.20. Father supportiveness as perceived by daughters ranged from a minimum of .611 (never) to a maximum of 4.0 (very often) with a mean score of 2.96. Overall, fathers perceived themselves as more supportive than their daughters perceived them to be. Daughters' perceptions of their fathers' support were also lower than their fathers' perceptions on each of the factors of support. The largest discrepancy between perceptions was on nurturant companionship, with a 2.64 mean score for perceptions on each of the factors of support. The largest discrepancy between perceptions was on nurturant companionship, with a 2.64 mean score for perceptions of fathers and 2.21 for perceptions of daughters. The smallest discrepancy between perceptions of father-daughter pairs was for verbal approval (fathers, 3.18; daughters, 3.11).

Based on the rating scale used in the research instrument, both fathers and daughters ranked fathers as fairly often supportive. Although there was a wide range of scores, median scores for both total supportiveness and factor areas were 3.08 for daughters' responses and 3.19 for fathers' responses.

Correlational analysis of father-daughter responses. The major purpose of this chapter is to determine whether there is significant association between fathers' and daughters' perceptions of general supportiveness. Paired father-daughter responses were compared on father supportiveness and on each of the factors constituting supportiveness. There was a significant, though moderate, correlation between fathers' and daughters' responses on each of the factors as well as on perceived father-supportiveness (Table 12.1).

By occupational status. Another purpose of this study was to determine whether fathers' and daughters' perceptions of father supportiveness would vary significantly according to the occupational or marital status of fathers or by the class level of daughters. Pearson product-moment correlations were computed to determine the relationship between fathers' and daughters' perceptions and the occupational status of fathers (Table 12.2). Perceptions of fathers and daughters were significantly correlated in both white-collar (r = .38) and blue-collar (r = .55) groups. Perceptions of blue-collar fathers and their daughters were significantly related on the factors of praise (r = .65) and nurturant

TABLE 12.1
Spearman Correlations of the Father-Daughter Rankings
on Father Supportiveness and Factors in Support

Total Support and Support Factors	rho	Number of Observations	
		Fathers	Daughters
Father Supportiveness	0.41**	105	105
Factors			
nurturance	0.32*	109	109
praise	0.34*	110	110
autonomy enhancement	0.24*	108	108
verbal approval	0.20*	109	109
nurturant companionship	0.40**	106	106

*$p < 0.05$· **$p < 0.01$.

companionship (r = .63). For white-collar fathers and their daughters only verbal approval failed to reach a significant level of correlation.

A chi-square test of relationship revealed that occupational status of fathers was not significant to fathers' and daughters' perceptions of father supportiveness (χ^2 = 3.05, 2 df, p = .218) overall, nor to any of the factors in support (Table 12.2).

By marital status of fathers. Correlations between married fathers' and their daughters' perceptions were significant (r = .44) for father supportiveness (Table 12.2) and for the factors of nurturance (r = .35), praise (r = .39), autonomy enhancement (r = .26), verbal approval (r = .21), and nurturant companionship (r = .39). The results of the analyses between divorced fathers and their daughters yielded no significant correlations between perceptions for father supportiveness or for any area of support.

When further subjected to chi-square analysis (Table 12.2), the relationship between fathers' and daughters' perceptions of fathers' supportiveness were found not to vary significantly according to the marital status of fathers (χ^2 = .10, 1 df, p = .746).

Class level of daughters. Correlations between freshman daughters and their fathers were positive and significant for father supportiveness (r = .66) (Table 12.2), and for praise (r = .55), autonomy enhancement (r = .55), verbal aproval (r = .47), and nurturant companionship (r = .54). Correlations between perceptions of sophomore daughters and their fathers were positive and significant for only two support factors: nurturance (r = .50) and nurturant companionship (r = .42). Correlations between perceptions of junior daughters and their fathers were positive and significant for father supportiveness (r = .68) and for the factors of nurturance (r = .40), praise (r = .53), verbal approval (r = .75), and

TABLE 12.2
Correlations of Father-Daughter Perceptions of
Father Supportiveness, by Demographic Variables

| | Number of Observations | | | |
	Fathers	Daughters	r	χ^2
Occupational status of fathers				3.05
blue collar	16	16	0.55*	
white collar	87	87	0.38*	
Marital status of fathers				.10
married	95	95	0.44*	
divorced	9	9	0.52*	
Class level of daughters				2.14*
freshman	21	21	0.66*	
sophomore	26	26	0.26*	
junior	26	26	0.68*	
senior	32	32	0.12*	

*$p < 0.05$.

nurturant companionship ($r = .55$). There were no significant correlations for father supportiveness or for any support factor between fathers and their senior daughters.

When tested for significance, it was found that the correlation between fathers' and daughters' perceptions of fathers' support did vary significantly for total support according to the daughters' class level ($\chi^2 = 9.94737$; $p < .025$) (Table 12.2).

DISCUSSION

Because few, if any, researchers have studied the congruence between fathers' perceptions of their support and daughters' perceptions of fathers' support, it is difficult to relate the present findings to previous results. However, certain trends in this research are discernible which have been explored to some extent in other studies. Block (1979), in his international study of parent and child self-reports of parental behavior, found that there were few discrepancies in fathers' and daughters' perceptions of fathers' parental behavior. The findings of this study indicated that father-daughter pairs held very similar perceptions of fathers' support. Block also found that fathers encouraged trustworthiness, truthfulness, and ladylike behavior in their daughters but were more likely to encourage independence and personal responsibility in their sons. Fathers were less strict with their daughters and treated them warmly, encouraging daughters to wonder and think about life. Daughters perceived fathers as affectionate and physically close, encouraging introspection and feminine behavior. Women reported their fathers were warm and involved but that they did not tend to encourage autonomy or independent achievement. The present study found that fathers were supportive, nurturant, and approving of their daughters. However, daughters' perceptions were not as favorable as fathers' in any support area. It appears either that fathers are not as supportive as they think they are or that fathers' and daughters' perceptions and/or definitions differ on what is occurring.

The largest discrepancies were in the nurturant and nurturant companionship factors, revealing fathers who thought they were more nurturant and better companions than daughters perceived them to be. Fathers' perceptions of autonomy enhancement were toward the "very often" range, with daughters' perceptions closer to the "fairly often" range. Both fathers and daughters reported fathers as "sometimes" to "fairly often" verbally approving. This was the lowest ranked factor in general support and both fathers and daughters were aware of the slight lack of verbal approval.

Stinnett, Farris, and Walters (1974) found that females, as opposed to their male counterparts, received more praise during childhood from both of their parents. This finding apparently holds true for older daughters also. This is consistent with the current study finding that daughters perceived praise from their fathers "often," though not as often as fathers perceived themselves giving praise to their daughters.

Fish and Biller (1973) report that high degrees of paternal nurturance and involvement during chidhood appear to enhance the personality adjustment of university females. Paternal rejection seems to contribute to difficulty in personality adjustment for college women. Although it is beyond the scope of the present study to test these conclusions, it can be stated that daughters are receiving nurturance from their fathers and this is possibly aiding in their personality adjustment during the college years.

McBroom (1981) found that social class alone had no significant effect on the sex-role orientations of university females. But when childhood relationships were good, social class was significant. The lower the social class, the more traditional the sex-role views. He concludes that social class of men forms the basis for the influence they exert on their daughters. The findings of the present study revealed no significant differences in support perceptions by either fathers or daughters according to the occupational status of fathers. However, as perceived by daughters, blue-collar fathers tended to be more nurturant than white-collar fathers and white-collar fathers tended to encourage autonomy more often than blue-collar fathers.

Hetherington (1972), Blanchard and Biller (1971), and Lamb, Owen, and Chase-Lansdale (1979) found that father absence does not seem to be as harmful to females as to males, but can contribute to difficulty in females' ability to interact with males. Lamb and his colleagues conclude that father absence appears to be most harmful early in the life of women, but the real effects become apparent during adolescence. The present study found that among father-daughter pairs, divorced fathers were perceived to be less nurturant than married fathers. However, divorced fathers constituted a very small percentage of the sample. A larger sample size of divorced father-daughter pairs would be needed to determine whether differences do exist with change in fathers' marital status.

We know of no research that explores the effects of college class level of daughters on perceptions of fathers' supportiveness. Furthermore, due to the wide variation of results found in this study, it is difficult to reach specific conclusions about class level of daughters. Senior daughters' and their fathers' perceptions of support were not associated in any factor. This finding could suggest that women, during one of the most crucial times in their lives of graduating from college, pursuing careers, and becoming independent functioning members of society, are not getting the support they need. This possibility is confirmed in other research. Lamb and his colleagues (1979) state that women remain close to their mothers as they grow older, but must earn approval and love from their fathers. Fathers' support is crucial. If fathers maintain traditional beliefs, they will not encourage "achievement-oriented" behavior but, rather, will communicate to their daughters that nontraditional behavior is not feminine and marriage should be the next step. It may also indicate that senior women are getting responses from fathers similar to that sons often get. That is, fathers may be allowing greater autonomy to foster independence and achievement in their daughters. For daughters, the effect may be more negative than positive. Lazoff (1974) found that involved, supportive, and encouraging fathers had a tremendous influence on enhancing autonomy in their daughters and that these women were successful in careers as well as in life. Unsupportive and uninvolved fathers had daughters who experienced much conflict in relationships as well as in life.

In this study, daughters more favorably perceived the importance of the father-daughter relationship than did fathers. Although, according to daughters, fathers overrate their perceptions of support, they underestimate the importance of their relationship to their daughters.

Daughters perceive fathers as less supportive than fathers perceive themselves, but still "agree" that the father-daughter relationship is important. Trends in other research support this possibility. Gilbert, Hanson, and Davis (1982) found that fathers were less likely to take part in developing skills and attitudes for effective living in today's world for their female children than for their male children. Lamb and his colleagues (1979) state that fathers are more involved in their sons' development than in their daughters'. They are not unconcerned about their daughters, but tend to view them as the responsibility of their wives.

Overall, university females tended to view fathers as supportive "fairly often." Fathers viewed themselves as supportive "fairly often" to "very often." These findings indicate that fathers think they are more supportive than they are perceived to be by daughters.

CONCLUSIONS

The findings of this study indicate a moderately high agreement between fathers and daughters on fathers' supportiveness. Overall, fathers appeared to be supportive of their daughters in the college years. Further investigations of fathers who have both sons and daughters to compare supportiveness for each child are needed to determine whether father supportiveness differs according to the sex of the child. Systematic efforts should be made to include fathers, mothers, and daughters in order to examine the influence the father-mother or mother-daughter relationship has on the father-daughter relationship.

It is important to underscore the importance of perpetual congruence of supportiveness. Perhaps the most salient finding of this study was the moderately high association of fathers' and daughters' perceptions—that is, fathers and daughters tended to agree on how supportive the father was of the daughter. This finding emphasizes that fathers and daughters may have close relationships that enhance the daughters' move toward independence from the parental family.

The importance of the father-daughter relationship during the launching period appears to be especially important today because of the changing roles of women. College-educated women are less likely than ever before to take on the traditional homemaker role. Further study is needed to determine whether father supportiveness increases or decreases the likelihood that daughters will follow careers and, if so, the types of careers the daughters will choose.

Although this study focused on young adult daughters, there is an apparent need for study of the father-daughter relationship at all ages. Longitudinal studies would best serve the purpose of determining the influence of the father in the development of the daughter. The multitude of problems in attempting longitudinal studies makes it unlikely that much information will be gained in this way. Nevertheless, life-span research, at least from birth through adolescence, is vital to understanding the father-daughter relationship.

REFERENCES

Armentrout, J. A., & Burger, G. K. (1972). Children's reports of parental child-rearing behavior at five grade levels. *Developmental Psychology, 7,* 44-48.

Biller, H. B., & Meredith, D. (1975). *Father power.* Garden City, NY: Doubleday.

Biller, H. B., & Weiss, S. D. (1970). The father-daughter relationship and personality development of the female. *Journal of Genetic Psychology, 114,* 79-93.

Blanchard, R. W., & Biller, H. B. (1971). Father availability and academic performance among third-grade boys. *Developmental Psychology, 4,* 301-305.

Block, J. (1979). Another look at sex differentiation in the socialization behaviors of mothers and fathers. In F. Denmark (Ed.), *Psychology of women: Future direction of research* (pp. 321-341). New York: Psychological Dimensions.

Bronfenbrenner, U. (1964). Some familial antecedents of responsibility and leadership in adolescents. In M. Petrullo & B. M. Bass (Eds.), *Leadership and interpersonal behavior.* New York: Holt, Rinehart & Winston.

Deaux, K. (1976). *The behavior of women and men.* Monterey, CA: Brooks/Cole.

Ellis, G. J., Thomas, D. L., & Rollins, B. C. (1976). Measuring parental support: The interrelationship of three measures. *Journal of Marriage and the Family, 38,* 713-721.

Fish, K. D., & Biller, H. B. (1973). Perceived childhood paternal relationships and college females' personal adjustment. *Adolescence, 8,* 415-420.

Gilbert, L. A., Hanson, G. R., & Davis, B. (1982). Perceptions of parental role responsibilities: Differences between mothers and fathers. *Family Relations, 31,* 261-269.

Goldberg, A., & Shiflett, S. (1981). Goals of male and female college students: Do traditional sex differences still exist? *Sex Roles, 7,* 1213-1222.

Hamilton, M. L. (1977). *Father's influence on children.* Chicago: Nelson Hall.

Heer, D. M., & Grossbard-Shectman, A. G. (1981). The impact of the female marriage squeeze and the contraceptive revolution on sex roles and the women's liberation movement in the United States, 1960 to 1975. *Journal of Marriage and the Family, 43,* 49-65.

Heilbrun, A. B. (1976). Identification with the father and sex-role development of the daughter. *Family Coordinator, 25,* 411-416.

Hetherington, E. M. (1972). Effects of father absence on personality development in adolescent daughters. *Developmental Psychology, 7,* 313-326.

Huber, J. (Ed.). (1973). *Changing women in a changing society.* Chicago: University of Chicago Press.

Johnson, M. M. (1963). Sex role learning in the nuclear family. *Child Development, 34,* 319-333.

Kopp, C. B., & Kirkpatrick, M. (Eds.). (1979). *Becoming female: Perspectives on development.* New York: Plenum.

Lamb, M. E. (1980). Paternal influences and the father's role: A personal perspective. *American Psychologist, 34,* 938-943.

Lamb, M. E., Owen, M. T., & Chase-Lansdale, L. (1979). The father-daughter relationship: Past, present, and future. In C. B. Kopp & M. Kirkpatrick (Eds.), *Becoming female: Perspectives on development* (pp. 89-112). New York: Plenum.

Lazoff, M. M. (1974). Fathers and autonomy in women. In R. B. Kundsin (Ed.), *Women and success.* New York: Morrow.

Lederer, W. (1964). Dragons, delinquents, and destiny. *Psychological Issues, 4,* 33.

Leuptow, L. B. (1980). Social structure, social change and parental influence in adolescent sex-role socialization: 1964-1975. *Journal of Marriage and the Family, 42,* 93-103.

Lynn, D. B. (1974). *Daughters and parents: Past, present, and future.* Stanford, CA: Stanford University Press.

Lynn, D. B. (1976). Fathers and sex-role development. *Family Coordinator, 25,* 403-409.

Maccoby, E. E., & Jacklin, C. N. (1974). *The psychology of sex differences.* Stanford, CA: Stanford University Press.

McBroom, W. H. (1981). Parental relationships, socioeconomic status, and sex-role expectations. *Sex Roles, 7,* 1027-1033.

McDonald, G. W. (1977). Parental identification by the adolescent: A social power approach. *Journal of Marriage and the Family, 39,* 705-719.

McDonald, G. W. (1980). Parental identification by the adolescent: A social power approach. *Journal of Marriage and the Family, 42,* 289-296.

Reuther, R. R. (1977). Home and work: Women's roles and the transformation of values. In W. Burghardt (Ed.), *Woman: New dimensions* (pp. 742-775). New York: Paulist Press.

Rodgers, R. R. (1966). *Cornell Parent Behavior Description: An interim report.* Ithaca, NY: Cornell University.

Safilios-Rothschild, C. (1977). The current status of women cross-culturally: Changes and persisting barriers. In W. Burghardt (Ed.), *Woman: New dimensions* (pp. 1-28). New York: Paulist Press.

Smith, T. E. (1981). Adolescent agreement with perceived maternal and paternal educational goals. *Journal of Marriage and the Family, 43,* 85-93.

Stinnett, N., Farris, J. A., & Walters, J. (1974). Parent-child relationships of male and female high school children. *Journal of Genetic Psychology, 125,* 99-106.

Thomas, D. L., Gecas, V., Weigert, A., & Rooney, E. (1974). *Family socialization and the adolescent.* Lexington, MA: D. C. Heath.

Walters, J., & Walters, J. J. (1980). Parent-child relationships: A review, 1970-1979. *Journal of Marriage and the Family, 42,* 807-822.

Weitz, S. (1977). *Sex roles.* New York: Oxford University Press.

PART III

Men in Family, Kin, and Friendship Networks

As we have noted in earlier sections of this book, many men not only have their most satisfying relationships within marriage and parenthood, but also may experience within their families the greatest sources of conflict and stress. Lawrence Gary in Chapter 13 reports from his own investigations of Black men that most of them do not perceive themselves as having a high level of conflict with Black women. However, for those who do report high conflict, being married is correlated with the highest level of conflict. And for those men who experience a high level of conflict with their mates, there are also reports of high levels of depressive symptoms, excessive drinking, drug abuse, suicide attempts, and violence. Gary, however, is quick to report that married Black men who have conflicts are now beginning to bring their marriage and family problems to the attention of mental health practitioners.

Contrary to most of the emphasis in this book upon the importance of marriage and parenthood for contemporary men, a case can also be made for the importance of other relationships men experience and value. These other meaningful relationships may exist within kinship and friendship networks. Graeme Russell in Chapter 14, for example, explores the special relationships that often develop for men who become grandparents. Russell explores grandfathers' reports of deriving considerable satisfaction from this relationship, being highly involved in it, and frequently spending time with their grandchildren. One explanation for this high level of involvement with grandchildren, according to Russell, is the grandfathers' reported regrets that they had not been more involved with their own children.

Other relationships that many men regretfully report in later life as not having developed more are adult friendships with other men. From some interviews with middle-class professional men, Peter Stein (Chapter 15) reports some of the barriers to the formation of adult friendships. He describes men's distress in even talking about their male friendships, but notes the great importance attached to the supportive friendships of these single and married men.

This book concludes with a study of identity change among older and younger men living in southern Appalachia. In many ways these men are "marginal men . . . undergoing a cultural transition from one set of values and behaviors to another set of values and behaviors" (Stonequist, 1961). In some ways, therefore, these men represent a microcosm of a larger but more diverse macrocosm of men today. This larger group of men, valuing their marriages and families, are experiencing new intrapersonal desires to change their values and behaviors. They are also experiencing new challenges and pressures from within their families to give more time and effort to their father and husband roles as "men in families."

REFERENCE

Stonequist, E. V. (1961). *The marginal man: A study in personality and culture conflict*. New York: Russell & Russell.

13

FAMILY LIFE EVENTS, DEPRESSION, AND BLACK MEN

Lawrence E. Gary

In recent years, considerable attention has been given to the dominant role played by men in the United States (Bell, 1981; Lewis, 1981). Because of the way in which our society is structured, it is argued that men receive an unfair share of its benefits. However, for Black men, racism has negated the so-called male advantage (Gary, 1981; Staples, 1978). In a recent article on Black men, Gary and Leashore (1982) reviewed government statistics and social indicators on income, health, employment, and so forth; they demonstrate that, compared to white men, Black men are at risk in the American society. For example, Black men have higher morbidity and mortality rates, experience greater unemployment, earn less, and have higher rates of incarceration and criminal victimization than do white men. These circumstances have crippling consequences for the mental health and the families of Black men and for the quality of life in Black communities.

When the well-being of Black men is threatened, the entire Black community is at risk. According to Haki Madhubuti (1981, p. 31):

> Properly functioning Black families will produce healthy male-female relationships. . . . Doctrines of right and wrong, concepts of love and caring are family centered. Human values, spiritual and material are first practiced and taught at a functional level by the family. The major social

Author's Note: *I would like to acknowledge the contributions of Ola M. Bell, Greta L. Berry, and Gayle D. Weaver in the development of this chapter. This research was made possible by Grant 5R01-MH-2555-1-06 from the National Institute of Mental Health.*

215

agency that any Black progressive movement (or nation) cannot do without is family.

This suggests that in order to examine male-female relations, one has to discuss this issue within the context of family life. The purpose of this chapter is to explore how conflict between the sexes predicts depressive symptoms among Black men. The specific research questions are as follows: What is the extent of conflict between Black men and women? Is there a relationship between conflict between the sexes and depression? Does conflict between the sexes bear a relation to depression that is independent of other stressful life events or variables?

BLACK FAMILIES ARE AT RISK

The need to examine the relationships between Black men and women is evident in the statistics and literature on family relationships. Census data for 1980 show that 40.3% of Black family units are headed by women, compared to 11.6% for whites in 1980 (U.S. Bureau of the Census, 1981b). For Black families, only 42.4% of children under 18 years of age live with both parents, compared to 82.9% for whites in 1980. In other words, the majority (56.8%) of Black children do not live in family units where both of their parents are present. Census data also suggest an increasing number of Black persons 18 years and older are not getting married and those who do are dissolving their marriages through divorce or separation. For example, in 1970, 64.1% of Black persons 18 years and older were married; in 1980, only 51.9% were married. In 1980, 29.8% of Black persons 18 years and older were single, compared to 20.6% in 1970 (U.S. Bureau of the Census, 1981). It is instructive to note that in 1980, the majority of Black males 15 years and older were not married. This was not the case for the majority male group. For example, in 1980, 63% of white males 15 years and older were married and present in the home, compared to only 42% for Black males (U.S. Bureau of the Census, 1981a).

Even when Black adults do marry, there is a higher probability that they will get divorced than will white adults. For example, the divorce ratio (per 1000 married persons with spouse present) in the Black community was 203, compared to 92 for whites in 1980. In 1970, the divorce ratio for Black people was 83; it was 62 in 1960 (U.S. Bureau of the Census, 1981a). When we look specifically at the adult female population, the evidence that there are some serious problems in male-female relations is even more revealing. In 1980, the divorce ratio for Black females was 257, compared to 110 for white females (U.S. Bureau of the Census, 1981a).

Other social indicators such as unwanted pregnancies, abortion rates, and incidence of family violence suggest that Black families are in trouble in the United States. More than half (55%) of all Black babies in the United States today are born out of wedlock, most of them to teenagers ("Births to the Unwed", 1981; Reid, 1982; U.S. Bureau of the Census, 1981a). Teenage fathers and Black males, in general, are implicated in the problems of teenage pregnancies and unwanted babies (Barrett & Robinson, 1982; Hendricks, 1981; Leashore, 1979). In 1976, 25.8% of all births to Black mothers between the ages of 15 to 44 years of age were unwanted pregnancies, compared to 9.5% for white mothers (U.S. Bureau of the Census, 1981b). Moreover, the abortion rate (per 1000 women) was 22.7 for white women in 1978; it was 60.4 for nonwhite women. Data on the abortion ratio (per 1000 live births) suggest that a Black woman is twice as likely as a white woman to have an abortion (U.S. Bureau of the Census, 1981b).

Homicidal violence is a major problem confronting Black communities. In 1980, an average of 53 of every 100 murder victims were white, 42 were Black, and 4 were persons of other races (U.S. Department of Justice, 1981). Over 9000 Black persons were murdered in 1980. Black people are responsible for most of the homicides in the Black community. For example, in regard to single victim/offender murder circumstances in the Black community, 94.8% of the murder offenders were Black in 1980 (U.S. Department of Justice, 1981). In 1980, whites constituted 51% of the total arrests for murder, Blacks made up 48%, and the other races were responsible for the remainder (U.S. Department of Justice, 1981). It is important to note that 51% of the murders committed in 1980 were perpetrated by relatives or persons acquainted with the victims. Killings within family relationship made up 16%, one-half of which involved spouse killing spouse (U.S. Department of Justice, 1981). These data also show that the Black woman is about 8 times as likely as the white woman to kill her mate. Violent crimes such as forcible rape, robbery, and aggravated assault and the consequences of economic and societal pressures make it difficult to establish and maintain functional and meaningful interpersonal relationships in the Black community. Increases in the incidence of alcoholism, drug addiction, depression, and so forth among Blacks warrant inquiry as to how these factors affect personal and family relationships.

RELATIONS BETWEEN BLACK MEN AND WOMEN

The statistics discussed above clearly suggest that the status of the Black family is at risk. When one's family life is seriously altered, there will be problems in interpersonal relations. Recent cases in the newspapers show the consequences of poor male-female relations in families. In Camp Springs, Maryland, as a result of a troubled relationship with his spouse, a Black man killed six people, including three children (Piantadoisi & Martin, 1981). A few years ago in Washington, D.C., a Black man who was angry with his girlfriend firebombed her apartment and several of their children died. In Philadelphia, a young Black man who graduated with honors in engineering from a college in upstate New York returned to Philadelphia to visit his girlfriend, who was the mother of his child. On visiting his girlfriend, he had an encounter with her new boyfriend and he was killed. In another area in Pennsylvania, a Black man, 42 years old, killed thirteen people, including seven children, five of whom were his.

The significance of male-female relationships in the Black community has also been the topic of discussion by various scholars in a wide range of disciplines (Akbar, 1976; Franklin, 1980; Gary, 1981; Grier & Cobbs, 1968; Hare, 1979a; Jackson, 1978; Jordon, 1977; Karenga, 1979; Noble, 1978; Poussaint, 1979; Rose-Rodgers, 1980; Scott, 1976; Smith & Millham, 1979; Staples, 1978, 1980, 1981; Stewart, 1980; Tucker, 1979; Turner & Turner, 1974; Wells, 1980; Welsing, 1974; Wilcox, 1979). These writers have identified a range of factors that influence interpersonal relationships between men and women. Issues such as *scarcity of Black men* (Braithwaite, 1981; Jackson, 1978; Staples, 1978); *division over authority within the family structure* (Franklin, 1980; Hammond & Enoch, 1976); *Black male chauvinism* (Noble, 1978; Shange, 1977; Wallace, 1979); *Black female emasculation of Black males* (Bond & Perry, 1969; Bracey, Meir, & Rudwick, 1971; Hare, 1964, 1971); *Black male-white female intimacy* (Franklin, 1980; Hare, 1979b; Noble, 1978; Wallace, 1979); and *friends* (Anderson, 1978; Bell, 1981; Liebow, 1967) have been discussed as sources of conflict between Black men and women. With the exception of a few scholars such as Franklin (1980), most writers argue that racism is the primary cause of the present conflict between the Black man and woman.

Although there has been a proliferation of written work and research on this topic, we have not learned very much about this important problem. In reviewing the literature on Black male and female relationships, I identified the following deficiencies: Most of the research is based on what Black women say about their relationships with men; too many of the studies on sex-role stereotypes are conducted on college students; most of the articles on this subject are not empirically based, but tend to be polemical in nature; the few empirical studies on this subject have tended to have small sample sizes and, in most cases, the subjects were selected by nonprobability procedures; these studies do not have a consistent research approach, thus creating problems of comparability; the research in this area tends to place too much emphasis on social structural variables.

STRESSFUL FAMILY EVENTS AND DEPRESSION

A major deficiency in the literature dealing with the relationship between men and women is that researchers have not paid adequate attention to the mental health consequences of this problem. Life stressors, including those related to family relationships such as change in arguments with spouse, in-law problems, a reconciliation with spouse, and change in family "get-togethers," can play a part in causing serious illnesses (Dohrenwend & Dohrenwend, 1981). Stress may be defined as "any unpleasant and disturbing emotional experience due to frustration." Stress often results from an alteration of or interference with an individual's usual pattern of behavior (Theodorson & Theodorson, 1969, p. 427). It is assumed that life stress can cause mental illness because illness is seen as a consequence of disequilibrium in the organism. For the most part, the life event approach is a major strategy for stress measurement (Kanner, Coyne, Schaefer, & Lazarus, 1981).

In general, there is ample research literature to indicate that increasing amounts of change in one's life (e.g., death of spouse, divorce, residential move, arrests, in-law problems, financial problems) are predictive of depression (Dohrenwend & Dohrenwend, 1981; Paykel, 1979; Rabkin & Struening, 1976). It is assumed that the more changes a person must make, the more psychological adjustment is necessary. In addition, the more adjustment becomes necessary, the greater the stress on the individual, leading to a variety of psychiatric and other types of illnesses (Holmes & Rahe, 1967). In examining social roles that are considered problematic or undesirable, Ilfeld (1977) found that these role circumstances accounted for more than 25% of the variance in the level of depressive symptoms. In comparison, selected demographic variables such as age, sex, marital status, and income accounted for only 8% of the variance. In their analysis of the relationship between depression scores and life change events, Markush and Favero (1974) report that for Blacks, the strongest association occurred for low-educated Black men between the ages of 35 to 54. Moreover, using data from a sample of drug abusers including 277 Black males, Borus and Senay (1980) found that elevated depressive scores were the results of acute life stress.

Although there is considerable disagreement on how to measure stressful life events, data consistently show that physical illnesses can contribute to the onset of depression (Dohrenwend & Dohrenwend, 1981). For example, in their study of correlates of depression in older adults, Murrell, Himmelfarb, and Wright (1983) conclude that by far the strongest relationship is with physical illness. Significant numbers of the subjects who reported illnesses such as kidney or bladder disease, heart trouble, lung trouble, hardening of the arteries, and stroke were above the depression cut-off point. Also, a number of studies in recent years have examined the relationship between economic trends and mental health. There is a consistent finding that the unemployed are more likely to be depressed than are persons who work (Brenner, 1973). In their review of social indicators and psychiatric illnesses, Rosen, Goldsmith, and Redlick (1979) suggest that persons who have high levels of contact with the criminal justice system and who are very mobile are high-risk groups for a variety of mental disabilities. Both U.S. Census data and reports from the U.S. Department of Justice indicate that a greater proportion of Black men than white men fit these characteristics (U.S. Bureau of the Census, 1981b, p. 176).

In recent years, there has been some discussion of the need to study not only major life events but also minor events as they affect mental health. For example, Kanner and his colleagues (1981) compared standard life events methodology for the prediction of psychological symptoms with one focusing on relatively minor events. They defined "hassles" as "irritating, frustrating, distressing demands that to some degree characterize everyday transactions with the environment" (p. 3). Examples of life hassles are status incongruity between spouses, sex-role conflict, demands of children and aged parents, work overload and underload, and role ambiguity. They discovered that hassles were a better predictor of psychological symptoms than were stressful life events; when the life events scores were controlled for, the relationship between hassles and symptoms remained significantly correlated. These findings suggest that in studying family stress and depression, it is important to analyze both minor and major life events.

The research reported here does not attempt to respond to all of the deficiencies in the literature on this subject. It is important to note, however, that the research is based on data collected from Black men. Subjects were noninstitutionalized; that is, they were not captive participants. Both minor and stressful life events will be explored in relationship to depression.

METHODS

PROCEDURES

In order to answer the research questions identified earlier, a cross-sectional survey of Black adult males was conducted. The target population for this study was 142 noninstitutionalized Black males who were 18 years of age and older living in the Washington, D.C., metropolitan area. Because of the general problem of securing "non-captive" Black males for social science research purposes, a variety of techniques were used to recruit subjects. The techniques were as follows: sampling through the use of a list of computer-generated random telephone numbers; posted announcements in selected barbershops; and referrals by respondents. A total of 142 subjects were identified and all agreed to participate in the study.

The age range was from 18 to 65 years, with the median age 33 years. With respect to marital status, 33% of the respondents were married, 21% were formerly married, and 46% were never married. With respect to education, 50% had received more than 12 years of education; one-fourth had received 12 years of education and another one-fourth had received less. Annual family incomes of 38% of the respondents were below $10,000; 44% had incomes between $10,000 and $24,999; and 18% had family incomes of $25,000 and above.

Personal interviews of approximately two hours were conducted by trained interviewers using facilities located at Howard University. The interview schedule consisted of open-ended and forced-choice questions.

MEASUREMENT OF VARIABLES

(1) Conflict between sexes index. The items used to obtain data on this measure were extracted from 13 questions addressing issues the respondents sometimes agreed or disagreed about with their spouses or mates. The specific wording on the interview was as follows: "I am going to read you some things about which men and their (wives, women) sometimes agree and disagree. Would you tell me which ones were problems between you and your wife during the past few weeks?" (See Table 13.1 for a list of the items.) The lowest possible score on the conflict index was 0, indicating no conflict, compared to the highest possible score of 13, indicating the opposite extreme. The mean scale score was 3.22. The item to scale correlation coefficients for this measure ranged from .19 to .64 and all were significant ($p < .05$). The alpha reliability coefficient for this scale was .60.

(2) Depressive symptoms. The Center for Epidemiological Studies-Depression Scale (CES-D) was used for this measure (Radloff, 1977). Widely used and extensively validated, this scale has 20 items developed to monitor depressive symptomatology during the past week. With a score range from 0 to 60, some researchers have used scores of 16 and above as indicators of clinical depression (Roberts, 1980; Weissman et al., 1977). A high score on the CES-D scale means a high level of depressive symptoms, whereas a low score indicates a low level of depression. The alpha coefficient for the CES-D scale with this sample was .82.

(3) Other measures. Demographic measures used in this study included the following: (a) age; (b) marital status; (c) educational status; (d) annual family income; and (e) household size. Other stressful life event variables were based upon the following measures: (a) employment status—whether or not the respondent is employed; (b) residential mobility—the number of times a person has moved in the past five years; (c) arrest records—the number of arrests by criminal justice agencies for a variety of reasons; and (d) illnesses—the number of illnesses in the past year.

RESULTS

THE EXTENT OF FAMILY CONFLICT

As shown in Table 13.1, the respondents did not view themselves as having a great deal of conflict with women. Fourteen subjects reported no conflict with their spouses or female friends. With respect to the specific problem areas, irritating personal habits, leisure time with friends, and being away from home and job were the major areas of conflict between Black men and women. Disciplining the children, religion, and female friendships were not viewed by these men as being major problem areas between them and their mates or spouses.

Table 13.2 presents data on the relationship between the conflict index and selected demographic variables. The data show no significant relationship between the conflict scale and the selected demographic variables.

DEPRESSION AND FAMILY CONFLICT

The mean score of the CES-D scale was 12.15 and the standard deviation was 8.44 for the sample. As mentioned earlier, researchers have generally used a score of 16 and above to indicate the presence of serious depressive symptoms. Based upon this cut-off point, 31% of the respondents had CES-D scores of 16 or more. In other words, one-third of the Black men in this study were suffering from depression.

A major research question for this chapter is whether there is a relationship between conflict with mates and depression. In this study, the data show that there was a significant relationship between scores on the CES-D scale and scores on the conflict index, $F(2, 75) = 8.07, p <$ .001. The mean depression score for the Black men who experienced low levels of conflict with mates was 6.72, compared to 14.21 and 12.23 for those in medium and high conflict categories, respectively.

Stepwise regression was used to examine how the conflict measure compared to other life events in its ability to predict depressive symptoms. Table 13.3 shows that of the five stressful life events variables, conflict between the sexes was the best predictor. The second best predictor was employment status. Mobility, number of arrests, and number of illnesses did not have any appreciable impact on depression scores.

TABLE 13.1
Frequency Distribution of Problems with Mate or Spouse[a]

Problem	Yes		No		Total	
	F	%	F	%	F	%
(1) Irritating personal habits	46	41	65	59	111	100
(2) How to spend leisure time	42	38	68	62	110	100
(3) Time spent with friends	41	37	71	63	112	100
(4) Your being away from home too much	39	40	58	60	97	100
(5) Your job	34	32	72	68	106	100
(6) Keep the house neat	27	28	70	72	97	100
(7) Not showing love	21	19	90	81	111	100
(8) Household expenses	21	22	76	78	97	100
(9) In-laws/her family	18	19	78	81	96	100
(10) Religion	14	12	98	88	112	100
(11) Discipling children	13	14	82	86	95	100
(12) Time spent with her friends	11	10	101	90	112	100
(13) Her being away from home too much	8	8	91	92	99	100

NOTE: Total valid cases were 88; mean = 3.22; SD = 2.46.
a. Not applicable and missing values excluded.

Table 13.4 presents data on the relationships among depression, selected demographic and stressful life variables, and conflict between the sexes. In this stepwise regression model, income, age, and marital status are included as control variables because they are believed to have some influence on depression, which is treated as a dependent variable in this particular analysis (Comstock & Helsing, 1976; Eaton & Kessler, 1981; Roberts et al., 1981). When income, conflict, marital status, employment status, and age are counted, 28% of the variance in the depression score is explained, with an F-ratio of 5.05, which is statistically significant at the .01 level. Income was the best predictor of depression scores. The second best predictor was conflict between the sexes. In examining the beta coefficients, the data suggest that conflict with mates bears a relationship to depression that is independent of other variables, including income and marital status.

DISCUSSION AND IMPLICATIONS

The results of this investigation show that the Black men in this sample did not perceive themselves as having a high level in conflict with Black women. But some men did experience considerable conflict with

TABLE 13.2
Demographic Variables and Conflict Between the Sexes Index

Variables	N	Mean	SD	F Ratio	df	Significance
Age						
less than 30	57	3.92	2.58	.48	2/87	.62
30-44	31	3.19	3.07			
45 and over	21	3.33	4.46			
Marital status						
married	45	4.24	3.89	2.46	2/86	.09
formerly married	12	2.16	2.12			
never married	32	3.13	2.32			
Education						
less than high school	17	4.77	4.67	1.19	3/86	.32
high school	25	3.64	3.60			
some college	20	3.05	2.50			
college/postgraduate	28	3.04	2.12			
Annual family income						
less than $8,000	15	2.47	2.13	1.65	3/81	.81
$8,000-$12,499	16	4.88	4.95			
$12,500-$19,999	28	3.68	3.38			
$20,000 or more	26	3.00	2.33			
Total persons in household including respondent						
respondent alone	18	2.17	2.01	2.17	3/86	.10
respondent and 1 person	21	3.62	3.60			
respondent and 2 or 3 persons	36	3.56	2.71			

NOTE: Mean = 3.22; N = 142.

their mates. Demographic variables did not have a significant impact on male-female conflict. However, some trends can be noted so that one can develop an exploratory profile of what predicts conflict in relationships between men and women. Age is a possible factor. For a man less than 30 years of age, one can expect a higher level of conflict than for a man who is 45 years of age or older. Of all the demographic variables, the men who were married had the highest level of conflict. The formerly married men had a lower level of conflict than any of the other demographic categories. Perhaps this explains why so many people are opting to dissolve marriages when there is conflict. As one would expect, as the educational level of the respondents goes up, the mean conflict score decreases. Employed men had less conflict with their mates than unemployed men. It is interesting to note that men who had annual family incomes of less than $8,000 had the lowest mean conflict

TABLE 13.3
Multiple Regression of Depression Scores, Selected Life
Events Variables and Conflict Between the Sexes Index

Variables	Multiple R	R^2 Change	Simple r	Beta
Conflict	.271	.073	.271	.234**
Employment status	.357	.055	.257	.214*
Mobility	.375	.013	.152	.132
Arrests	.381	.004	.152	.070
Illnesses	.385	.003	.041	−.058
Total R^2		.148		

NOTE: $F (5, 66) = 2.29$, N.S.
*Significant at $p < .05$; **significant at $p < .01$.

scale among the various income categories. Mobility (number of moves in the past five years) had an interesting impact on conflict. Those men who moved four or more times had the highest mean conflict score among any of the demographic variables. Second, those men who lived in families with four or more persons also tended to have high levels of conflict.

The data indicate that among those Black men who experienced considerable conflict with their mates, there was a tendency for them to report a high level of depressive symptoms. Some of the antisocial or deviant behavior, such as excessive drinking, drug abuse, suicide attempts, and violence, which are prevalent in the Black community, may be a manifestation of the level of family confict that many Black men are experiencing in their daily lives (Gary & Leashore, 1982; Staples, 1978; Stewart & Scott, 1978).

There is some evidence that some Black men are beginning to bring their interpersonal and family problems to the attention of mental health practitioners. For example, Jones and his colleagues (1982) conducted a survey of psychiatrists who were treating Black men. They found that the major presenting problems were depression, work difficulties, problems relating to others, family difficulties, anxiety, and marital conflict, in that order. The data in this study seem to support their findings. This research shows that family conflict and depression were significantly related to each other. According to Jones et al. (1982), the Black male patients in psychotherapy were typically married and 31 to 40 years of age. In examining the beta coefficients in this analysis, it is clear that there were men in this study who needed the assistance of mental health specialists in order to help them to resolve family difficulties that are responsible for their depressive feelings.

TABLE 13.4
Multiple Regression of Depression Scores, Selected Variables
and Conflict Between the Sexes Index

Variables	Multiple R	R^2 Change	Simple r	Beta
Income	.341	.116	−.341	−.388**
Conflict	.459	.094	.289	.253**
Marital status	.496	.036	−.053	−.249**
Employment status	.522	.027	.247	.170*
Age	.529	.007	−.201	−.093
Total R^2		.280		

NOTE: $F (5, 65) = 5.05$, $p < .01$.
*Significant at $p < .05$; **significant at $p < .01$.

In order to develop programs and policies for improving relationships between the sexes in the Black community, conceptual clarity is needed as to what the problem is and what causes the problem. As Franklin (1980, p. 47) stated:

The familiar rationale offered for Black male-female [conflict], white racism, is deemed logically inadequate. . . . To be sure, not all Black males and females experience undue difficulty in social interaction. . . . It is suggested that the conflict stems from the diverse manner in which some Black males and females define situations, interpret each other's behaviors, and direct action toward each other.

This implies that one needs to recognize the diversity within the Black community and also to examine a range of variables in regard to identifying factors that influence interpersonal relationships. Nonstructural variables must be viewed as important factors in any serious study of this problem.

Black churches, fraternities, and sororities need to sponsor programs that focus on the management of interpersonal relations. Appropriate emphasis should be placed on racial ideology, spirituality, community activism, social networks and friends, and communication skills. What is being suggested is that more male bonding is a necessary first step in preparing young Black men for adult roles. Boys (and girls) need to see Black men sit down and discuss substantive issues. In a recent article, "The Value of Older Men, Fruit of the Loom and Snoring," Campbell (1982) outlined the positive role of men in Black families.

There are other areas for improving male-female relationships: (1) We have to teach men how to stroke each other. Showing appreciation through both physical and intellectual compliments is important for both men and women; (2) we have to teach men how to develop good communication skills (share feelings, discuss expectations, and so on), (3) we have to teach young men how to be resourceful; (4) we have to teach young men how to deal with crises. More consideration has to be given to teaching problem-solving skills, including making young men aware of community resources such as ministers, mental health centers, counseling centers, psychologists, and so forth; and (5) we have to teach young Black men the importance of having goals and the articulation of some specific values. These suggestions are not exhaustive. For the most part, the solution to the problem of male-female relations must be seen as coming from the heart and soul of Black people.

REFERENCES

Akbar, N. (1976). Rhythmic patterns in African personality. In L. King et al. (Eds.), *African philosophy: Assumption and paradigms for research on Black persons.* Los Angeles: Fanon Center.

Anderson, E. (1978). *A place on the corner.* Chicago: University of Chicago Press.

Barrett, R., & Robinson, B. (1982). Teenage fathers: Neglected too long. *Social Work, 27,* 484.

Bell, R. (1981). *Worlds of friendship.* Beverly Hills, CA: Sage.

Births to the unwed found to have risen by 50% in 10 years. (1981, October 26). *New York Times.*

Bond, J., & Perry, P. (1969). Has the Black man been castrated? *Liberator, 9,* 4-8.

Borus, W., & Senay, E. (1980). Depression, demographic dimensions, and drug abuse. *American Journal of Psychiatry, 137,* 699-704.

Bracey, J., Meir, A., & Rudwick, E. (Eds.). (1971). *Black matriarchy: Myth or reality?* Belmont, CA: Wadsworth.

Braithwaite, R. (1981). Interpersonal relationships between Black males and females. In L. Gary (Ed.), *Black men* (pp. 83-87). Beverly Hills, CA: Sage.

Brenner, M. (1973). *Mental illness and the economy.* Cambridge, MA: Harvard University Press.

Campbell, B. (1982, June 30). The value of older men, Fruit of the Loom and snoring. *Washington Post,* p. C1.

Coleman, L. (1973). *Beulah land.* Garden City, NY: Doubleday.

Comstock, G., & Helsing, K. (1976). Symptoms of depression in two countries. *Psychological Medicine, 6,* 551-563.

Dohrenwend, B. S., & Dohrenwend, B. (Eds.). (1981). *Life events and life stress.* New York: Neale Watson.

Franklin, C. (1980). White racism as the cause of Black male-female conflict: A critique. *Western Journal of Black Studies, 4,* 42-49.

Gary, L. (Ed.). (1981). *Black men.* Beverly Hills, CA: Sage.

Gary, L., & Leashore, B. (1982). The high risk status of Black men. *Social Work, 27,* 54-58.

Gourash, N. (1966). Help-seeking: A review of the literature. *American Sociological Review, 25.*

Grier, W., & Cobbs, P. (1968). *Black rage.* New York: Basic Books.

Hammond, J., & Enoch, J. (1976). Conjugal power relations among Black working class families. *Journal of Black Studies, 1,* 107-128.

Hare, N. (1964). The frustrated masculinity of the Negro male. *Negro Digest,* pp. 5-9.

Hare, N. (1971). Will the real Black man please stand up? *Black Scholar, 2*(10), 32-35.

Hare, N. (1979a, November). Black male-female relationships. *Sepia,* p. 82.

Hare, N. (1979b). Sexual life between Black and white. *Black Male-Female Relationships, 1*(1).

Hendricks, L. (1981). Black unwed adolescent fathers. In L. E. Gary (Ed.), *Black men* (pp. 131-138). Beverly Hills, CA: Sage.

Hendricks, L., Howard, C., & Gary, L. (1981). Help-seeking behavior among urban Black adults. *Social Work, 26*(2), 161-163.

Holmes, T., & Rahe, R. (1967). The social readjustment rating scale. *Journal of Psychosomatic Research, 11,* 213-218.

Ilfeld, F. (1977). Current social stressors and symptoms of depression. *American Journal of Psychiatry, 134,* 161-166.

Jackson, J. (1978). But where are the men? In R. Staples (Ed.), *The Black family: Essays and studies.* Belmont, CA: Wadsworth.

Jackson, L. (1975). The attitudes of Black females toward upper and lower class Black males. *Journal of Black Psychology, 1,* 53-64.

Jones, B., Gray, B., & Jospitre, J. (1982). Survey of psychotherapy with Black men. *American Journal of Psychiatry, 139,* 1174-1177.

Jordon, J. (1977). *Things that I do in the dark.* New York: Random House.

Kanner, A., Coyne, J., Schaefer, C., & Lazarus, R. (1981). Comparison of two modes of stress measurement: Daily hassles and uplifts versus major life events. *Journal of Behavioral Medicine, 4,* 1-39.

Karenga, R. (1979). On Wallace's myths: Wading thru troubled waters. *Black Scholar, 10*(8-9), 36-39.

Leashore, B. (1979). Human Services and the unmarried father: The forgotten half. *Family Coordinator, 28,* 529-534.

Lewis, D. (1975). The Black family: Socialization and sex roles. *Phylon, 36,* 221-237.

Lewis, R. (Ed.). (1981). *Men in difficult times: Masculinity today and tomorrow.* Englewood Cliffs, NJ: Prentice-Hall.

Liebow, E. (1967). *Tally's corner.* Boston: Little, Brown.

Madhubuti, H. (1981). Why Black men need family. *Black Male-Female Relationships, 2,* 31-35.

Markush, R., & Favero, R. (1974). Epidemiologic assessment of stressful life events, depressed mood and the psychophysiological symptoms: A preliminary report. In B. Dohrenwend & B. Dohrenwend (Eds.), *Stressful life events: Their nature and effects.* New York: John Wiley.

Murrell, S., Himmelfarb, S., & Wright, K. (1983). Prevalence of depression and its correlates in older adults. *American Journal of Epidemiology, 117,* 173-185.

Noble, J. (1978). *Beautiful, also are the souls of my Black sisters: A history of black women in America.* Englewood Cliffs, NJ: Prentice-Hall.

Paykel, E. (1979). Recent life events in the development of the depressive disorders. In R. A. Depue (Ed.), *The psychobiology of the depressive disorders: Implications for the effects of stress* (pp. 245-262). New York: Academic Press.

Piantadoisi, R., & Martin, W. (1981, May 3). Six slain at house in Maryland county. *Washington Post,* pp. A1, A5.

Poussaint, A. (1979). White manipulation and Black oppression. *Black Scholar, 10*(8-9), 52-55.

Rabkin, J., & Struening, E. (1976). Life events, stress and illness. *Science, 194*, 1013-1020.

Reid, J. (1982). Black America in the 1980's. *Population Bulletin, 37*, 11-13.

Radloff, L. (1977). The CES-D scale. *Applied Psychological Measurements, 1*(3), 385-401.

Roberts, R. (1980). Reliability of CES-D scale in different ethnic contexts. *Psychiatric Research, 2*, 125-134.

Roberts, R., Stevenson, J., & Breslow, L. (1981). Symptoms of depression among Blacks and whites in an urban community. *Journal of Nervous and Mental Disease, 169*, 774-779.

Rosen, B., Goldsmith, F., & Redlick, R. (1979). Demographic and social indicators: Uses in mental health planning in small areas. *World Health Statistics Quarterly Report, 32*, 12-101.

Rose-Rodgers, L. (1980). Dialectics of Black male-female relationships. In L. Rose-Rodgers (Ed.), *The Black woman* (pp. 251-263). Beverly Hills, CA: Sage.

Sandry, P. (1981). *Female power and male dominance on the origins of sexual inequality.* Cambridge: Cambridge University Press.

Scott, J. (1976). Polygamy: A futuristic family arrangement for African-Americans. *Black Books Bulletin*, pp. 13-19.

Shange, N. (1977). *For colored girls who have considered suicide when the rainbow is enuf.* New York: Emerson Hall.

Smith, L., & Millham, J. (1979). Sex role stereotypes among Blacks and whites. *Journal of Black Psychology, 6*, 1-6.

Staples, R. (1978). Masculinity and race: The dual dilemma of Black men. *Journal of Social Issues, 34*(1), 169-183.

Staples, R. (1980). *The world of Black singles.* Westport, CT: Greenwood.

Staples, R. (1981). Black manhood in the 1970's: A critical look back. *Black Scholar, 12*(3), 2-9.

Stewart, J. (1980). Relationships between Black males and females in rhythm and blues music of the 1960's and 1970's. *Western Journal of Black Studies, 4*, 186-196.

Stewart, J., & Scott, J. (1978). The institutional decimation of Black American males. *Western Journal of Black Studies, 2*, 82-92.

Theodorson, G., & Theodorson, A. (1969). *Modern dictionary of sociology.* New York: Thomas Y. Cromwell.

Tucker, R. (1979, November 3). Therapy to quell the rage: Love, sex and Black macho. *Washington Post.*

Turner, B., & Turner, C. (1974). Evaluations of women and men among Black and white college students. *Sociological Quarterly, 15*, 442-456.

U.S. Bureau of the Census. (1981a). Marital status and living arrangements, March 1980. In *Current population reports* (Series P-20, No. 365) (pp. 3, 8-9, 38). Washington, DC: Government Printing Office.

U.S. Bureau of the Census. (1981b). *Statistical abstract, 1981.* Washington, DC: Government Printing Office.

U.S. Department of Justice. (1981). *Uniform crime reports for the United States.* Washington, DC: Government Printing Office.

Wallace, M. (1979). *Black macho and the myth of the superwoman.* New York: Dial.

Weissman, M., Sholomskas, D., Pattenger, M., Porusoff, B., & Locke, B. (1977). Assessing depressive symptoms in five psychiatric populations: A validity study. *American Journal of Epidemiology, 106*, 203-214.

Wells, L. (1980). *Essence's quality of life survey results* (Vol. 1). Unpublished data, University of Maryland, College Park.

Welsing, F. (1974). The cress theory of color confrontation and racism. *Black Scholar, 5,* 32-40.

Wilcox, P. (1979). Is there life for Black leaders after ERA? *Black Male-Female Relationships, 2*(1), 53-55.

Wright, N. (1981, August 13). Crime must be checked within the Black community. *Washington Afro-American.*

14

GRANDFATHERS: MAKING UP FOR LOST OPPORTUNITIES

Graeme Russell

He was about 60 and well over 6 feet tall, and had a sense of presence about him as he led his family into the restaurant. Everyone stopped eating and turned their heads when his loud voice beamed through their conversations as he sought to have the table near the window—"the one with the best view." His wife, daughter, son-in-law, and three-year-old granddaughter (it was obvious from their physical characteristics what the relationships were) followed him as he strode to the table.

He was obviously a farmer and one who enjoyed a drink or two. His stomach easily protruded over his platted leather belt, which held his well-worn trousers just above his hips. His face was red, changing color to a hat-protected white just below his balding hair line.

He remained standing while he directed his family to their seats. Too impatient for the drink waiter to come to their table, he took orders for drinks from the others and strode purposefully through the crowded restaurant to the bar. Again, his voice dominated over the chatter at the tables when he spoke to the barman.

"We will have two beers and three cokes, thank you."

(The barman's reply was inaudible.)

"No, not for this little one. By golly, we don't want to teach *you* bad habits, do we?"

(The barman's reply was again inaudible.)

"Did you pick yourself a winner at the horses yesterday? Thank you."

Author's Note: *I wish to acknowledge the contribution made by Jacqueline Smith to the design of this study and the assistance given in data collection and analysis by Judy French and Lisa Connolly.*

The waiter then followed the man back to the table carrying the drinks. This was an impossible task for the farmer, because "this little one" to whom he didn't "want to teach bad habits" was a six-week-old baby. He had carried the baby in his arms from the time that he had entered the restaurant. He had maintained an affectionate gaze, "gooed" and "gaaed" intermittently, sang a bar or two from a couple of favorite nursery rhymes, and tickled her toes—all while negotiating to have the best table, ordering drinks, and then later throughout the meal. It was the grandfather who interrupted his eating and conversations to attend to the baby's cries and demands for attention. And, it was the grandfather who actively sought the attention of the baby! (Russell, n.d.)

My father can't take his hands off him. As quiet as he was, all Al wants to do now is take Amir to the park, play baseball with him, throw him in the air, chase him around, spend a lot of time with him. (Kareem Abdul Jabbar's description of his father's reaction to his grandchild, taken from his autobiography *Giant Steps*)

It is very difficult to draw any conclusions at all about whether nurturance and involvement, like that displayed in the two examples above, is characteristic of grandfatherhood. Very little research has been conducted on grandfathers, and not much more on grandmothers. These two grandfathers, however, do fit very well both with the current emphasis on the study of expressive males (e.g., fathers who share the responsibilities for child care; Russell, 1983), and with recent theoretical perspectives in life-span development. The suggestion has been made that in old age men tend to express more "feminine" qualities (Gutmann, 1975) and that sex roles become less rigid for both sexes (Sinnott, 1977). The evidence to support such a theory, however, is rather mixed. Although studies of changes in personality characteristics (e.g., Livson, 1976) are generally consistent with the theory, those on divisions of labor for household tasks are not (see McGee & Wells, 1982). It may be, however, that older men will express nurturance and sensitivity in ways other than in the performance of household tasks. In particular, they might see grandparenting as an opportunity to express these feelings by participating in the care and socialization of their grandchildren.

Grandparents have rarely been considered in either individual or family developmental research (Troll, 1980), and it is often assumed that grandparenting simply "fills a vacuum . . . for aged, essentially infirm and otherwise unoccupied individuals" (Troll, 1983, pp. 64-65). But, as has been pointed out by others, with the increase in life expectancy for males (now 68 years in the United States) and females (now 76 years), grandparenthood is a common and continuing experience for both sexes. Troll (1983) reports that the modal age of becoming grandparents is around 49-51 years for women and 51-53 years for men. Further, it is now generally accepted that grandparenthood is a highly significant and integral part of the lives of older people.

In her recent review of grandparenting literature, Troll (1983) draws four general conclusions: First, that grandparents play an important part in family dynamics, but that their part is usually secondary to that played by parents; second, that the most important role of grandparents is that of maintaining the family system. Troll also speculates that grandparents may operate as "family watchdogs," continually monitoring family functioning and stepping in only when they perceive that they are needed.

Another of Troll's conclusions is that the nature of grandparent involvement and grandparent-grandchild relationships is influenced by the development status of both grandparents and grandchildren. To expect some kind of universal response to grandchildren, of course, is far too simplistic. People become grandparents at different stages of their lives: some when they are still deeply engrossed in paid work, some when they are in early retirement, and some when they are much older and less physically able. Considerations of development status also make research designs quite problematic and limit considerably the conclusions that can be drawn. Studies that control for all possible variables are yet to be conducted. A recent study by Cunningham-Burley (1984), although doing better than most by controlling for the development status of the grandchild and grandparenthood (all were first-time grandparents), was not able to control for the developmental status of the grandparents (something that was obviously too difficult to do given the constraints of research budgets).

Troll's fourth conclusion is that grandparent interactions and roles are diverse and depend largely on individual preferences and life circumstances, with factors such as social class, ethnicity, and sex also having an influence. However, Troll's review included only two studies (Hagestad, 1978; Neugarten & Weinstein, 1964) that specifically considered sex differences and the possibility that grandfatherhood might differ in major ways from grandmotherhood. That grandfathers have been ignored seems surprising when it is considered that the classic paper of Neugarten and Weinstein (1964) was based on 70 grandparent *couple* interviews.

Neugarten and Weinstein (1964) reported several important sex differences and speculated on possible reasons for these. They found that grandmothers were more likely to be surrogate parents and grandfathers reservoirs of family wisdom, and that grandfathers were less likely to feel that a significant aspect of grandparenthood is how it provides a source of biological renewal (e.g., "It makes me feel young again") or biological continuity (e.g., "It's carrying on the family line"). Despite these findings, much of the research has emphasized general dimensions of the meaning of grandparenthood, while ignoring possible sex differences and the hypotheses emanating from Neugarten and Weinstein's work.

Two notable exceptions to the consistent lack of emphasis on grandfathers are the studies by Hagestad (1978) in the United States and Cunningham-Burley (1984) in the United Kingdom. Hagestad studied 80 young adults and their grandparents and found major differences between grandmothers and grandfathers. Grandfathers, in comparison to grandmothers, were found to be more instrumental in their relationships, and tended to place more emphasis on influencing their grandchildren on matters of work, education, and money; to differentiate more between grandsons than granddaughters; to be less warm in their relationships with their grandchildren; and to have difficulties in their relationships with their granddaughters associated with problems in adjusting to cultural changes and the redefinition of male and female roles.

Cunningham-Burley (1984) conducted joint interviews with a sample of eighteen couples before and after the birth of their first grandchild. While the data reveal that men did not speak as readily about grandfatherhood and that they were not as involved as their spouses were in the early months, Cunningham-Burley also concludes that her data probably underestimate the degree of significance that grandparenthood had for the men and the degree of satisfaction they derived from it. Cunningham-Burley also reports that on the five occasions the grandchildren were present during interviews, it was the grandfathers who seemed to spend more time with the grandchildren, and that they were more absorbed in this interaction than they were in the interview.

The study to be reported on in this chapter, like those of Neugarten and Weinstein (1964), Hagestad (1978), and Cunningham-Burley (1984), emphasizes grandfatherhood and the similarities and differences between grandfathers and grandmothers. This study, however, provides three important extensions to these earlier studies. First, it examines differences between maternal and paternal grandfathers from the same family system. These differences have been ignored by most researchers, despite Kahana and Kahana's (1970, p. 120) finding in a study on grandchildren's perspectives that "the grandparent's place in the kinship system is an important determinant of their relationships with their grandchildren." Their findings also indicate that maternal grandfathers have more contact than paternal grandfathers, and they are more likely to be nominated by grandchildren as their favorite grandparents.

The second important extension is that this study includes the perspective of the second generation (i.e., the parents of the grandchildren). Although there have been numerous studies of the role of grandparents from the perspective of the grandchildren, few appear to have recognized the potentially important role the parents themselves might play in mediating the grandparent role (see Robertson, 1975; Hagestad, 1978, 1981). A final extension on previous research is that this study examines the quality of relationships between the first and second generations in families (e.g., between fathers and sons or between mothers- and daughters-in-law), and the perceived impact that grandchildren have on these.

The chapter is divided into six parts. The first provides an overview of the method, including the characteristics of the sample. The second examines the nature of grandparent involvement with grandchildren in terms of frequency of contact and types of activities that they engage in together. The third focuses on grandparents' beliefs about grandparenthood. Of particular interest are beliefs about roles and responsibilities, and perceptions of the significance of grandparenthood. Positive and negative evaluations of the experience of being a grandparent provide the focus for the fourth section. The fifth section examines adult parent-child relationships and the influence that grandchildren have on these. The final section presents a summary and conclusions, including suggestions for directions for future research.

RESEARCH METHOD

THE SAMPLE

Recruitment. Families were recruited as part of a broader study of intergenerational family relationships in different family contexts. The sample included 23 sets of parents with young children, and the maternal (n = 23 grandmothers; n = 16 grandfathers—16 couples) and paternal grandparents (n = 22 grandmothers; n = 16 grandfathers—15 couples) from the same family systems. Families were recruited through the second generation (the parents of the grandchildren). The only criteria

were that they had at least one preschool-aged child and that at least one
of each of the maternal and paternal grandparents lived in close proximity and was available to be interviewed. Grandparents not interviewed
had previously died. The present chapter focuses primarily on data
collected from the 32 grandfathers.

Characteristics. The mean age of the grandfathers was 61.6 years
(range 43-77). In terms of social status, the sample represented a wide
cross section. A total of 35% had completed high school and only 22%
had completed university degrees. The current or previous occupations
of the subjects covered a broad range, including printer, truck driver,
small business owner, teacher, painter, accountant, lawyer, and doctor.
The mean occupational status ranking (Congalton, 1969; this is a 7-
point scale for which 1 = high-status occupations) for the sample was 4.5.
Of the 32 grandfathers, 10 had retired from their employment. There
were no significant differences between maternal and paternal grandfathers on these or other characteristics.

Grandfathers had an average of 5 grandchildren (range 1-15), with
22% having only granddaughters, 17% only grandsons, and 61% having
both grandsons and granddaughters. (Small numbers in the first two
groups precluded any meaningful comparisons for sex of grandchild.)
The ages of their grandchildren ranged from 6 weeks to 28 years. All
grandfathers, however, did have preschool-aged grandchildren, because,
as was stated above, families were recruited only if they had at least one
preschool-aged child. The average age of the youngest child was 1.9
years and for the eldest child it was 5.1 years. Families had an average of
2.2 children. Interviews emphasized grandparenting in relation to the
grandchildren in these families.

INTERVIEWS

Interviews were conducted in the homes of grandparents. Following
the procedure outlined in Russell (1983), data on patterns of grandparent interactions were collected in joint interviews (where there were
couples). All other data to be reported here relating to beliefs, meanings,
evaluation of grandparenting, and the quality of family relationships
were collected in individual interviews with respondents.

GRANDPARENT-GRANDCHILD INTERACTION

TIME SPENT TOGETHER

Grandfathers reported that they spent an average of 3.5 hours per week with their grandchildren, compared with an average of 4.7 hours reported by grandmothers. Grandfathers were also less likely to report that they had regular telephone contact with their grandchildren. For 67% of the grandparent couples, it was most commonly the case that grandfathers visited grandchildren with their spouses, or their grandchildren visited them when they were both at home. Only 25% of grandfathers and 22% of grandmothers did not have regular weekly contact with their grandchildren. This latter finding is consistent with earlier findings that only 25% of a sample of U.S. grandparents over 65 did not see their grandchildren at least once a week (Louis Harris and Associates, 1975).

Grandparents were also asked how much time they spent each week taking responsibility for their grandchildren. The average figure for grandfathers was 2.2 and for grandmothers it was 2.7 hours per week. Only two grandfathers, however, reported that it was common for them to spend time alone (i.e., without their spouses being there) with children, taking sole responsibility for them. Of the sample, 25% regularly (every two to three weeks) had their grandchildren stay at their houses overnight. Three sets of maternal grandparents spent considerably more time than others with their grandchildren because they provided daytime child care while the parents were at their jobs.

In agreement with Kahana and Kahana's (1970) reports from grandchildren, maternal grandfathers were found to spend more time with their grandchildren (maternal = 4.6; paternal = 2.4), and more time in child minding with their spouses (maternal = 2.9; paternal = 1.5).

Thus, in terms of frequency of interaction and time spent, grandchildren appear to be highly significant for both grandfathers and grandmothers. Although grandfathers reported spending less time with their grandchildren than grandmothers did, visits with grandchildren were obviously not seen as an exclusively female activity that men opted out of when they could. Nevertheless, little support was found for a highly involved grandfather who spent a lot of time alone with his grandchildren. As was stated above, only two grandfathers reported regularly caring for grandchildren. In this sense, these findings for grandfathers parallel those previously reported for fathers. It has been found that fathers rarely take sole responsibility for their young children (Russell, 1983). These data, however, do not provide information on the ways in which grandmothers and grandfathers divide responsibilities for their grandchildren when they are both at home, or how much time each might spend alone with them, going for walks or taking them out to parks or other places.

TYPES OF SHARED ACTIVITIES

Grandparents were asked to use a five-point scale to rate how frequently (from 1 = never to 5 = very frequently) they engaged in a series of common activities with their grandchildren when they saw them. The activities that grandfathers reported they engaged in most frequently were the following: have a cuddle (mean = 4.0); sit and talk/listen (3.3); play with children inside with their toys (3.1); read a story book (3.1); play ball games with them outside (2.9); play rough-and-tumble games (2.7). In comparison to grandmothers, grandfathers were more likely (p < .05) to report playing rough and tumble games, but less likely to: read a storybook; play with children inside with their toys; play educational/ cognitive games; help with drawing/craft activities; and sit and talk and listen. Again, these findings of differences between grandfathers and grandmothers parallel those found for parents with young children (Russell, 1983).

Significant differences were again found between maternal and paternal grandfathers. Maternal grandfathers were more likely (p < .05) to do the following with their grandchildren: go for a walk to a park, read a story book, watch TV, and be involved in gardening. On the other hand, paternal grandfathers were more likely to engage in rough-and-tumble play, and to play amusement/fun games. These differences are probably explained by the earlier finding that grandchildren spend more time with their maternal grandfathers and more time being cared for by their maternal grandparents. As such, maternal grandfathers would be expected to engage in activities of a more routine nature, whereas paternal grandfathers, because their visits are briefer, would be more likely to engage in activities of a spontaneous nature.

Grandfathers were also asked what they enjoyed doing most with their grandchildren. The most commonly mentioned activities were talking and listening, taking children for walks, having a cuddle, playing with them, just having the grandchildren around, and watching them grow and develop.

TEACHING SPECIAL SKILLS

A final question about the nature of grandfather-grandchild interaction inquired as to whether there were any skills that grandfathers were especially trying to teach their grandchildren. A total of 53% said that they were not trying to teach any special skills and, indeed, a few became quite irritated upon being asked such a question. As one grandfather said, "No, I'm not going out of my way to teach them any skills. I think the grandparent's part is to talk to them, just to impart a little knowledge, not to force things onto them." Of those who said they were trying to impart skills, the most commonly mentioned were physical skills (e.g., ball games, swimming), painting, drawing, and reading; three said that they were trying to teach home-maintenance skills (e.g., carpentry). It was obvious, therefore, that grandfathers did not see this as an important part of their current role. One possible reason for this, of course, is that the children in these families were very young. Responses to this question might be very different in a study of older children.

STYLES OF GRANDPARENTING

Grandparents were asked to rate on a five-point scale (from 1 = not at are like to 5 = very much like) how well a series of five statements described their present role as a grandparent. The statements rated most highly were "I am very interested and help out when asked, but try not to intrude" (means: grandfathers = 4.5; grandmothers = 4.8); "My children and grandchildren come to me for advice" (grandfathers = 3.3; grandmothers = 3.6); and "I like to be someone special and give my grandchildren little treats" (grandfathers = 3.3; grandmothers = 4.1). The statements rated least highly were "I am highly participant in the care and rearing of my grandchildren" (grandfathers = 2.6; grandmothers = 2.9) and "I only see my grandchildren on special occasions such as birthdays" (grandfathers = 1.2; grandmothers = 1.2). As can be seen from the above results too, sex differences were obvious on only one item.

Grandfathers were less likely to describe their role in terms of "being a special person who gives treats" ($t(75) = 1.8, p < .1$).

Significant maternal/paternal grandfather differences were found on two of these items. Maternal grandfathers rated themselves as being more highly participant in the care and rearing of their grandchildren (maternal = 3.0; paternal = 2.2, $t(30) = 2.8, p < .01$), whereas paternal grandfathers reported a greater involvement in giving advice (maternal = 2.7; paternal = 3.9, $t(30), p < .01$).

Finally, grandparents were asked to rate the nature of their relationships with their grandchildren using the same five-point scale as the one described above. Both grandfathers and grandmothers described their relationships as "comfortable" (means: grandfathers = 4.4; grandmothers = 4.5), "warm and close" (grandfathers = 4.0; grandmothers = 4.5), and "open and honest" (grandfathers = 4.5; grandmothers = 4.8). Grandfathers, however, were less likely to describe their relationships in terms of "sharing interests" (grandfathers = 3.2; grandmothers = 4.6, $t(75) = 6.0, p < .001$) and "spending a lot of time together/talking on the phone a lot" (grandfathers = 3.1; grandmothers = 4.3, $t(75) = 3.8, p < .001$). This latter item was the only one for which there were significant differences between the two groups of grandfathers. Maternal grandfathers rated the item more highly (maternal = 3.6; paternal = 2.9, $t(30) = 2.6, p < .02$).

These findings provide mixed support for previous research (for example, see Hagestad, 1978) that has shown that grandmothers have closer or warmer relationships with grandchildren than grandfathers do. Significant sex differences were not found on any of the warmth/closeness dimensions; the differences occur only on shared interests and spending time together. Differences between these and Hagestad's findings could, of course, be explained either by the differences in ages of grandchildren (the grandchildren in Hagestad's study were young adults), or differences in cohort. It may be that present-day grandfathers do have closer relationships with their young grandchildren than those from previous cohorts. The finding of few differences between maternal and paternal grandfathers is also somewhat inconsistent with Kahana and Kahana's (1970) suggestive finding that grandchildren have a poorer-quality relationship with their paternal grandfathers. While this view is obviously not shared by the present grandfathers, if may yet be that this is the longer-term consequence of their having less contact with their grandchildren.

BELIEFS ABOUT GRANDPARENTING

The most researched aspect of grandparenting is unquestionably the beliefs and meanings that grandparents and grandchildren have about the roles of grandparents. It is generally assumed that these beliefs and meanings will have an impact on the approaches people take to grandparenting. But, as was argued earlier, the second generation is likely to play an important part in mediating the style of grandparenting and the grandparent-grandchild relationship. This possibility was taken into account in this study by asking both generations what they believed to be the roles and responsibilities of grandparents.

ROLES AND RESPONSIBILITIES

Grandparents and parents were given the items listed in Table 14.1 and asked to rate how important they were for the roles and responsibilities of grandparents (from 5 = extremely important to 1 = not important at all). Items included in the questions were based on findings from previous studies, together with those from a pilot study in which family members were asked open-ended questions about their perceptions of the roles and responsibilities of grandparents. Mean ratings for grandparents and parents are presented in the table. As can be seen from these figures, the items rated most highly by grandfathers were "helping out when asked"; "to be a source of advice"; "to provide economic support in times of need"; "to be available to care for grandchildren when needed"; and "to establish a warm/close relationship." In contrast, fathers and mothers of the grandchildren placed more emphasis on "establishing a warm/close relationship" and "providing children with another set of experiences/teaching skills," and markedly less emphasis than grandfathers did on "providing economic support" and "being available to care for grandchildren when needed." Both generations, however, gave the lowest priority to "being active participants in the rearing and disciplining of grandchildren."

Additional analyses revealed that in comparison to grandmothers, grandfathers placed less importance on "having a warm/close relationship," $t(75) = 4.4$, p $<$ .001, and "having fun without the constraints of discipline," $t(75) = 3.7$, p $<$ .001, and more importance on "being a source of advice," $t(75) = 3.5$, p $<$ .001. Significant differences between maternal and paternal grandfathers were also found on two items. Paternal grandfathers placed more importance on "being a source of advice" (paternal = 4.0; maternal = 3.1, $t(30)$ = 3.9, p < .001), and on "providing economic support" (paternal = 4.1; maternal = 3.2, $t(30)$ = 3.5, p < .001).

Grandfathers, but more especially paternal grandfathers, see their role, therefore, in terms of being a family resource and support. This includes economic support as well as being a source of advice, or, in Neugarten and Weinstein's (1964) terms, being a "reservoir of family wisdom." Having close relationships with their grandchildren was also seen as important. More critically, it appears that there is an emphasis on adopting a passive style, standing back and being prepared to help out when a need arises or when they are asked to contribute. The grandfathers in this sample did not place much importance on being a "fun" person or on being a person who teaches the younger generation a set of skills. This latter finding is consistent with data presented earlier showing that few grandfathers were actively involved in teaching skills. In contrast to the findings of Neugarten and Weinstein (1964), grandmothers did not rate the parent surrogate item ("active participants in the rearing and disciplining of grandchildren") more highly than grandfathers did.

Although grandfathers gave a high priority to the establishment of a warm and close relationship, they did not rate this as highly as the second generation did. Disagreements between the generations are also evident on the items which relate to support and advice. The younger generation appear to prefer to be less dependent on their parents for economic support and child care than their parents would like them to be. Overall, it seems that grandparents give more emphasis to being supportive and continuing to function as parents toward their adult children, whereas members of the younger generation are much more focused on the importance of grandchildren having warm and close relationships with their grandparents.

SIGNIFICANCE OF BEING A GRANDPARENT

As was mentioned above, several researchers have focused attention on the study of the meaning or significance that grandparenthood has for grandparents (for recent reviews and findings, see Johnson, 1983; Kivnik, 1981, 1983; Troll, 1980, 1983). Kivnik (1983), using qualitative

TABLE 14.1

Mean Ratings for Grandparents' and Parents' Perceptions of the Relative Importance of Grandparenting Roles and Responsibilities

	Grandfathers	Grandmothers	Fathers	Mothers
Be interested/help out when asked, but do not intrude	4.1	4.4	3.6	3.9
Be available to mind children when needed	3.7	3.9	2.6	3.2
Be someone special who small treats	3.1	3.2	3.2	3.5
Be an active participant in rearing and discipline	2.3	2.2	2.4	2.5
Be a source of advice for parents and grandchildren	3.7	3.0	3.4	3.4
Provide economic support in times of need	3.7	3.7	2.8	2.7
Provide grandchildren with set of experiences/teach skills	3.1	3.3	3.8	3.8
Establish a warm and close relationship	3.6	4.2	4.3	4.4
Have fun without the constraints of discipline	3.1	3.8	3.4	3.8

NOTE: Items were rated on a 5-point scale, from 1 = not important at all to 5 = extremely important.

and quantitative methods, has delineated five dimensions of grandparenthood meaning: centrality (grandparenting is central to people's lives); valued elder (giving advice and being a resource person); immortality through clan (e.g., grandchildren carry on the family line); reinvolvement with personal past (e.g., reliving experiences with own grandparents); and indulgence (giving treats and being lenient). Kivnik also suggests two further meaningful dimensions of grandparenthood that did not emerge from her analysis: family relationships and relationships between grandparents and grandchildren. Although the present study did not set out to test Kivnik's theory, some of the items included here overlap with those in her study.

Grandparents were given the items shown in Table 14.2 and were then asked to rate their significance for them as grandparents (from 5 = extremely significant to 1 = not significant at all). The most significant aspects for both grandfathers and grandmothers were "feeling proud of the achievements of my grandchildren"; "the joy and satisfaction I get from my relationships"; and "providing support for my children's families." The other three aspects were rated as being less significant, with "helps me forget about being old" being rated to be the least significant of all. In support of Neugarten and Weinstein (1964), grandfathers rated this item as being less significant than grandmothers did , $t(75) = 3.1$, p $< .05$. Only one item showed a significant difference between grandfather groups. Paternal grandfathers rated "feeling proud" more highly (paternal = 4.5; maternal = 3.7, $t(30) = 2.5$, p $< .02$).

Taking the findings presented here for the questions on "roles and responsibilities" and "meaning" together, it is obvious that strong support is given to Kivnik's dimension of valued elder. The present data, however, suggest that some account needs to be taken of the advice and support that grandparents give to their adult children, and to possible sex differences. Only moderate support was found for the significance of indulgence, and this was stronger for grandmothers than for grandfathers. Finally, the finding that the items rated most highly here relate to the dimension of the grandparent-grandchild relationship lends strong support to Kivnik's arguments for the inclusion of this dimension into an expanded conceptual model of the significance of grandparenthood. More extensive comparisons with Kivnik's (1983) findings are limited, however, because of the lack of overlap between the items and because of Kivnik's failure to report sex differences.

EVALUATION OF GRANDPARENTING

With all the recent emphasis on the study of the meaning of parenthood, little attention has been given to the experiences of being a grandparent or to the affective component of the role (see Neugarten and Weinstein, 1964, who did examine ease of role performance). Questions were asked here which required grandparents to give both positive and negative evaluations of their roles and experiences.

POSITIVE EVALUATIONS

Grandparents were asked to rate how happy or satisfied they felt with grandparenting and with their relationships with their grandchildren (ratings from 1 = very unhappy to 7 = extremely happy). Mean ratings for grandfathers on both items were very high: For satisfaction with

TABLE 14.2
Mean Ratings of Grandparents' Perceptions of the
Relative Significance of Various Aspects of Grandparenting

	Grandfathers	Grandmothers
Being a grandparent helps me forget about being old.	2.1	2.8
My grandchildren give me a link with the future.	3.3	3.0
It gives me the opportunity to help and teach my grandchildren.	3.2	3.3
Feeling proud of the achievements of my grandchildren.	4.1	4.3
The joy and satisfaction I get from my relationships with my grandchildren.	4.0	4.5
Providing support for my children's families.	3.6	3.7

NOTE: Items were rated on a 5-point scale, from 1 = not important at all to 5 = extremely important.

grandparenting the mean was 6.1 and for satisfaction with their relationships with their grandchildren it was 6.2. No differences were found between grandfathers and grandmothers or between maternal and paternal grandfathers on these ratings. Grandfathers were also asked to rate the degree of satisfaction they felt with their role as a parent (mean 5.7) and with their relationships with their own children (mean 6.2). Comparing these two sets of figures, it appears that these grandfathers generally experience a high level of satisfaction with being grandparents.

Grandparents were also asked an open-ended question about what they really enjoyed about being a grandparent. All had something very positive to say, but the nature of the responses varied considerably. Responses were coded into eight categories: enjoyment of their grandchildren's company and affection (33% of the total number of responses given by grandfathers, and 36% of those given by grandmothers, were in this category); watching the grandchildren grow and develop new skills (18% of grandfathers; 21% of grandmothers); feeling a sense of pride about grandchildren (13% of grandfathers; 1% of grandmothers); the ways in which they give meaning and status to life (9% of grandfathers; 11% of grandmothers); doing things with them or for them (9% of grandfathers; 13% of grandmothers); having the time to be involved and interested (6% of grandfathers; 9% of grandmothers); having the fun without the responsibility (6% of grandfathers; 3% of grandmothers); reliving the bringing up of our own children (6% of grandfathers; 5% of grandmothers). Major differences were not found between maternal and paternal grandfathers. Some examples of the responses given by grandfathers are listed below.

I enjoy the company of them immensely. I enjoy the fact that my grandson is more than an intelligent fellow. I enjoy seeing them healthy and happy.

I love taking them out for day trips. Babysitting them, and having the responsibility of them without their parents being around. I also enjoy being their confidantes.

The way they call me "Poppy." The way that they speak and their inquisitive nature. The questions they ask, talking to them and the funny things that they say.

Seeing her growing and developing. It's like an awakening. I'm much more conscious of it than with my own children.

I enjoy the way that they stimulate my self-pride. I also enjoy the way that they seem to respect me.

I enjoy watching my grandaughter growing up. She'll be Miss World in 1999!

I enjoy the way that they make life fuller. Life would be very dull without them.

I have lived as long as I have just to see the grandchildren.

I love babies and children, and sitting back and seeing the family line carried on.

Several grandfathers also said that they gained more satisfaction from their grandchildren than they did from their own children when they were young. This was explained in terms of their now having the time to sit, relax, and listen, and to enjoy the originality and energy of the children. Structured questions were asked that examined these types of comparisons between parenting and grandparenting.

Grandparents rated how well each of four statements described their feelings (from 1 = not at all like to 5 = very much like their feelings). Responses indicated that both grandparents found it easier being a grandparent than a parent (mean ratings: grandfathers = 4.6; grandmothers = 4.8); grandfathers were less likely to say they enjoyed their children more than their grandchildren (grandfathers = 1.8; grandmothers = 2.9, $t(75)$ = 3.4, p $<$ .01), and more likely to say they regretted not having spent more time with their children when they were younger (grandfathers = 2.8; grandmothers = 1.9, $t(75)$ = 3.0, p$<$ .01) and that they would like to spend more time with their grandchildren (grandfathers = 3.2; grandmothers = 2.5, $t(75)$ = 2.2, p $<$ .02). This latter item was rated even more highly by paternal grandfathers (paternal = 3.7; maternal = 2.6, $t(3)$ = 2.2, p $<$ .05). Grandfathers then appear to have some regrets about their lack of involvement with their own children, and many obviously saw their involvement with their grandchildren as a way of compensating for this. They also appear to gain more satisfaction from their grandchildren, and are keen to spend even more time with them than they currently do.

NEGATIVE EVALUATIONS

Two questions were included in the interviews which gave grandfathers the opportunity to report negative aspects of grandparenting. In the first they were asked what they really disliked about being a grandparent, and in the second what they found most difficult about it. The overwhelming response to the first question was that there wasn't anything much that they really disliked about the role—75% of grandfathers gave a response of this type (compared with 80% of grandmothers). Those who disliked it were more inclined to say the following types of things: "it makes me feel old" (13% of both grandfathers and grandmothers); "the grandchildren annoy me by screaming and being disobedient" (9% of grandfathers); "the added expense and worry" (3% of grandfathers and 7% of grandmothers).

Answers to the question about what grandparents found most difficult were coded into six categories: no difficulties at all (given by 41% of grandfathers and 23% of grandmothers); holding back and not giving advice or stepping in to discipline (20% of grandfathers; 40% of grandmothers); not being able to do things because of physical health (10% of grandfathers; 12% of grandmothers); difficulties in communicating with grandchildren because of generation differences (15% of grandfathers; 5% of grandmothers); not being able to see them as often as would like (9% of grandfathers; 10% of grandmothers); and not having enough patience (5% of grandfathers; 10% of grandmothers).

Consistent with the findings of Neugarten and Weinstein (1964), the majority of grandfathers did not report having strong negative feelings about grandparenting, and only about two-thirds of this sample reported any major difficulties. These responses did, however, reveal an element of conflict between the two generations in terms of the approaches that each take to bringing up children. The above results also indicate that grandfathers did not seem to experience as much difficulty in this regard as grandmothers did.

This issue was pursued in more detail elsewhere in the interview. Grandparents were asked whether or not they felt their grandchildren were being brought up differently from the way in which they had brought up their own children. A total of 63% of grandfathers and 74% of grandmothers said that there were major differences. The differences most commonly noted related to discipline and child centeredness. A specific question was also asked about whether current parents were harder or softer in their approaches to child rearing. Only 5% of grandfathers and no grandmothers at all thought that the current generation was harder. In contrast, 53% of grandfathers and 61% of grandmothers perceived that the current approach was softer and more child centered. Some examples of the responses are presented below:

> They treat them more as adults from the word go. They ask opinions on things and consider them more as equals. Discipline is not as severe, it seems to be working, so my approach might not have been warranted. [Grandfather]

> They are more democratic. We came from the older school where they did what they were told and that was it. [Grandfather]

These data on negative evaluations, therefore, add weight to the interpretation of the grandfather role as being more passive and supportive. The finding that grandmothers find it more difficult to hold back and not interfere in discipline also provides indirect support for Neugarten and Weinstein's (1964) report that grandmothers are more likely to emphasize being surrogate parents and being concerned about the socialization of the grandchildren. Further, the finding that grandparents consciously hold back from intervening in the upbringing of their grandchildren confirms the generational stake hypothesis (Bengtson & Kuypers, 1971), and the findings of others (e.g., Hagestad, 1978; Troll & Bengston, 1979) that there are sensitive areas in family relationships that people tend to avoid for the sake of maintaining family ties.

ADULT PARENT-CHILD RELATIONSHIPS AND GRANDPARENTING

Most analyses of grandparenting ignore the possible critical importance of the relationship between the two generations of adults and the impact that grandchildren might have on these. Grandparents might see their role in relation to their grandchildren as an extension of their own parenting. Their perceptions and beliefs about their parental responsibilities with their adult children, therefore, could mediate the nature of their approach to grandparenting and they might give greater priority to their relationships with their own children rather than to their grand-children. Involvement with grandchildren, therefore, might be seen primarily in terms of supporting their adult children, and to maintaining parental relationships with them. It seems far too narrow an approach to take, like some have (e.g., Kivnik, 1983), to consider grandparent-hood simply within the context of a relationship between two individuals—a grandparent and a grandchild. This argument is sup-ported by data collected here about grandparents' beliefs about their role as parents.

DOES PARENTING CONTINUE?

Grandparents were asked if they thought that parenting ever stopped, and if it didn't, what the current nature of their parenting role was. All but one of the 32 grandfathers said that parenting continued. Answers to the question about the current nature of the role were coded into six categories: to be a source of knowledge/advice, more in a worldly sense (24% of responses were in this category); continuing to worry and have strong feelings about children (22%); to be available for emotional support (20%); help out when needed, but don't interfere (14%); con-tinue a strong parent-child relationship (12%); to provide economic support in times of need (6%). Examples of grandfathers' responses are given below.

> Not really, when they get married they still come to you and ask for help. You still share their problems.
>
> I'm still a parent, but don't interfere. If they get into trouble, I help as best I can. They can always come home and talk to me.
>
> Never. I still worry when I know they are on the roads. I still get annoyed with them for the same things they do wrong as when they were young— their lack of respect etc. I will always be the same toward them as when they were young.

Grandmothers were also strong in their views that parenting respon-sibilities continued. They, however, were less likely to emphasize being a source of knowledge/advice in a worldly sense (12% of their responses were of this type), and much more likely to emphasize continuing to worry and having strong feelings about children (45% of their responses were of this type). Three comments made by grandmothers are listed below.

> No. One's maternal instinct is always there. You can't break the ties of love.
>
> No, it seems to be an inborn drive, it's your reason for living, for our being here. Parents like to feel that they are needed especially when they get older.
>
> No, I still regard them as our children, and feel responsible even though they become more equal. I have a strong desire to help them if they need it.

THE IMPACT OF GRANDCHILDREN ON ADULT PARENT-CHILD RELATIONSHIPS

A series of structured questions were used to assess the quality of adult parent-child relationships and the perceived impact that having grandchildren had had on these relationships. Cicierelli (1983) has reviewed findings on the quality of adult parent-child relationships and concluded that, in line with the generational stake hypothesis, parents report feeling closer to their children than their children do in return; and daughters feel closer to their parents than sons do. Previous research (e.g., Hagestad, 1978) also suggests that grandchildren have a tendency to strengthen relationships between female members of families—between mother and daughter and between mother-in-law and daughter-in-law, for instance—and reinforce the role of women as kin-keepers (see Bahr, 1976).

Questions asked in this study required parents and grandparents to rate (using the five-point scale described above) how well the statements listed in Table 14.3 described their current relationships, and what impact having grandchildren had had on their relationships. Mean ratings for each are shown in Table 14.3.

Several features are obvious from this table. The first is the general dominance of relationships between female members of the family. The mother-daughter relationship in particular and the mother-in-law/daughter-in-law relationship are consistently rated as being the closest and warmest. Paternal grandmothers, for example, have closer relationships and more contact with their daughters-in-law than paternal grandfathers do. The paternal grandfather appears to be the most distant of

TABLE 14.3
Grandparents' and Parents' Mean Ratings of the Quality of Their Relationships with Each Other and Their Perceptions of the Impact Grandchildren Have Had

| | Grandparents | | | | Daughter | | Son | |
| | Maternal | | Paternal | | | | | |
	Father	Mother	Father	Mother	Father	Mother	Father	Mother
Current Relationship								
Comfortable/friendly								
parent/child	4.9	4.9	4.5	4.5	3.7	4.2	4.2	3.7
parent/child-in-law	4.4	4.3	4.5	4.6	3.3	3.6	3.6	3.5
Warm and close								
parent/child	4.0	4.5	4.1	4.4	3.2	4.2	3.6	3.1
parent/child-in-law	3.8	3.7	4.0	4.6	2.2	3.3	2.6	2.8
Open and honest								
parent/child	4.7	4.8	4.4	4.7	3.8	4.1	4.3	3.8
parent/child-in-law	4.4	4.3	4.4	4.7	3.8	3.8	3.3	3.5
Share interests and views								
parent/child	4.7	4.5	4.3	4.5	3.9	4.3	3.3	3.4
parent/child-in-law	4.2	4.0	3.6	4.5	3.5	3.8	3.5	3.5
Spend lot of time together								
parent/child	3.7	4.4	3.4	4.0	3.2	4.1	2.9	3.2
parent/child-in-law	3.6	3.5	3.3	4.0	2.1	3.0	2.3	2.5
Impact of Having Grandchildren								
Spent more time together								
parent/child	2.4	3.6	3.1	3.0	2.9	3.3	2.5	2.9
parent/child-in-law	2.4	2.9	3.1	3.0	2.8	3.1	2.6	2.9
Feel closer								
parent/child	2.4	2.5	3.0	3.2	2.8	3.2	2.7	2.9
parent/child-in-law	2.6	2.7	3.0	3.3	2.8	3.1	2.6	2.9
Have more in common								
parent/child	2.8	2.7	3.3	3.7	2.8	3.0	2.3	2.5
parent/child-in-law	2.8	2.6	3.3	3.9	3.1	2.8	2.4	2.5

NOTE: Reading the table: For example, 4.9 in row 1, column 1 refers to the maternal grandfather's perception of how comfortable/friendly his relationship with his daughter is, while his son-in-law's perception of his relationship with him is represented by the figure 3.6 in row 2, column 7. Items were rated on a 5-point scale, from 1 = not at all like to 5 = very much like.

all. When the perceptions of both members of each dyad are considered, it appears that the only really close relationship he has is with his son.

Consistent with previous research are the findings that children feel closer to their same-sex parents, and that relationships are rated to be much warmer by parents than by children. This latter generational discrepancy is even more evident for in-law relationships. Fathers- and mothers-in-law tend to rate their relationships with their sons- and daughters-in-law in a much more positive manner than their sons- and daughters-in-law do. Grandparents' responses, therefore, tend to conform with the old adage that "we haven't lost a daughter/son, but have gained a son/daughter."

One of the aspects of interest in this study was whether or not having grandchildren might bring the two generations closer together, and strengthen the bonds between parents and adult children. As was evident from the above, both generations rated their relationships with their same-sex parents or children as very strong, and these certainly were the dominant relationships within the family system. As such, there is likely to be less room for changes in these relationships than for in-law relationships.

Findings presented in the above table indicate that having grandchildren has meant that the mother-daughter and mother-daughter-in-law relationships are strengthened in terms of time spent together and perceived closeness. Both groups perceive this to be the case. There appears to be little impact on the relationship between maternal grandfathers and their sons-in-law. However, having grandchildren seems to have some impact on relationships between paternal grandparents and their sons and daughters-in-law. Paternal grandparents consistently rate these relationships as having changed in terms of time spent, closeness, and having more in common. The greatest changes of all are perceived by grandfathers in their relationships with their sons. It appears from the figures presented in the table, however, that their sons do not share this feeling nearly as strongly.

These findings that grandparents perceive more positive changes in their relationships with their children are again consistent with the generational stake hypothesis. Perhaps there is another reason, however, for why sons and sons-in-law in particular do not feel closer to their fathers and fathers-in-law as a result of having children. Present day fathers perceive major differences between the two generations in terms of patterns of involvement—40% of the fathers said that a major difference was that they were more involved than their own fathers had been. Therefore, they might feel that they do not have much in common in the parenting domain with their fathers and fathers-in-law.

SUMMARY AND CONCLUSIONS

Findings presented in this chapter lend strong support to the small number of previous studies that have shown that males derive considerable satisfaction from grandparenting and rate this as a highly significant aspect of their lives. Although they spent less time with their grandchildren than grandmothers did, these grandfathers with young grandchildren were highly involved, and 75% had regular weekly contact. They were also highly active in their interactions when they saw their grandchildren. The most common activities were having a cuddle, talking and listening, playing with toys inside, reading storybooks, playing ball games, and rough-and-tumble games. Sex differences were found to parallel findings for sex differences in parent-child interactions. Grandfathers were less likely than grandmothers to engage in more conventional play with toys, games, and reading, and art/craft activities, but were more involved in physical and outdoor activities.

In general, visits with grandchildren were engaged in as couple activities, and it was not characteristic of this sample of grandfathers for them to spend time having the total responsibility for minding grandchildren. Again, these findings were interpreted as paralleling those previously reported for divisions of labor between parents with young children. As such, this study might be viewed as failing to give strong support to the theories of Gutmann (1975) and Sinnott (1977) about men becoming more "feminine" in older age. These data, however, left open the question of the degree to which grandparents divided up responsibilities when they were both with their grandchildren. Further research, using interview as well as observational methods, is needed to examine more closely questions of divisions of responsibilities, and of the quality of grandfather-grandchild relationships. Research of this type would also provide data on the extent of grandfather nurturance and sensitivity, and provide a more direct test of Gutmann's and Sinnott's theories. Future investigations will also need to include the age of the grandchild as a variable, as many of the present findings might be specific to having younger grandchildren.

Although grandfathers were less likely than grandmothers to rate having a warm, close relationship with their grandchildren as being an important aspect of grandparenting, the weight of evidence indicated that grandfathers rated the actual quality of their relationships as highly as grandmothers did. They were just as likely to describe their relationships as warm and close and just as likely to say that they were satisfied with them. Moreover, it was obvious from responses to several different questions that grandfathers placed a high priority on the warmth and affection that they shared with their grandchildren. Activities that they reported they enjoyed most included "having a cuddle," and "sitting, talking, and listening to them." Their most frequent responses to a question about what they really enjoyed about being a grandparent were "the enjoyment of the grandchildren's company and affection" and "watching the grandchildren grow and develop." Other responses given by these grandfathers indicated that they also placed a high priority on the satisfaction they derived from the sense of pride they felt about their grandchildren.

Although a high level of involvement and feelings of pride and joy from having warm relationships with grandchildren was a dominant aspect of grandfathering, other findings suggest a more traditional component as well. The evidence is consistent with grandfathers viewing their role in a dual way, in much the same way as the farmer in the example at the beginning did. They had frequent contact with their grandchildren and obtained considerable satisfaction from their interactions with them. But they also gave a high priority to being available to support their adult children in times of social and financial need, and to be available to give advice when worldly problems arose. This aspect of their role is probably best described in Neugarten and Weinstein's terms as a "reservoir of family and worldly wisdom."

On the other hand, the weight of evidence suggests a much more active style for grandmothers and one that is much more oriented toward the care and socialization of the grandchildren. They saw themselves as sharing more in their grandchildren's interests, and placed more emphasis on doing things for their grandchildren and giving them special treats. Although like grandfathers, they saw it important to be prepared to help but not intrude, 40% of grandmothers admitted that they had difficulty in doing this.

Some differences were evident between the first and second generations in their ideas about grandparenting. Grandparents were more likely to emphasize their role as a potential support and source of advice, whereas their children emphasized having a close and warm relationship with the grandchildren. The younger generation therefore appears to feel that either they should not be, or do not want to be dependent on the grandparents for economic and social support. It also appeared that grandparents would have liked to have been consulted more or to have been asked for help in times of need (e.g., financial, for child care) more than was the case.

Findings presented here were entirely consistent with those of previous studies in showing greater closeness between women in the family system, and between same-sex parent-child dyads. And, in agreement with the generational stake hypothesis, grandparents rated their relationships with their children as being warmer than their sons and daughters did. This generational difference in perceptions of warmth of relationships was even more evident for parent/child-in-law dyads. Evidence was also found for changes in adult parent-child relationships as a consequence of having grandchildren. As would be expected, both groups reported spending more time together, but this was more common for females. Paternal grandparents reported more changes than maternal grandparents, with major changes being more evident for the paternal grandfather's relationship with his son. It should be kept in mind that these are retrospective data and studies of the process of becoming grandparents (see Cunningham-Burley, 1984) might reveal entirely different patterns.

Another consistent finding was that there were quite significant differences between maternal and paternal grandfathers. A theme runs through these data indicating that paternal grandfathers spend less time with their grandchildren, that they are more traditional in their interactions, more likely to see it as their role to advise and support their families, and more likely to wish that they could spend more time with their grandchildren. Despite these differences, however, paternal grandfathers rated the quality of their relationships with their grandchildren just as highly as maternal grandfathers did. There is a need for future research to examine these differences more closely and examine their longer term implications. Studies are also needed to examine the effects of having grandchildren of different sexes, and explore the possibility that paternal grandfathers are more involved and have closer relationships with grandsons (see Hagestad, 1978).

Another question worthy of future investigation concerns the relationship between grandfather-involvement and father-involvement. Findings indicated that 40% of the fathers said that one of the major differences in approaches between the two generations was that they were more involved than their own fathers had been. On the other hand, grandfathers reported that they regretted not having been more involved with their own children, and that they enjoyed their grandchildren more than they had enjoyed their own. Many grandfathers appeared to view being involved with their grandchildren as a way of making up for opportunities that they felt they had lost with their own children. This also raises the question, however, of what impact the *current* approaches of the two generations of males might have on each others' levels of involvement with children. Might a highly nurturant father place demands on a grandfather to adopt a similar style? Or might a highly nurturant grandfather who emphasizes his lost opportunities influence his son or son-in-law? Could this create more conflicts between the two generations, or would it bring them closer together? If present day fathers continue to become more involved and take more responsibility, will this have the effect of reducing the distance between the paternal grandfather and others in the family system? Will it operate to loosen the current strong ties between women in families? Future investigators will need to look more closely at the links between the three generations and monitor changes in these as a function of changes in patterns of divisions of labor.

REFERENCES

Bahr, H. M. (1976). The kinship role. In I. F. Nye, H. M. Bahr, S. J. Bahr, J. E. Carlson, V. Gecas, S. McLaughlin, & W. L. Slocum (Eds.), *Role structure and analysis of the family*. Beverly Hills, CA: Sage.

Bengtson, V., & Kuypers, J. (1971). Generational differences and the generational stake. *Aging and Human Development, 2,* 249-260.

Cicirelli, V. G. (1983). Adult children and their elderly parents. In T. H. Brubaker (Ed.), *Family relationships in later life*. Beverly Hills, CA: Sage.

Congalton, A. A. (1969). *Status and prestige in Australia: Studies in Australian society*. Melbourne: Cheshire.

Cunningham-Burley, S. (1984). "We don't talk about it . . . ": Issues of gender and method in the portrayal of grandfatherhood. *Sociology, 18,* 325-338.

Gutmann, D. (1975). Parenthood: A key to the comparative study of the life cycle. In N. Datan & L. H. Ginsberg (Eds.), *Life span developmental psychology*. New York: Academic Press.

Hagestad, G. (1978). *Patterns of communication and influence between grandparents and grandchildren in a changing society*. Paper presented at the Ninth World Congress of Sociology, Uppsala, Sweden.

Hagestad, G. (1981). Problems and promises in the social psychology of intergenerational relations. In R. W. Fogel, E. Hatfield, S. B. Keisler, & E. Shanas (Eds.), *Aging: Stability and change in the family*. New York: Academic Press.

Louis Harris and Associates. (1975). *The myth and reality of aging in America*. New York: National Council on Aging.

Johnson, C. L. (1983). A cultural analysis of the grandmother. *Research on Aging, 5,* 547-567.

Kahana, R. A., & Kahana, E. (1970). Grandparenthood from the perspective of the developing child. *Developmental Psychology, 3,* 98-105.

Kivnik, H. Q. (1982). Grandparenthood: An overview of meaning and mental health. *Gerontologist, 22,* 59-66.

Kivnik, H. Q. (1983). Dimensions of grandparenthood meaning: Deductive conceptualization and empirical derivation. *Journal of Personality and Social Psychology, 44,* 1056-1068.

Livson, F. B. (1976). Coming together in the middle years: A longitudinal study of sex role convergence. Prepared for *The double standard of aging: A question of sex differences.* Symposium conducted at the Twenty-Ninth Annual Meeting of the Gerontological Society, New York.

McGee, J., & Wells, K. (1982). Gender typing and androgyny in later life. *Human Development, 25,* 116-139.

Neugarten, B., & Weinstein, K. (1964). The changing American grandparent. *Journal of Marriage and the Family, 26,* 199-204.

Robertson, J. F. (1975). Interaction in three-generation families: Parents as mediators: Toward a theoretical perspective. *International Journal of Aging and Human Development, 6,* 103-110.

Russell, G. (1983). *The changing role of fathers?* St. Lucia, Queensland: University of Queensland Press.

Russell, G. (n.d.) *Sharing the caring.* Unpublished manuscript.

Sinnott, J. D. (1977). Sex-role inconsistency, biology, and successful aging. *Gerontologist, 17,* 459-464.

Troll, L. E. (1980). Grandparenting. In L. W. Poon (Ed.), *Aging in the 80's.* Washington, DC: APA Publication.

Troll, L. E. (1983). Grandparents: The family watchdogs. In T. H. Brubaker (Ed.), *Family relationships in later life.* Beverly Hills, CA: Sage.

Troll, L. E.. & Bengtson, V. (1979). Generations in the family. In W. Burr, R. Hill, F. I. Nye, & I. Reiss (Eds.), *Contemporary theories about the family* (Vol. 1). New York: Free Press.

15

MEN AND THEIR FRIENDSHIPS

Peter J. Stein

The topic of adult friendships represents an underresearched area of sociology. Only recently have social scientists begun to examine this crucial area of human interaction (Blau, 1973; Brain, 1976; Lewis, 1978; Davidson & Duberman, 1979; Parlee, 1979; Bell, 1981, Hess, 1981, Stein, 1981).

A friend is "one joined to another in intimacy and mutual benevolence independently of sexual or family love" (*Oxford Dictionary*, 1965). It is a unique form of social bonding. Mary Parlee (1979, p. 60) writes that "unlike marriage or the ties that bind parents and children, it is not defined or regulated by law." Friendship is different from other social roles that we are expected to occupy, in that friendship "has its own subjective rationale, which is to enhance feelings of warmth, trust, love and affection between two people" (Parlee, 1979). While work, citizenship, marriage, and parenthood continue as obligatory adult social roles, friendship, in contrast, constitutes "an optional social role. People are expected to fulfill the demands of work and family life and the judgment of their success or failure as adults rests primarily on the attainment and maintenance of these roles and not on the number of friends they have or on the quality of their friendships" (Blau, 1973, p. 60). It is an optional role in that it lies outside of the structured roles and institutions of our society, but it also makes it a fragile role for which fewer norms and expectations exist. Friendship roles are more subject to individual negotiations and dependent on individual resources for satisfactory ongoing friendships.

Author's Note: *I am very grateful to several professional friends who have helped me rethink this crucial topic: Bob Lewis, John Darling, Natalie Hannon, and Nick Alex. I gratefully acknowledge the assistance of Terri Lobosco and Pamela Mazurek in the typing of this chapter.*

261

DIFFERENCES IN THE EXPERIENCES
OF FRIENDSHIP FOR
MEN AND FOR WOMEN

As with experiences and behavior in other areas, the friendship experiences of men and of women in American society differ. Both men and women are subject to and experience the overall normative definitions of friendships among adults in our society, but the specification of norms differs for men and for women. Empirical studies indicate important differences in the extent to which men and women are integrated into support networks and differences between men and women regarding intimacy, sociability, affiliative styles, degrees of self-disclosure, and empathy (Pleck, 1975; Maccoby & Jacklin, 1974; Davidson & Duberman, 1979).

Such studies have also shown that men have fewer friendships and experience greater difficulties in the formation of friendships. Several authors have documented the problems men face in their attempts to establish more meaningful friendships with other men. Both Robert Lewis (1978) and Joseph Pleck (1975) identify the major barriers to male friendships: (1) male competitiveness, which inhibits the development of friendships and the sharing of vulnerabilities and weaknesses; (2) the lack of skills and the relative lack of positive role models from which to learn about friendships and the handling of intimate relationships; (3) men's homophobia regarding the show of affection and tenderness toward other men; and (4) men's false need to be "in control," which prohibits self-disclosure and intimate sharing of issues and feelings.

In a recent study of adult development based on interviews with 40 men, Daniel Levinson (1978, p. 335) notes:

In our interviews friendship was largely noticeable by its absence. As a tentative generalization we would say that close friendship with a man or woman is rarely experienced by American men. The distinction between a friend and acquaintance is often blurred. A man may have a wide social network in which he has amicable, "friendly" relationships with many men and perhaps a few women. In general, however, most men do not have an intimate male friend of the kind that they recall fondly from boyhood or youth. Many men have had casual dating relationships with women, and perhaps a few complex love-sex relationships, but most men have not had an intimate, non-sexual friendship with a woman. We need to understand why friendship is so rare, and what consequences this deprivation has for adult life.

How can we account for these findings? The literature on socialization and social learning provides some answers. Maccoby and Jacklin (1974, pp. 205-211) report that young boys have more interaction with peers in games where interaction is based on players' skills rather than on liking and disliking. For example, boys will include others in their play to make a team complete. Girls report that they like the people they interact with and are more likely to choose playmates on the basis of personal attraction. Both American and cross-cultural data report that by the age of seven, girls focus their playtime relationships on one or two best friends while boys spend playtime in larger groups. In childhood and adolescence, girls' friendship patterns are more intimate, more exclusive, and have greater self-disclosure and telling of secrets. Among adolescents, male-male friendships were less intimate than female-female friendships (Douvan & Adelson, 1966). Booth found in a study of adults (1972) in two urban communities that while some men have more friends than women, the men's friendships are less close and spontaneous. Another study (Adams, 1968) found less intimacy among men friends than among women friends. Moreover, Booth (1972) also reported that men with "a high need for affiliation and affect" were judged by other men as having negative qualities. Sociability and communication about matters peripheral to the self are supported, but intimacy, the sharing of feelings and thoughts central to oneself, in those relationships is less acceptable for men than for women in our society.

But not all studies support the negative findings regarding the extent and quality of men's friendships. For example, Booth (1972) found that one group of men, "healthy, in white collar occupations and married," did have more friends than a similar group of women. Another study, based on a sample of 450 young and middle-aged men, indicated that men were not isolated or lacking in friends (Farrell & Rosenberg, 1977). About 80% reported seeing friends on a regular basis. There were changes in friendship experiences over the life course. For example, marriage and parenthood reduced contacts with male friends but increased couple-oriented activities. Farrell and Rosenberg's research indicates the importance of life-cycle stage in the formation and nature of friendships.

Moreover, though identifying the problems men face in friendship formation, Pleck (1975) indicates that men are seeking to establish more meaningful relationships with each other and that brotherhood is possible. Such changes are occurring in dyadic relations, in group settings, and in other contexts. For example, "Men's groups are emerging as a new social form in which many men are searching for a new kind of relationship with each other" (Pleck, 1975, p. 242). As another step toward that goal, Lewis (1978) describes a series of workshops developed to encourage "openness and intimacy" between men. He reports finding that "many of the barriers to self-disclosure melt away in these workshops where permission is given to disclose oneself . . . surrounded by the acceptance and warm support of other men" (p. 117).

A STUDY OF MALE FRIENDSHIPS

In an attempt to understand the development of male friendships better, I analyzed a series of interviews with 40 single and married men. The data presented here are part of a larger study of adult men and women focusing on issues of marriage and singlehood, work, lifestyles, and cross-sex and same-sex friendships.[1] This chapter focuses only on issues of men's friendships with other men.

Despite the structural barriers and interpersonal limitations to male friendships mentioned above, a number of men in our study found male friendships to be important and were committed to developing and sustaining friendships with other men. Their experiences included care and support of each other, reciprocity, acceptance, relative openness, and the mutual sharing of feelings and activities. Discussions of friendship were not easy—the men interviewed at times gave halting answers, stumbled in their attempts to discuss it, coughed, at times seemed uneasy, and sometimes changed their minds about their answers. Nevertheless, they all agreed on the importance of male friendships in their lives.

For example, it took one man a while to define friendship: "It's hard to pin down . . . definitions are changing. A friend is one who tries; who wants to care, support, and help as much as he can [pause] . . . friends forgive shortcomings, without trying to ignore them (uh) they try to be helpful. . . . A friend is someone trying to be free of the old familiar restrictions" (Jim, 36, writer, divorced father, living with Doris).

Many felt that support among friends should be reciprocal. Most of the men stressed the idea that friends take turns helping each other and "being available for each other." One man indicated that "David and I do things for each other without counting. . . . He is also someone whom I can help or can help me get things done. The thing to remember is what you did together. . . . A friend is someone I am concerned about as much as he is about me" (Tom, 44, administrator, married). Reciprocity involves the sharing of activities and feelings. For another man, "My friends help me be more open and support my saying what I feel . . . it's reciprocal . . . I used to think I could make someone be my friend, but now it's a matter of my being somewhat friendly and their being friendly, and it's cumulative" (Mike, 41, attorney, divorced, father of two children, living with roommate).

The men interviewed expected their friends to be generally accepting of them. Such acceptance usually developed over time and involved the giving and taking of trust. The importance of trust and acceptance was cited as important in both dyadic friendships and among members of men's groups. Several men said that friends were men who "accepted you and didn't make a judgment about you right away." One man said, "A good friend can realize your shortcomings, can see some counter-productive behavior, but still accepts you as a friend . . . is tolerant. I think it is friendly to mention shortcomings. I may not like it, but I am able to accept it, particularly since I know it's coming out of our friendship, not as antagonism" (Walter, 34, social worker, single, living alone). For another man, feeling comfortable with friends is important: "With a friend, I feel at ease and don't have to get into my role playing. I feel comfortable with them. . . . I can say what's on my mind and they'll listen. . . . They'll be comfortable with me" (David, 42, biologist, divorced, now living with Lynda).

FRIENDSHIPS IN MEN'S GROUPS

The men interviewed stressed the development of friendships not only in dyadic contexts but also as members of men's groups and friendship networks. Of the 40 men interviewed, 30 had at one time or another belonged to a men's group. These groups are similar in format and structure to women's consciousness-raising groups. Groups usually meet for about two and a half hours at a time, every three or four weeks. Meetings are usually in the evenings, in one of the members' homes. Topics for discussion include various aspects of the male role, including work and careers; relationships with women; fathering, both current and proposed; relationships with parents, friends, and colleagues; health; political issues; neighborhood issues; and discussions of movies; plays, and books. Some groups have agreed on topics and readings; others have no predetermined agendas and deal with any topics raised at the meeting. In some cases group members do things together, such as going to movies of common interest, political discussions, or restaurants. Two groups had periodic trips such as camping or playing softball or basketball. There is some fluidity of membership, but each group has a core membership of six to eight, with a total membership of eight to twelve men.

What were the experiences of the men with these groups? Each of the thirty men, who collectively belonged to six different men's groups, praised their experience. On the whole they found the men's groups to be very important sources of support. They provided settings in which these men could talk about a number of different topics, be listened to, and get feedback from other members about the specific issues. The settings fostered an atmostphere of sharing and openness and trust that are crucial for the development of all friendships. There was an explicit norm in each group that issues raised during the meetings would be treated with confidentiality. In one instance when confidentiality was breached, members took great care to reemphasize its importance at the next meeting and to support the offended member. Most of those interviewed felt that their men's groups provided supportive environments for both problem solving and the sharing of feelings and emotions.

Members also reported experiencing personal and interpersonal changes as a result of the feedback received in the groups. For one member, "The guys in the men's group really got me started with the idea of changing jobs. They helped me realize how stuck I was and my unhappiness with the situation. We spent a long time discussing my feelings about work and what I wanted in a new situation" (Frank, 38, former historian, now working for a public foundation). In the same men's group, Barry related the painful story of his marital separation and the kind of support his male friends provided: "I started crying at one of the meetings, but the guys were there to help me. . . . I was afraid that they would laugh and call me a fool, but Jim started talking about the pain he felt years earlier around his separation, and I stopped feeling alone" (Barry, 35, psychologist, married five years before his separation and eventual divorce). What Barry learned was that "as we began to talk about problems and feelings we began to realize that individuals trying to solve their own problems often experienced loneliness and frustration. . . . It was important to find out that others faced the same problems I did."

The theme of support was echoed in all of the interviews. Such support included helpful comments from others, men to call in case of emergencies, a group to do things with, sharing good times and fun, and for one member even a source for an emergency financial loan (with no interest). Jan, who has been living with Sarah for three years and is planning to marry and raise a family, finds his men's group a good place in which to explore future plans: "We talk about all kinds of things—women, work, marriage and kids. About four of the guys are or were married and are fathers and it's really interesting hearing about their experiences . . . the fun they have with their kids as well as the hassles."

These friendships did not develop overnight. They involved a growing sense of commitment on the part of these men. Very few respondents said that they had an easy time developing friendships; for most a marked effort was involved in reaching out and sharing information and feelings with other men. It involved a conscious effort to take an active role in seeking friends and cultivating friendships. Some respondents felt relatively comfortable initiating and pursuing friendships; others played a more passive role. A sense of reciprocity appeared to be crucial in sustaining friendships, along with a sense of concern and interest on the part of the other. For example, Mike talked about some of the difficulties he experienced with friendships, particularly "my unwillingness to open myself to others." He had always felt that "openness is inconsistent with my well-being. . . . It's really important to guard yourself. Now I'm trying to unlearn that."

The reciprocity and concern take time to develop. Phil indicated that "there's one guy, Jim, who I always have a good time with when we get together. We joke around a lot, lots of laughs, a good time. But we seem to have a difficult time getting together on a regular basis. For a while we took turns canceling get-togethers . . . he was busy, I had a writing deadline, and so on. There were long gaps in between, and it bothered me."

Other obstacles to the development of male friendships emerging from the interviews included feelings of competitiveness with other men, greater achievement drives, and a fear of getting too close. One man reported that "in our group there are several guys who are really making it and I sometimes feel inferior to them in terms of the money I make and the lack of security I have in my job. They are climbing up the ladder, and I sometimes feel that I'm treading water. But talking about it helps and I've discovered that they too have their uncertainties and doubts."

Despite these problems the membership in men's groups was, on balance, a positive experience for all. Phil's comment offers an accurate summary: "I now have a new group of friends who feel essentially the way I do, and who offer support for my lifestyle, work, interests, and my life in general. It's good to have a group of male friends" (Phil, 42, social worker, single).

CONCLUSION

My interviews with one sample of middle-class professional men indicate the importance of supportive male friendships in their lives. The major elements in these friendships have been identified and their developmental nature discussed. It is difficult to generalize such patterns to other groups of men, but the processes of friendship formation are clearly crucial: reciprocity, trust, and the development of intimacy.

The variation in the compositions of the samples used by the different researchers in this area appears to account for some of the contradictory findings. Variables of age, education, income, occupation, marital status, parental status, ethnicity, and psychological resources and development have not been systematically controlled and compared. Moreover, the Farrell and Rosenberg study (1977) and my own interviews indicate the importance of longitudinal studies for identifying the processes involved in the formation, development, and diminishment of male friendships. Methodological improvements in studies would yield richer data about the full development of friendships and their importance for adult men and women. In difficult times, and in trouble-free times, friendships are indeed crucial sources of support.

NOTE

1. The original sample included men and women ranging in age from 25 to 50. The average age of the men was 36; of the women, 30. Most were college graduates, almost one-half held advanced degrees, and most worked in the professions. About two-thirds were single. Sample members lived in New York City and Boston and a majority were single at the time of the interviews. About 90% of sample members were white; the rest were either Black or Hispanic. For earlier analyses of these issues, see Stein (1976, 1981).

REFERENCES

Adams, B. (1968). *Kinship in an urban setting*. Chicago: Markham.
Bell, R. R. (1981). *Worlds of friendship*. Beverly Hills, CA: Sage.
Blau, Z. (1973). *Old age in a changing society*. New York: Franklin Watts.
Booth, A. (1972). Sex and social participation. *American Sociological Review, 37*, 183-192.

Brain, R. (1976). *Friends and lovers*. New York: Basic Books.

Brenton, M. (1975). *Friendship*. New York: Stein & Day.

Davidson, L., & Duberman, L. (1979). *Same-sex friendships: A gender comparison of dyads*. Unpublished manuscript.

Douvan, E., & Adelson, J. (1966). *The adolescent experience*. New York: John Wiley.

Farrell, M., & Rosenberg, S. (1977). *Male friendship and the life cycle*. Paper presented at the meetings of the American Sociological Association.

Hess, B. H. (1981). Friendship and gender roles over the life course. In P. Stein (Ed.), *Single life* (pp. 104-115). New York: St. Martin's.

Lazarsfeld, P., & Merton, R. (1954). Friendship as a social process. In M. Berger, T. Abel, & C. H. Page, *Freedom and control in modern society* (pp. 18-66). New York: Van Nostrand.

Levinson, D. (1978). *The seasons of a man's life*. New York: Knopf.

Lewis, R. A. (1978). Emotional intimacy among men. *Journal of Social Issues, 34*(1), 108-121.

Maccoby, E. E., & Jacklin, C. N. (1974). *The psychology of sex differences*. Stanford, CA: Stanford University Press.

Parlee, M. B. (1979, October). The friendship bond. *Psychology Today*, pp. 48-54, 113.

Pleck, J. H. (1975). Man to man: Is brotherhood possible? In N. Glazer-Malbin (Ed.), *Old family/new family* (pp. 229-244). New York: Van Nostrand.

Stein, P. J. (1976). *Single*. Englewood Cliffs, NJ: Prentice-Hall.

Stein, P. J. (Ed.). (1981). *Single life: Unmarried adults in social context*. New York: St. Martin's.

16

IDENTITY CHANGE AMONG OLDER AND YOUNGER MEN

Mick Coleman
Jack O. Balswick

Despite the rapid modernization of the southern Appalachias during the past three decades, social scientists, the mass media, and the Appalachian people themselves have all continued to promote the region as a distinct subculture. Ford (1962) and Photiadis (1970, 1977) have characterized this subculture as emphasizing the values of individualism, localism, traditionalism, life in harmony with nature, familism, fatalism, and fundamental religious beliefs. Furthermore, Photiadis (1977) contends these values originated from the beliefs of the original settlers of the region and the types of interaction created by the physical geography of the mountains. There are conflicting reports as to how justified these characterizations of southern Appalachia are. Colliver and Warner (1979) found that while individualism, self-reliance, traditionalism, fatalism, and fundamental religious beliefs were indeed stronger than when measured in the 1950s, they were no different from those held by non-Appalachian residents of the same state.

Stonequist's (1961) "marginal man" describes the crisis experienced by individuals undergoing a cultural transition from one set of values and behaviors to another set of values and behaviors. The modernization of the southern Appalachias in coexistence with its continued promotion as a distinct subculture could represent a situation in which the "marginal man" would appear. For example, the traditional "mountain man" image continues to be associated with the southern Appalachias. Does the Appalachian male today accept this image as accurately defining his behavior? Or is the "mountain man" in fact a "marginal man?" If so, does he really differ in his marginality from that of other American males who must adjust to changes in the wider

American society? The purpose of this study was to address these questions.

METHOD

SAMPLE

Males who represented at least a third generation Northeast Georgia Mountain family were recruited for participation in the study. Of the 71 volunteers, 59 reported that their great-grandfather or great-grandmother had also lived in the region.

Volunteers were recruited from a factory, educational system, vocational school, and personal contacts of the volunteers. A cross section of occupations was obtained (e.g., student, teacher, factory worker, farmer), and all participants were of the Caucasian race. Of the 45 married males, 33 reported that their wives were also from the Northeast Georgia Mountains.

The age range of the sample was from 17 to 65 with a median age of 29. Since change in the southern Appalachian region studied had been most dramatic since the 1950s, the medium age of 29 was used to divide the sample into comparison groups of younger and older males.

DEPENDENT MEASURES

To measure identity with the Appalachian Mountains, one item was taken from Photiadis's (1970) study, the remainder being developed by the researchers. Likewise, all items measuring identity with traditional family norms were developed by the researchers.

Balswick's (1975) Expressiveness Scale was used to measure the expressions of love, anger, happiness and sadness. The Expressiveness Scale was developed through analytic techniques and has proven useful in previous research (e.g., Dosser, 1981).

A similar format to that employed by Dosser (1981) was used to measure degree of social and personal disclosure across the target person's wife/girlfriend, male friend, and female friend. The social and personal disclosure items were taken either from Dosser's study or developed by the researchers.

The male's conceptualization of what it means to be a "mountain man" was of particular interest. Thus three short responses were requested to the question, "What is a North Georgia Mountain Man?" Finally, Photiadis's (1970) Life Preference Scale was used to rank the male's preferred ways of life.

PROCEDURE

The questionnaires were delivered to and collected from the male volunteers by various contact people. The contacts were given no instructions other than that they were not to assist the participants in completing the questionnaires. Written instructions were provided to allow the participants to complete the questionnaires at their leisure. Approximately 20-30 minutes were needed to complete all items.

Statements regarding anonymity and the purpose of the study were printed on the face sheet to ensure adequate motivation in the completion of the questionnaires. Likewise, the senior researcher, although never directly meeting the participants, identified himself as a native of the Northeast Georgia Mountains.

RESULTS

As can be seen in Table 16.1, both the younger and older Appalachian males strongly identified with Appalachia as a unique geographic and cultural region. There was less identification with traditional family norms.

Photiadis's (1970) procedure was used to determine the rank order of the eight life preferences across all men. As can be seen in Table 16.2, 54% of all the men placed "family" within the ranks of 1 and 2. "Material conveniences," "outdoor living," and "religion" were also ranked highly as life preferences. "Friendship" was ranked as an intermediate life preference, and "work," "recreation," and "achievement" were all ranked as low life preferences. Thus, 60% of all males placed "achievement" within the bottom ranks of 7 and 8.

Each response to "What is a North Georgia Mountain Man?" was coded into one of seven categories: "strong-dominant," "family man," "character-honesty," "hard-working," "regional identity," "personal

TABLE 16.1
Percentage of Younger and Older Appalachian Males Identifying
with Physical/Cultural and Traditional Family Norms

Statements	% Agree	% Disagree
The North Georgia Mountain area is the one place you can be happy even if you don't have much		
younger males	.98	.02
older males	.100	.00
The North Georgia Mountains have a major influence on the way people who live here think and act.		
younger males	.89	.11
older males	.94	.06
The North Georgia Mountain people should do more to preserve their customs and habits.		
younger males	.92	.08
older males	.92	.08
North Georgia Mountain people are not like other people in the country.		
younger males	.74	.26
older males	.61	.39
Husbands should always be the main breadwinners of their households.		
younger males	.60	.40
older males	.78	.22
It is important for one to know who his ancestors were and where they came from.		
younger males	.86	.14
older males	.81	.19
It is important that children do not move away from their families.		
younger males	.51	.49
older males	.20	.80
Even today, to be really happy one must marry and have children.		
younger males	.32	.68
older males	.47	.53
The main concern of women should be to care for their husband, home, and children.		
younger males	.74	.26
older males	.72	.28
Parents should not allow their children too much independence.		
younger males	.43	.57
older males	.39	.61

NOTE: Younger males, N = 35; older males, N = 36.

TABLE 16.2
Percentages of All Men at Each Rank
for Eight Life Preferences

Rank Ordering of Life Preferences	Ranks							
	1	2	3	4	5	6	7	8
Family	.24	.30	.18	.11	.02	.02	.11	.02
Material conveniences	.15	.12	.22	.18	.14	.11	.08	.00
Outdoor living	.19	.12	.19	.14	.12	.09	.09	.06
Religion	.23	.14	.09	.06	.15	.05	.11	.17
Friendship	.04	.11	.14	.22	.23	.09	.14	.03
Work	.06	.09	.08	.11	.12	.29	.19	.06
Recreation	.05	.06	.08	.13	.15	.20	.18	.15
Achievement	.05	.03	.03	.08	.06	.15	.11	.49

growth-freedom," and "other/missing data" (see Table 16.3 for examples of responses under each category).

As can be seen in Table 16.4, the younger and older men had points of agreement and disagreement in their definitions of a "mountain man." Younger males most frequently defined a "mountain man" with "strong-dominant" (35%) and "personal growth-freedom" (17%) terms, with "regional identity" (6%) the most infrequent theme. Older males most frequently defined a "mountain man" with "character-honesty" (39%) and "strong-dominant" (24%) terms, with "personal growth-freedom" (4%) and "regional identity" (4%) the most infrequent themes.

Both age groups had similar means for all four feelings on Balswick's Expressiveness Scale (see Table 16.5). Dosser's (1981) study of university men was thus used for comparison purposes. The means for love, sadness, and happiness for the total sample of Appalachian men were somewhat lower than that found by Dosser. However, both younger and older Appalachian males obtained higher means for the expression of anger.

As can be seen in Table 16.6, younger men were significantly higher in personal disclosure than older men across the target persons of wife/girlfriend ($t = 2.70$, $p < .01$), male friend ($t = 2.39$, $p < .05$), and female friend ($t = 2.17$, $p < .05$). In contrast, older males were significantly higher in social disclosure to their female friends ($t = -2.17$, $p < .05$) than younger males. No significant differences were found between the two groups for social disclosure to wife/girlfriend ($t = -.79$, $p > .05$) or male friend ($t = -1.30$, $p > .05$).

TABLE 16.3

Examples of Responses to

"What Is a North Georgia Mountain Man?"

Category	Responses
Strong-dominant	Mean; takes care of nature; sex; drinking; independent; capable; quiet-deliberate; ill at ease with outsiders; hunts and fishes; tough; adaptable; boss; strong; self-sufficient; set in ways; self-bossed; outdoors type; strong-minded.
Family man	Head of home; takes care of home; provider; responsible for care and security of family; family's center.
Character-honesty	Kind; good; God fearing; loyal to family and friends; concerned about environment and country; quality; living example to his principles; honest and truthful; dependable; humble and worthy of respect; considerate; high moral and spiritual values; dedicated to what he does; simple minded; straightforward; speaks mind; reliable.
Hard-working	Hard worker; a person who will work to make a living.
Regional identity	Loves mountains; good as the land raised on; proud of his heritage.
Personal growth-freedom	Happy; freedom from others; smart; do what you want to; person enjoying life; "me"; not a hick; at peace with self; right with nature; happy with peace of mind; what he believes he is; interested in what is going on about him; full of laughter; healthy; inner peace.
Other	Grown boy; equal to women; affection; the same as any other man.

DISCUSSION

For both the younger and older males, identity with the Appalachian Mountains as a distinct geographic and cultural region was quite strong (see Table 16.2). This finding is of little surprise given the ideology of traditionalism that exists in the region studied. Life fairs, craft shows, and such popular books as *Foxfire* (Wigginton, 1975) have all contributed to the image of a traditional lifestyle in contemporary southern Appalachia. The degree to which this geographic and cultural identity is ingrained in the personal identity of the males studied or is tied to their need for continuity in a changing Appalachia can be assessed through the remaining dependent measures.

TABLE 16.4
Percentages of Younger and Older Appalachian
Males' Perception of a "Mountain Man"

Response Category	Younger Males (N = 31)	Older Males (N = 34)
Strong-dominant	.35	.24
Character-honesty	.12	.39
Personal growth-freedom	.17	.04
Hard-working	.11	.10
Family man	.09	.12
Regional identity	.06	.04
Other missing data	.10	.07

PREFERENCE FOR WAY OF LIFE

Both age groups of Appalachian males only moderately identified with traditional family norms (see Table 16.1). Likewise, both groups responded infrequently with traditional "family man" terms to the question, "What is a North Georgia Mountain Man?" (see Table 16.4). However, in ranking life preferences "family" (i.e., "to have a lot of time to be with your family") was clearly considered of major importance. Although the Appalachian males were thus accepting of the fact that traditional family norms are no longer viable in modern southern Appalachia, they nevertheless desired more family contact. The high ranking of family contact may reflect the frustration of these men in facing the realities of modern Appalachian life that weaken traditional family ties and structures. However, whether desire for a greater amount of family contact is stronger for Appalachian males than other American males is an issue that will require further study.

Contact with nature has also been a traditional Appalachian value, although the influx of industry had led to a decline in outdoor living as a reality. This inconsistency between Appalachain ideology and reality may again explain the ranking of "outdoor living" as a highly preferred way of life. It is worth noting that a similar ranking might be expected for other rural American males (such as farmers) who, due to economic pressures, are being forced to decrease the amount of time they spend in outdoor living.

The South as a whole has characteristically endorsed religion as an important institution. It is thus not surprising that the Appalachian males ranked this high as a life preference.

TABLE 16.5
Comparison of Means on Balswick's Expressiveness Scale
for Appalachian Males and Dosser's University Males

Feelings	Appalachian Males			Doser's University Males (N = 142)
	Total Sample (N = 71)	Younger Males (N = 35)	Older Males (N = 36)	
Anger	8.78	8.46	9.00	8.42
Love	9.95	9.88	10.22	11.04
Sadness	8.58	9.00	8.16	8.91
Happiness	10.25	10.22	10.28	11.04

A common characteristic of the Appalachian male has been his low motivation for achievement (Ball, 1970; Ford, 1962; Hennon & Photiadis, 1979). Even within the peripheral Appalachian area of northeast Georgia, work and achievement were found to hold relatively little importance as life preferences. However, the high life preference for material conveniences reflects the modern lifestyle to which this area has long been introduced but that traditional Appalachian values such as familism and outdoor living, make difficult of obtainment.

The intermediate ranking of friendship represents a departure from the traditional Appalachian emphasis on individualism. This finding may be due to the economic development of the region studied, its subsequent long-term exposure to the modern values of outsiders, and the Appalachain male's increased dependence upon others (e.g., factory work) for economic survival.

The low ranking of recreation as a life preference can be considered from two points. First, recreation is antithetical to the image of a "strong-dominant" mountain man that was endorsed by both age groups. Secondly, "recreation" in the particular region studied has long been tied to the intrusion of recreational enterprises that have made demands on the area's resources and people.

THE MOUNTAIN MAN DEFINED

The younger and older Appalachian males displayed points of agreement and disagreement in their definitions of a "mountain man." Both groups frequently defined a "mountain man" with stereotyped "strong-dominant" terms. However, older males most frequently de-

TABLE 16.6
Means and Standard Deviations for
Personal and Social Disclosure Across Target Persons

Target Person	Younger Males		Older Males		
	$\overline{X}$	SD	$\overline{X}$	SD	
Personal Disclosure					
wife/girlfriend	15.13	2.68	13.62	1.64	**
	(N = 23)		(N = 34)		
male friend	12.56	2.33	11.20	2.36	*
	(N = 32)		(N = 34)		
female friend	11.43	2.14	10.06	3.02	*
	(N = 30)		(N = 33)		
Social Disclosure					
wife/girlfriend	15.70	2.50	16.32	3.22	
	(N = 23)		(N = 34)		
male friend	15.40	2.57	16.26	2.78	
	(N = 32)		(N = 34)		
female friend	14.30	1.68	15.56	2.88	*
	(N = 30)		(N = 34)		

$*p < .05;$ $**p < .01.$

fined a "mountain man" with "character-honesty" terms, and younger males responded this way less frequently. Younger males frequently defined a "mountain man" with "personal growth-freedom" terms, but older males used this type of definition infrequently. These differences are reminiscent of the attitudes that characterize the "generation gap" of the larger American society but should be lacking in Appalachia with its traditionally espoused familism ideology.

Both age groups infrequently defined a "mountain man" with "regional identity" terms. This infrequent response represents a social identity. In contrast, the most frequent definitions of a "mountain man" were concerned with his personal identity (e.g., strong-dominant, character-honesty, personal growth-freedom). This finding is most likely due to the structure of the questionnaire. When questioned in a more structured form both younger and older males identified with the Appalachian Mountains as a distinct geographic and cultural region (see Table 16.2). However, when asked to subjectively define a "mountain man" (i.e., self), it should not be surprising that personal definitions would be forthcoming. Whether social or personal identity is of most concern to the southern Appalachian male is another issue that will require further study.

In summary, the life preferences and personal identities of the Appalachian males studied only selectively tied in with traditional Appalachian values and a traditional "mountain man" image. In each case a modernization element prevented a clear picture of a traditional "mountain man" from developing. Moreover, these modernization elements resembled those faced by most American males who are adjusting their personal and family lives to changes in a high-technological society.

EXPRESSIVENESS AND DISCLOSURE

Although the total sample means for the Appalachian male's expressiveness of anger, love, sadness, and happiness were similar to Dosser's (1981) university male population, the direction of difference was as would be expected. The "strong-dominant" image endorsed by the Appalachian males would negate the expression of love, sadness, and happiness. Anger would be the one feeling a "strong-dominant mountain man" would be expected to express, and anger was indeed the one feeling expressed by both age groups of Appalachian males more than Dosser's university population.

Younger and older Appalachian males differed in their personal disclosure across target persons. The younger group displayed a significantly greater willingness to disclose personal information to their wives/girlfriends and male and female friends than did older males. The finding is in keeping with the younger group's more liberal "personal growth-freedom" definition of a "mountain man."

In regard to social disclosure, only the older Appalachian males' disclosure to their female friends was significant. This may be due to the operation of different cohort norms governing gender relations. The older males were reared in a more traditional Appalachia containing fewer norms for interacting with females outside the family. When faced with the demand for greater social involvement with non-kin females (e.g., factory work), they could be expected to be more dependent on the norms of the larger American society. In contrast, social disclosure would be a minor issue to the younger Appalachian males studied, given their greater willingness to disclose personal information across all target persons. That no difference was found between the two age groups for social disclosure to wife/girlfriend or male friend is not surprising given the more established norms that exist for these types of transactions.

CONCLUSION

The Appalachian males in this study often identified with a traditional image of a "mountain man." However, in each case the influence of modernization led to a qualification of that image. The endorsement of the "mountain man" stereotype may thus reflect more on the cultural ideology associated with the promotion of a traditional southern Appalachia than with the existence of any "mountain man" subculture reality. In short, the southern Appalachian male today may, in part, be said to represent a "marginal man." Furthermore, the experiences of the southern Appalachian male in many ways reflect those of his contemporaries in American society in general. It is thus possible that the southern Appalachian "mountain man" represents a prototype of the marginality displayed by all American males living in a rapidly changing society. Research using a non-Appalachian rural male population is clearly needed to determine the degree of difference between Appalachian and other American males on the issues addressed in this study.

On the other hand, it is important not to downplay the "mountain man" image. The men in this study reside in an area that, although having become part of the larger American culture, is still heavily influenced by a traditional "mountain life" ideology. Perhaps the Appalachian males studied could thus best be described as a product of an idealized "subculture" that, while attempting to maintain a continuity with its heritage in the face of continued change, has forced its male members to adopt radically conflicting behaviors and values most characteristic of the prototypical "marginal man." The use of such a mixture of traditional and modern behaviors and values could serve as what Photiadis (1977) has termed "buffers" against the frustrations associated with change in the Appalachias, allowing its male members to make needed adjustments to the larger American society. Further research into how a drastic disruption of these "buffers" would influence the southern Appalachian male's role identity and sense of self-esteem could be of value in allowing for a better understanding of how the American male in general adopts to his changing physical and social world.

REFERENCES

Ball, R. A. (1970). The southern Appalachian folk subculture as a tension-reducing way of life. In J. D. Photiadis & H. K. Schwarzweller (Eds.), *Change in rural Appalachia: Implications for action programs.* Philadelphia: University of Pennsylvania Press.

Balswick, J. O. (1975, August). *The development of an emotion scale and an expression of emotion scale.* Paper presented at the meeting of the American Sociological Association, San Francisco.

Colliver, M. C., & Warner, P. D. (1979, August). *Appalachian values: A longitudinal analysis.* Paper presented at the meeting of the Rural Sociological Society, Burlington, VT.

Dosser, D. A. (1981). *Sex differences and situational factors in emotional expressiveness: A reconsideration of male inexpressiveness.* Unpublished doctoral dissertation, University of Georgia, Athens.

Ford, T. R. (1962). *The southern Appalachian region: A survey.* Lexington: University of Kentucky Press.

Hennon, C. B., & Photiadis, J. (1979). The rural Appalachian low-income male: Changing role in a changing family. *Family Coordinator, 28,* 608-615.

Photiadis, J. (1970). *Selected social and sociophychological characteristics of West Virginians in their own state and in Cleveland, Ohio.* Morgantown, WV: Appalachian Center.

Photiadis, J. (1977). *An overview of the process of social transition in rural Appalachia.* Morgantown, WV: West Virginia University, Office of Research and Development.

Stonequist, E. V. (1961). *The marginal man: A study in personality and culture confict.* New York: Russell & Russell.

Wigginton, E. (1975). *Foxfire books* (3 vols.). Garden City, NY: Doubleday.

ABOUT THE CONTRIBUTORS

Linda Ade-Ridder, Ph.D., is an Assistant Professor in the Department of Home Economics and Consumer Sciences, Miami University, Oxford, Ohio. She received her Ph.D. degree from Florida State University in 1983. Her professional interests include therapy with individuals and families, marriage in later life, abuse within families, and women's roles in families and society.

Kristine M. Baber received her doctorate in human development and family relations at the University of Connecticut. She currently is Assistant Professor of Child and Family Studies at the University of New Hampshire, where she is continuing research on delayed childbearing and changing gender roles.

Jack O. Balswick, Ph.D., is Professor of Sociology and Family Development at Fuller Theological Seminary. He is well known for his work on the inexpressiveness of men. He has authored four books, *Social Problems in the United States, Why I Can't Say I Love You, The Greek Cyprist Family in a Changing Society,* and *Ascension at the Crossroads: A Case Study of a Church Caught in the Turbulence of Rapid Social Change.*

Timothy H. Brubaker, Ph.D., is a Professor in the Department of Home Economics and Consumer Sciences and an Associate of the Family and Child Studies Center, Miami University, Oxford, Ohio. He is the editor of *Family Relationships in Later Life* (Sage Publications, 1983) and coauthor of *Family Caregivers and Dependent Elderly: Minimizing Stress and Maximizing Independence* (Sage Publications, 1984). His research interests focus on the division of responsibility for household tasks, long-term relationships, and service delivery to the elderly and their families.

Bram Buunk, Ph.D., is a Professor in Psychology at the University of Nijmegen, the Netherlands. In 1984 he was a Fulbright Scholar at the University of California, Los Angeles. His major interests are focused on sexual jealousy and styles of coping with extramarital involvement of spouses.

Mick Coleman, Ph.D., is Lecturer, Department of Human Services, at the University of North Carolina, Charlotte. At the time the research project was conducted, he was a doctoral student in the Department of Child and Family Development, University of Georgia, Athens.

Michael E. Connor, who received his Ph.D. in clinical psychology from the University of Hawaii, is an Associate Professor of Psychology at California State University, Long Beach. Additionally, he is a clinical psychologist in private practice working primarily with children and offering parenting training programs to adults of all ages. His major research interests focus on positive attributes of black men who are fathers, issues in dual careers, successful male/female adult relationships, and "positive" aging processes.

Jenny De Jong-Gierveld, Ph.D., is a Full Professor in the Department of Research Methods, Free University, Amsterdam, the Netherlands. Currently, her work involves the project "Research into Loneliness," with a focus on the development of measurement instruments for this phenomenon. Her publications are also in the areas of the well-being of older unmarried people, singles, and singlehood.

Peggy S. Draughn, Ph.D., is Associate Professor of Home Economics at Louisiana State University. She has published research in work and family in the *Journal of Marriage and the Family* and the *Home Economics Research Journal*. She holds degrees from the University of Southern Mississippi and Florida State University.

Albert S. Dreyer, Ph.D., is Professor of Human Development in the School of Family Studies, University of Connecticut. His primary professional interest is parent-child relations. He recently coauthored a chapter in the *Review of Child Development Research*, Vol. 7, on psychological perspectives of the family.

Stephen F. Duncan is a doctoral student in family studies at Purdue University, West Lafayette, Indiana. His research thus far has been devoted to the exploration of why men remain single or delay marriage and identifying ways to help them overcome marriage obstacles. He himself happily has been part of a "delayed" marriage for over two years.

Lawrence E. Gary, Ph.D., is the Director of the Institute for Urban Affairs and Research and Professor of Social Work and Urban Studies at Howard University. His research interests include mental health, social support systems, especially the family, and substance abuse. He has published numerous articles in professional journals such as *Community Mental Health, Journal of Black Studies, Psychological Reports, Public Health Reports*, and *Social Work*. He is the author of several books, including *Mental Health: A Challenge to the Black Community* and *Black Men*.

Philip B. Gordon, Ph.D., is Assistant Professor in the School of Home Economics, Indiana University of Pennsylvania. He holds a doctorate from Ohio State Universtiy. His research interests are in the areas of family decision making and family violence.

Shirley M.H. Hanson, Ph.D., is a Professor and Chairperson of the Department of Family Nursing at the Oregon Health Sciences University School of Nursing in Portland, Oregon. She formerly taught at the University of Washington and Seattle University in Seattle, Washington, and at the Intercollegiate Center for Nursing Education in Spokane, Washington. Her present research focuses on fatherhood, single-parent families, and health and families. Her recent publications include *Dimensions of Fatherhood, Health and Single Parent Families*, and *Collaborative Research*.

Michael E. Lamb, Ph.D., is Professor of Psychology, Psychiatry, and Pediatrics at the University of Utah, Salt Lake City. His research on fathers and children is among the best-known research in this field. Some of his latest books include *Fatherhood and Family Policy*, with Abraham Sagi (Lawrence Erlbaum Associates, 1983), and *The Future of Fatherhood.*

James A. Levine, Ph.D., is Director of the Fatherhood Project at Banks Street College, New York City. He is author of *Who Will Raise the Children?; Day-Care and the Public School;* and *Child Care and Equal Opportunity for Women.*

Robert A. Lewis, Ph.D., is Head and Professor of the Department of Child Development and Family Studies at Purdue University, West Lafayette, Indiana. Since receiving his doctorate in sociology from the University of Minnesota in 1969, he has been engaged in research and teaching in family studies and family sociology at the Universities of Minnesota, Georgia, Pennsylvania State, and Arizona State University, where he was Director of the Center for Family Studies. He also did research and taught graduate courses at the University of Uppsala, Sweden, in 1977. He has published numerous articles in family journals and books, especially on the topics of marital quality and marital stability, mate selection, couple development, and critical family transitions. He coedited a special issue of *The Family Coordinator*, "Men's Roles in the Family," in 1979 with Joseph H. Pleck. He has also edited three other books: *Men in Difficult Times* (Prentice-Hall, 1981), *Assessing Marriage: New Behaviorial Approaches*, with Erik E. Filsinger (Sage Publications, 1981), and *Men's Changing Roles in the Family*, with Marvin B. Sussman (Haworth, 1985).

John Lewis McAdoo, Ph.D., is an Associate Professor in the School of Social Work and Community Planning at the University of Maryland at Baltimore.

Patrick C. McKenry, Ph.D., is Associate Professor of Family Relations and Human Development, Ohio State University. He received his Ph.D.

from the University of Tennessee and has published in the areas of sex roles, adolescence in family context, and divorce.

Bruce Nordstrom, Ph.D., is in the Sociology Department at St. Olaf College, Northfield, Minnesota, where he teaches a class on men's lives. The chapter included in this volume is part of a book he is writing on men and their families, work, friendships, and personal changes.

Joseph H. Pleck, Ph.D., is Program Director, Male Role Program, Center for Research on Women, Wellesley College, Wellesley, Massachusetts. He received his doctorate in clinical psychology at Harvard University in 1973. His work focuses on male roles, sex roles, and sex-role attitudes, and on family roles, work and family issues, and work schedules. His recent books include *The Future of Fatherhood, Working Wives, Working Husbands, Research in the Interweave of Social Roles* (with Helena Lopata), and *The Myth of Masculinity.*

Sharon J. Price received her Ph.D. from Iowa State University. She is currently Professor of Child and Family Development at the University of Georgia, Athens. Her recent publications have been on the topics of divorce, conjugal power, and family perceptions.

Nancy M. Rudd received her Ph.D. from the University of Illinois. She is currently Associate Professor of Home Management and Housing, Ohio State University. Her research interests include women's economic development and consumer decision making.

Graeme Russell, Ph.D., is currently employed as a Senior Lecturer in Behavioral Sciences at Macquarie University, Sydney, Australia. His major interests are in fathers and families in which mothers and fathers share the responsibilities for child care, multimethod approaches to the study of families, and sex-role development. His publications include *The Changing Role of Fathers?* and *A Practical Guide for Fathers.*

Robert E. Salt, M.S., is a doctoral student in family studies at Purdue University. He has been studying various aspects of men's family roles

for over five years, since beginning his graduate work at the University of Maine. He has recently published an article, "Legal Changes and the Role of Fathers: American Experiences" (Haworth, 1985). He has presented papers at meetings of the National Council on Family Relations and the American Association of Marriage and Family Therapy on policy implications of paternal touch and on therapy with fathers. He has led a men's group at Purdue University, focusing on family changes for returning male students. He is also planning a course in gender studies for next year at Purdue University. He has been a consultant and host of a three-part television series for teenage parents and a multimedia production on the prevention of rape.

Peter J. Stein, Ph.D., is Professor of Sociology at William Paterson College, where he teaches courses in gender roles, marriage and the family, introduction to sociology, and the sociology of sports. He is the author of *Sociology* (2nd ed.), with Beth Hess and Elizabeth Markson; *Single Life;* and "Men in Families" in the Winter 1984 issue of *Marriage and Family Review*, a special issue entitled "Women and the Family: A Decade Review," edited by Marvin Sussman and Beth Hess.

Mary L. Waggenspack is Director of Volunteers, Traveler's Aid Society, in New Orleans. She earned the B.S. and M.S. in home economics from Louisiana State University. The chapter included in this book is based on her unpublished thesis, "Father's General Supportiveness as Perceived by University Female Students and Their Fathers."